# Film Business
by Lillian Ross

# Film Business

from *The New Yorker*, 1948–2003

# by Lillian Ross

# THE FiLm DeSK

ISBN: 979-8-9864463-3-2
Library of Congress Control Number: 2023937526

1st edition of 1,500, 2023, Film Desk Books, New York
Jim Colvill and Jake Perlin, publishers

© Lillian Ross, 1948, 1949, 1950, 1954, 1963, 1965, 1966, 1969, 1970, 1972, 1976, 1981, 1982, 1984, 1985, 1993, 1996, 2001, 2002
All work originally published in *The New Yorker*

Introduction © Richard Brody, 2023

The publishers extend their grateful appreciation to Richard Brody, Jane Gelfman, Cathy Gleason, Susan Morrison, Nicolas Pedrero-Setzer, Laura and Oliver.

Designed by Brian McMullen
Printed at Sheridan Books, Inc. in Michigan

Also published by The Film Desk:

François Truffaut by Lillian Ross,
from *The New Yorker*, 1960–1976

John Huston by Lillian Ross,
from *The New Yorker*, 1949–1996

Phillippe Garrel—*L'Enfant secret*

Pasolini in New York

Duras/Godard Dialogues

The World of Jia Zhangke
by Jean-Michel Frodon

Film as a Subversive Art
by Amos Vogel

Facing Blackness
by Ashley Clark

Diary of a Film
by Jean Cocteau

| | |
|---|---|
| Introduction by Richard Brody | 9 |
| Come In, Lassie! | 23 |
| Rush | 43 |
| Feeling Lost | 47 |
| Mr. Hulot | 51 |
| In Charge | 55 |
| Reasons of the Eye | 59 |
| Godard Est Godard | 65 |
| Anatomy of a Commercial Interruption | 73 |
| Producer | 137 |
| The Faces of the Husbands | 143 |
| McLuhan's Child | 149 |
| Revels | 155 |
| Truffaut, Part V | 163 |
| Kurosawa Frames | 169 |
| Some Figures on a Fantasy | 201 |
| Generator | 249 |
| With Fellini | 255 |
| Oliver Stone Has Lunch with His Mom | 263 |
| Huston Chronicle | 267 |
| Wes Anderson in Hamilton Heights | 271 |
| Nothing Fancy | 275 |
| Tony Again | 291 |

introduction
by Richard Brody

THERE'S AN ESSENTIALLY CINEMATIC aspect to Lillian Ross's writing, as she herself said. In her autobiographical book *Reporting Back*, from 2002, she described her process: "As I write, I'm always trying to build scenes into little story-films." She said, of another piece, that she considered the details that she observed and heard in one reporting venture "very similar to shots for a movie that had to be edited together to make a whole." The very existence of this book owes itself to her movie-based methods: "While reporting a story, I find myself automatically translating what I see and hear into film-like scenes. So I naturally have been drawn to writing pieces about the directors who were of interest to me."

The recognition, from early in her career, that the center of gravity in the world of movies is indeed the director puts Ross—or, I should say, Lillian, because I had the honor of being acquainted with her, owing to the time that our work at *The New Yorker* overlapped—at the forefront of film-centric writers of her generation. The pieces in *Film Business* reflect her attunement to the art of movies—an attunement that's also something of a philosophy of life, as befits the work of a writer who, self-consciously, from early in her career, approached nonfiction writing as an essentially literary, novelistic venture—and who made that discovery while working on her first major piece about movies, "Come In, Lassie!," from 1948, with which this collection begins.

Ross, who was born in Syracuse, New York, in 1918, joined *The New Yorker* in 1945 after a stint as a reporter at the short-lived, ambitious daily *PM*. Her earliest work involved writing for the Talk of the Town section—writing pieces that would then be rewritten by male staffers. (At the time, that section's pieces were published unsigned, as they would be until 1994, though archives establish authorship and books of her Talk pieces appeared, starting in 1966.) Soon, she was writing longer, and signed, pieces of reporting. In 1947, she traveled to Mexico, to profile the Brooklyn-born bullfighter Sidney Franklin; as she put it, "On my way back from Mexico, I stopped in Hollywood."

It was no casual visit; she was aware of the pressure being placed on the movie industry by the House Un-American Activities Committee and knew that writers had been blacklisted by the studios as a result. She wrote, "Almost immediately, wherever I turned, I sensed what my story would be. Nervousness and uncertainty were all around me." The climate of fear that prevailed was triggered by the committee's subpoena power—it held in contempt of Congress witnesses who refused to testify. But, as Ross relates, those hearings would have been of far slighter note without the collusion of unofficial authorities—the Red-baiting and scandal-mongering demagogy of journalists, the amplified fury of pressure groups, and the studio bosses themselves, who were very fast to knuckle under to such pressure. (The blacklist, after all, wasn't mandated by law but instituted by the studios.)

Ross reports thoroughly, in pointed details, on the climate of fear that reigned in Hollywood as a result (actors were cautioned not to talk politics in interviews, and, when meeting journalists, were joined by one or more studio P.R. people to vet questions and answers); on the industry's vulnerability at that time, with viewership and production declining; and on the overt Republican-Party politics at the heart of the machinations. Ross makes clear the impingement on the very subjects of movies that the campaign effected; bankers and industrialists as villains were out of the question, for instance, and even the word "labor" was considered trouble. (The overwhelming popularity of Lassie, who was being shoehorned into movies incongruously, suited the dog's studio bosses well, as one told Ross: "Lassie doesn't make speeches.") Ross also observed, and further anticipated, the artistic brain drain that was likely to result from such restrictions: "A number of actors and producers, including Charlie Chaplin, are planning to go to England, France, or Italy, where they believe that they will be free to make the kind of pictures they like."

One of the most keenly crafted scenes in the piece is centered on the production of the film noir *Key Largo*, and a lunchtime discussion of politics and persecution by the movie's cast—including the married couple Humphrey Bogart (who had narrowly skirted trouble for some of his anti-HUAC advocacy) and Lauren Bacall ("What will happen if the American Legion and the Legion of Decency boycott all his pictures?"), and Edward G. Robinson, plus the movie's director, John Huston, who described the censorship battles that he was fighting over the movie's script.

The reporting trip to Hollywood proved immensely consequential for Ross, for *The New Yorker*, and, indeed, for the history of American letters—and that lunch was a key reason. First, it was in the course of writing the piece overall that Ross discovered what she described as her method, her basic principle of nonfiction writing: "...I discovered literary forms that grew out of the nature of the material." In particular, by way of her encounter with Huston, she also developed what is, in effect, an experiential auteurism, as they forged a friendship that was itself cinematic, as she later wrote— "Hanging out with him was always high-spirited fun; it invariably felt as though I were part of one of his dramatic, intriguing movie scenes." In 1950, Huston invited her back to Hollywood, to observe the entire production of *The Red Badge of Courage*. She reported on the experience, from the preproduction work on casting, writing, and location scouting, through the shoot, the edit, and the release.

The result was one of the great tours de force of American nonfiction, a five-part series published in *The New Yorker*, in 1952, under the title "Production Number 1512" and then collected as a book that she titled *Picture*. It's one of the most distinctive nonfiction books ever written, and Ross knew, nearly from the start, that she was onto something. Soon after she arrived in California and became immersed in the environment of the production, she wrote to William Shawn, then the managing editor of *The New Yorker* (and, later, her partner, as she wrote in the 1998 memoir *Here But Not Here*), "I don't know whether this sort of thing has ever been done before, but I don't see why I shouldn't try to do a fact piece in a novel form, or maybe a novel in fact form.... It's almost as though the subject material calls for that kind of form."

In *Picture*, Ross gave explicit voice to her discovery of the convergence of the director and his art, writing that "the style of the Huston pictures, Huston being one of the few Hollywood directors who manage to leave their personal mark on the films they make, was the style of the man" and going into detail on the connections. She also discovered that his personal mark meant little to the studio, M-G-M, with its impersonal commercial imperatives. In the course of the nearly two-year process that took Huston from the late stages of preproduction through the release of the film in 1951, she traced the conflict between Huston's artistry and the studio's power—the inevitable clash between the director's ideas and the producer's and studio executives' demands for changes, reshoots, and reedits based on their sense of what would make the film commercially successful. As it turned out, the movie was a box-office failure—and it was also an artistically adulterated work, a mere remnant of the creation that Huston had in mind, had put in his script, and had even shot.

Ross's vision of the oppressive hand of studio overlords that botched the art and even the commerce of talented directors came packed with a crucial counterpart: the ideal of independence. It was embodied by yet another luminary whom she encountered in 1948, in the course of her reporting from Hollywood under political siege: Charlie Chaplin. In 1950, when he was visiting New York to cast his next feature, *Limelight*, she visited him at his hotel and wrote a Talk of the Town story about the meeting, "Feeling Lost" (included here). It is, among other things, a sharply etched portrayal of disproportion. Ross's meeting with Charlie Chaplin resonates with her awed awareness of the imbalance of the daily ordinariness of a man in a hotel room and the worldwide fame that he bears—a fame that's nearly coextensive with the popularity of the cinema itself. Chaplin's reminiscence about arriving in New York in 1916 after what he modestly calls his "first success" ("The police had sent me word on the train that I wasn't to go in to Grand Central, because of the crowds waiting to see me there, so I had to get off at 125th Street") suggests the philosophy that Ross teases out from the art of movies, namely, that the art is inseparable from its commercial aspect, not by way of calculation or formula, but, on the contrary, by dint of the cinema's magnification of personality—a technical power that amplifies its artists' psychological bond with their audiences.

Chaplin made movies as he saw fit because he could afford to do so—because he had amassed a mighty fortune, by way of the commercial success of his films, that enabled him to own his own studio and to work at his own pace, by his own lights. He fretted a bit about the new film, saying, "I can't afford to wait too long on it, because I use my own money," which comes off as a humble brag, one that he was quite entitled to, given the ambition, the audacity, and the accomplishment of his films—and given the confession that he'd lost money with the defiantly corrosive, sardonically funny *Monsieur Verdoux*, which, Ross reports, "he considers his best work"—in which he portrays a petit-bourgeois Bluebeard. By contrast, Hollywood figures who hadn't reached such stratospheric heights of success or independent wealth had to justify themselves relentlessly to the studios, and often in vain; as the ambitious producer Walter Wanger told Ross, in 1948, "If you want to stay in this business, if you want to make pictures that contribute to the country's welfare, you've got to make pictures that make money."

Though Ross's perspective on the art of the cinema, as reflected in *Film Business*, is indeed inseparable from the business of film, she knew where the talent was. In June, 1954, Jacques Tati's latest film, then newly released in New York, received a five-sentence, respectfully dismissive review from *The New Yorker*'s film critic John McCarten; several weeks later, Ross, in a Talk piece about Tati, "Mr. Hulot," on the occasion of his visit to the city for the film's opening, uninhibitedly calls him "one of the funniest men alive" and, without editorializing about the film itself, merely by letting Tati speak at length and thereby give voice, on the page, to his extraordinary personality, frames the brief story as a portrait of a formidably original and self-evidently significant artist.

On the other hand, success at the box office only did harm to the reputation of one of the greatest of all directors, Alfred Hitchcock, who was long considered, above all, a deft showman of déclassé genres who put Hollywood gloss on cheap thrills. (Not one of his films was in the top twenty-six in the 1962 *Sight and Sound* critics' poll of the greatest films of all time.) Even in 1963, when Ross talked with him at the time of the release of *The Birds*, his artistic status in the United States was largely confined to the auteurist enthusiasms of Andrew Sarris, at the *Village Voice*, and the precocious Peter Bogdanovich, who, in his early twenties, had been recruited by the Museum of Modern Art to put on a Hitchcock retrospective. Perhaps Ross caught Hitchcock fever from the French New Wave, of which she was an early enthusiast, embarking in early 1960 on the first of her five pieces about François Truffaut (collected in a separate Film Desk volume). In any case, she flat-out called Hitchcock "a great director." (In the issue of *The New Yorker* following Ross's piece, the critic Brendan Gill would disrespectfully dismiss *The Birds*, in a one-paragraph review, as "a sorry failure.")

Without openly contradicting Gill, Ross, first, gives Hitchcock a chance to state his philosophy of cinema—which is to say, she grants him the status of a preeminent artist who *has* such a philosophy ("Most movies are just pictures of people telling stories. My movies are the pictures telling stories"). He speaks of his New Wave connections, the impending book of interviews with him that Truffaut was crafting—and, in praising Truffaut, doubles down on his philosophy (and proves to be in synch with Ross's own) by reminding him, Ross, and the world that the essence of cinema is found in its fundamental character as a mass medium: "The movies are the only art form that is truly global. I like to think of my pictures' being able to convey the same thing to different audiences in cities and towns and villages all over the earth. Extraordinary, to have the power to make those millions of unseen people laugh or cry out of fear! I must say I enjoy being in charge of people's emotions." It's as if, in a handful of lines, Ross rendered Hitchcock as canonical as Chaplin, as world-historical as Chaplin, and gave him the platform that elevated him to a supremacy in the art that his awareness of its conjoined powers—the aesthetic ones, of the image, and the practical ones, of its social and psychological place in the world—had earned him. (What's more, Ross's endearingly droll depiction of Hitchcock's epicurean and sybaritic side also hints that, like Chaplin, he connected with audiences who thereby made him rich enough, independent enough, to make movies his own way.)

Yet it isn't wealth as such, but the connection, that, for Ross, marks the essence of a great director's artistic power, as seen in her fascinating, fascinated portrait of Jean-Luc Godard, from the time of his visit to the third New York Film Festival, in 1965. Godard had three films at the festival: *Alphaville, Le Petit Soldat,* and the short film "Montparnasse et Levallois" (which was part of the compilation film *Paris vu par....*); above all, he had a personal allure, an aura akin to that of a rock star, which exerted itself above all on young moviegoers. In conversation, Godard displays the combination of off-the-cuff brilliance, quiet intellectual audacity, and un-self-sparing candor that made his career-long plethora of interviews an entire parallel track of artistic creation. Even as he discusses his own checkered box-office results (declaring that only three of his movies had made money), he's reminded that his autographs were said to bring ten dollars apiece at a university, and Godard responded, "Yes. I have heard the kids in America say about *Breathless* that it was for the first time they are seeing their own life in a picture."

The transformative power of Godard's own daring reconceptions of cinematic form (themselves a subject of the discussion) leads Ross to her own reconfigurations of nonfiction form. Just as she was inspired by the modernistic classicism of late-forties and early fifties Hollywood artistry to develop a literary manner of cinematic inspiration, now, in light of Godard's freewheeling transformations of Hollywood-classic styles and his intellectually uninhibited innovations, Ross turned a Talk piece into a virtual cinematic object, written in the style of a loose screenplay, with its scenes set Francophonically as "extérieur" or "intérieur," dialogue apportioned to characters ("Woman:...," "Godard:..."), rapid montages of fragments of overheard dialogue, descriptions of what the camera would see from different angles (and even imaginary collections of film clips), and fantasy-like manipulations of action in fast-forward motion suggesting a soundtrack desynchronized from the images.

If this playful yet jangled manner suggests both the mindbending power of Godard's films (even of his personal presence) and the feedback-like distortions emanating from the public's reaction to his presence, it also suggests Ross's awareness and embrace of a new world of cinema that Godard was playing a large role in creating and that was in evidence not only on-screen but at the festival's events, amid its public, filtered outward into the life of the times, including journalistically. She put this new, cinematized nonfiction format to heavy-duty use in the longest piece in *Film Business*, a 1966 profile of the director and producer Otto Preminger, titled "Anatomy of a Commercial Interruption." Here, Ross deploys an even more elaborate screenplay-like format to altogether ironic effect.

Preminger, one of the most distinctive and creative studio directors, was also a daring and practical producer who went far out on a limb to preserve the integrity of his work, which often reflected his socially progressive views. He also won a significant measure of artistic freedom by dint of his commercial successes (and of the many Oscar nominations that he, his films, and their casts and crews garnered), gaining contractual right to final cut on some of his films, including epic legal drama *Anatomy of a Murder*, from 1959, in which his own education as a lawyer (he never practiced) bore artistic fruit. The studio that distributed the film, Columbia Pictures, sold broadcast rights to the film—and when it was shown on television, it was interrupted many times (thirteen in its New York broadcast, Preminger counted) for commercials. Preminger sued Columbia on the grounds that the interruptions violated his right to final cut and harmed the film's future commercial prospects. The court proceedings of this suit, and the life that Preminger led amid his courtroom appearances in downtown Manhattan, provides the stuff of Ross's virtuosic panorama of the director's temerity, chutzpah, and sheer force of will. (The strikingly unusual format of this profile also coaxes out, with a stifled guffaw, the similarities of a screenplay to a trial transcript.)

Living in an art-filled townhouse on the Upper East Side and working from an art-filled office in Columbia's New York headquarters, Preminger was quite as much of a Hollywood grandee as Chaplin and Hitchcock—but one whose personal touch wasn't as distinctive, whose artistry wasn't as original, and who depended more on the studio's backing to make his movies. As a result, Ross's admiration is tinged with skepticism; while manifestly admiring Preminger's work, and marveling at the magisterial force of reason that he musters to press his irrationally passionate case, she takes an ironic view of his fierce defense of his artistic independence—the sort that had to be complained for and battled for rather than merely taken. The pathos of Huston's frustration with *The Red Badge of Courage* is balanced—and enshrined—in his readiness to shrug and move on (as he did, immediately, to *The African Queen*). Preminger's deployment of the overwhelming resources of money, time, and energy on the lawsuit, for what he considers a matter of principle, comes off as a kind of vanity, a disproportionate obsession—albeit an extraordinarily florid and picturesque one that yields wide-ranging and idiosyncratically detailed insights into the personalities and practices of civil court and the private life of the director himself.

Yet, amid the high-handed flaunting of his Hollywood persona in the ritualized formality of court, Ross brings to the fore one visionary aspect of the lawsuit: Preminger's prediction, on the witness stand, that "in the next ten years there will be no interruptions in any motion picture." He was, of course, partly right; the primordial cable-TV channel that took Manhattan by storm in the nineteen-seventies was, after all, called Home Box Office (check the acronym) that showed movies uncut and without interruptions, beginning the long march of television toward the level of prestige then associated with the best of Hollywood.

There was a dearth of female filmmakers in Hollywood in the nineteen-sixties; what might have ensued, in the seventies, had Ross encountered

Elaine May, Barbara Loden, Claudia Weill, or other women who left their directorial mark on the times remains a matter of imagination. For that matter, Ross, who wrote about Truffaut and Godard during their New York visits, didn't write about Agnès Varda (who was at the New York Film Festival in 1966 and 1969), but she did the next-best thing: she published, in 1969, "Producer," a Talk story about Mag Bodard, one of the few female film producers in France at the time, who made her mark as the driving force behind *The Umbrellas of Cherbourg*, directed by Jacques Demy (Varda's husband), and then, while Varda's own career was stalled after the commercial failure of *Cleo from 5 to 7*, produced a new film of Varda's, *Le Bonheur*, which Bodard spoke of candidly: "For me, this film was very, very important. It was a film made by a woman, and it is exactly what goes on inside the head of every woman, except that she doesn't realize it."

In the nineteen-seventies, Ross caught Truffaut in a melancholy mood as he, at the age of forty-four, admitted to feeling the pressure of time to make the many films he had in mind. (His concerns were sadly prescient: he died in 1984, at the age of fifty-two.) She paid admiring attention to Akira Kurosawa when he came to New York in 1981 for a retrospective; in 1985, she spent time with Federico Fellini and Giulietta Masina (the great actress and his frequent star, who was also his wife) when they were schlepped to a Connecticut estate as the guests of the chairperson of the Film Society of Lincoln Center. She rightly discerned a new Hollywood luminary, and the future of the art, in her 2001 portrait of Wes Anderson, then thirty-two, amid his cast of luminaries in *The Royal Tenenbaums* during its shoot at a mansion-like townhouse in upper Manhattan. In 2003, she portrayed another kind of Hollywood independence rooted in world renown, in an extensively observed Profile of a late starter, Clint Eastwood, who had launched his directorial career at the age of forty and was then a vigorous seventy-two. (She was a vigorous eighty-four.)

For me, the most moving piece in *Film Business*, alongside Ross's boldly indignant 1948 confrontation with the blacklist, is her 1982 Profile of Francis Ford Coppola, "Some Figures on a Fantasy," which is the second-longest piece in the book (behind the Preminger article). If, in her account of Preminger, Ross depicts in motion a perhaps enviable but ultimately dubious form of success—hubris without comeuppance—her depiction of Coppola is perched on the edge of tragedy and has its comeuppance built into the hubris that gives it its drama, a heroic hubris that arises from Coppola's passion for his art. The Profile is centered on Coppola's outburst of creative fury—and his reckless drive for creative independence—in making his 1982 film *One from the Heart*. In making that movie, Coppola strove for new heights of technical innovation and aesthetic originality; remarkably, Ross's piece matches it in audacity of form. Though her article about Preminger is more conspicuously unusual in its narrative method, her portrait of Coppola is accomplished with a dramatic sleight of hand that lends it something of a *Citizen Kane*-like dimension of retrospective, reconstructive clarity and of wide-embracing, full-range perspective.

Already in the Kurosawa piece, Ross had detailed the unusual process that Coppola—who spoke with the elder director about it at a reception—was developing in order to revolutionize moviemaking: "Video, Coppola explains, is about to evolve into what he calls the electronic cinema, and *One from the Heart*"—which was already shot but not yet released—"was an experiment in its use." In writing a Profile of Coppola, Ross doesn't appear to have spent much time with him until *One from the Heart* was already completed. She doesn't report from the shoot of the film or the editing room, and the first of her post-production encounters with Coppola that she discusses occurred on January 15, 1982, when he came to premiere the film at Radio City Music Hall.

Ross's story about *One from the Heart* is, above all, the story of the release of *One from the Heart*—which is to say that it's an amazingly intricate and detailed story about the American movie business at the time. Ross details, with a reportorial deep dive, the relationships between budgets and profitability, the complications of distribution deals, and the ancillary markets and income sources that contribute to a film's commercial viability. Ross takes pains to talk numbers and contracts, Hollywood practices and the journalistic shorthand that accreted around them (and that are now commonplaces: "Movie distributors like to publicize their products in terms of their 'grosses'...") Indeed, under the guise of a Coppola portrait, Ross delivers one of the most meticulously analytical accounts of the flow of money and power in so-called New Hollywood, the movie era that was dominated by a new generation of directors that included Coppola as well as his close friends Steven Spielberg and George Lucas, who, along with their films, figure in the story.

Indeed, they loom over the story: Ross cites *Variety*'s report that the two of them were, at the moment, responsible for the top five grossing films of all time—*Star Wars*, *E. T.*, *The Empire Strikes Back*, *Jaws*, and *Raiders of the Lost Ark*—along with the merchandising madness that these movies engendered. ("Among other things," Ross writes, "there is an *E.T.* talking doll—capable of saying 'Ouch,' 'Home,' and two other words—which the manufacturer estimates will bring in fifteen million dollars in 1982 all by its extra-terrestrial self.") Into that teen-and-child-centric movie marketplace, Coppola was injecting *One from the Heart*, which cost twenty-seven million dollars to make, and which, Coppola said, would have to do sixty-eight million dollars at the box office—more than half the gross of *Jaws*—to turn a profit. The movie in question is one that Coppola described as "a fable about love and show business"; it's a romantic drama, set in Las Vegas (a highly stylized and artificial version thereof), but one for which he had high aesthetic and intellectual ambitions: "We're going to tell this simple story in a fantasy way, so we'll make our own fantasy of Las Vegas, which for me is a metaphor for America itself, and like the *Mahagonny* of the world." I don't recall Lucas and Spielberg citing that opera by Brecht and Weill in relation to their mega-hits. The air of doom, the phantom menace of failure in advance, is built into the article's very subject, because Coppola, an artist who insisted on making movies of self-conscious artistry and on eluding all commercial-based constraints on his directorial efforts, was competing in the same ring as these heavyweight box-office champs.

What's more, Coppola had long sought the elusive and tantalizing ideal of independence. He wanted a studio of his own, and he bought one, which he renovated at great expense and named Zoetrope, to go with the name of his production company, American Zoetrope. He invested heavily in the electronic system that would enable him to launch his experiments in electronic cinema, starting with *One from the Heart*. But he didn't just want to make *One from the Heart* and to make it in his own studio, he also wanted to own the film, and, in talking with Ross, he bundled all of his cravings for control in a couple of sentences that suggested the trouble he'd got himself into: "I believe that an artist has a right to own what he creates, but I can't get my hands on the capital that I need to do the creating. I was running a movie studio that had no money." Not only did Coppola have to put up his studio as collateral for the loans that he needed in order to own the film, he and his wife, Eleanor, also had to put up their home, at which the telephone was shut off for nonpayment. The pathos of the piece is centered on Coppola's self-awareness, ranging between the blithe and the agonized, of the excessive risks of his venture, which he likened to a bet.

In its forty-page sprint reported nearly in real time, "Some Figures on a Fantasy" is as thorough and definitive a requiem for the New Hollywood age of the unfettered directorial hero as Steven Bach's 1985 book *Final Cut*, about the turbulent creation and epochal catastrophe of Michael Cimino's 1980 film *Heaven's Gate*, has long been considered. In this piece, Ross gives a vital account not just of the deflation, in the age of Ronald Reagan's presidency, of New Hollywood's artistic ambitions, but of the civic change that it represents. She portrays an era in which the conquering heroes of world cinema weren't the peers of Alfred Hitchcock but of Walt Disney, a time when the mighty successes of toy-like and toy-centric movies ensured that the studios, after a seeming brief interregnum of audacity, would be as timid and as mercenary as ever. In alluding to the box-office champions, Ross also suggested that they were catering to an infantilized audience all too happy to flee from reality into uncritical and lulling fantasies. Ultimately, Ross's view of Hollywood and its place in American society in 1982 is as indignantly and scathingly political as her 1948 vision of a Red-scared industry pressured into Lassie-tude.

Richard Brody<br>
2023

## Come In, Lassie!
February 21, 1948

Hollywood is baffled by the question of what the Committee on Un-American Activities wants from it. People here are wondering, with some dismay and anxiety, what kind of strange, brooding alienism the Committee is trying to eliminate from their midst and, in fact, whether it was ever here. They are waiting hopefully for Chairman J. Parnell Thomas, or Congress, or God, to tell them. They have been waiting in vain ever since last November, when eight writers, a producer, and a director—often collectively referred to these days as "the ten writers"—were blacklisted by the studios because they had been charged with contempt of Congress for refusing to tell the Thomas Committee what political party, if any, they belong to. In the meantime, business, bad as it is, goes on. The place is more nervous than usual, but it is doing the same old simple things in the same old simple ways. The simplicities of life in Hollywood are not, of course, like those anywhere else. This is still a special area where you get remarkable results simply by pushing buttons; where taxi-drivers jump out of their cabs, open their doors, and politely bow you inside; where you can buy, in "the world's largest drugstore," a good-looking clock for $735; where all the lakes in the countryside are labeled either "For Sale" or "Not for Sale"; and where guests at parties are chosen from lists based on their weekly income brackets—low ($200–$500), middle ($500–$1,250), and upper ($1,250–$20,000). During the last few months, party guests have tended to be politically self-conscious, whatever their brackets, but this is not especially embarrassing in Hollywood, where it is possible to take an impregnable position on both sides of any controversy. At an upper-bracket party not long ago, a Selznick man introduced to me as Merve told me that he was appalled and outraged by the blacklisting of the ten writers. "It's a damn shame," Merve said, beaming at me. "Those human beings got a right to think or believe anything without letting Washington in on their ideas. They can't put their ideas into Hollywood pictures. Nobody can."

Just then, we were approached by Sam Wood, the producer, who was feeling grumpy, according to Merve, because his latest picture, *Ivy*, had cost $2,000,000 to make and was expected to gross only $1,500,000.

"Glad to see you, Sam," said Merve. "Listen, Sam, I want you to tell this young lady what you think of the way Congress investigated us here in Hollywood."

"I say Congress ought to make everybody stand up publicly and be counted!" Mr. Wood shouted. "I say make every damn Communist stand up and be counted. They're a danger and a discredit to the industry!"

Merve continued to beam. "Make *every* radical, every Communist, every Socialist, and every Anarchist stand up and be counted," he said expansively. "We ought to get every one of them out of the industry."

The political self-consciousness at parties is, on the whole, rather cheerful. "I never cut anybody before this," one actress remarked happily to me. "Now I don't go anywhere without cutting at least half a dozen former friends." At some parties, the bracketed guests break up into sub-groups, each eying the others with rather friendly suspicion and discussing who was or was not a guest at the White House when Roosevelt was President—one of the few criteria people in the film industry have set up for judging whether a person is or is not a Communist—and how to avoid *becoming* a Communist. Some of the stars were investigated several years ago, when the Un-American Activities Committee was headed by Martin Dies, and the advice and point of view of these veterans are greatly sought after. One actor who is especially in demand at social gatherings is Fredric March, who suddenly discovered, when called to account by Mr. Dies, that he was a Communist because he had given an ambulance to Loyalist Spain. Dies rebuked him, and it then turned out that Mr. March had also given an ambulance to Finland when she was at war with Russia. "I was just a big ambulance-giver," Mr. March said to his sub-group at a recent party, loudly enough for other sub-groups to hear. "That's what I told Dies. 'I just like to give ambulances,' I told him, and he said, 'Well, then, Mr. March, before you give any more ambulances away, you go out and consult your local Chamber of Commerce or the American Legion, and they'll tell you whether it's all right.'"

Some groups play it safe at parties by refusing to engage in any conversation at all. They just sit on the floor and listen to anyone who goes by with a late rumor. There are all sorts of rumors in Hollywood right now. One late rumor is that the newest black-market commodity in town is the labor of the ten writers, who are reported to be secretly turning out scripts for all the major studios. Another is that one producer is founding a film company and will have all ten of the blacklisted men on his staff. Rumors that the F.B.I. is going to take over casting operations at the studios are discounted by those who have lived in Hollywood for more than fifteen years. The casting director at Metro-Goldwyn-Mayer, a fidgety, cynical, sharply dressed, red-cheeked man named Billy Grady, Sr., who has worked in Hollywood for nearly twenty years, thinks that it would serve J. Edgar Hoover right if the casting of actors were handed over to the F.B.I. "Hoover thinks *he's* got worries!" Grady shouted at me in a Hollywood restaurant. "What does a G-man do? A G-man sends guys to Alcatraz! Ha! I'd like to see a G-man find a script about Abraham Lincoln's doctor in which we could work in a part for Lassie. What do you find inside of Alcatraz? Picture stars? Directors? Cameramen? No! The goddamn place is full of doctors, lawyers, and politicians. This is the fourth biggest industry in the country, and only three men in this industry ever went to jail. There are fifty thousand people in this industry, and all they want is the right to take up hobbies. Spencer Tracy takes up painting. Clark Gable takes up Idaho. Dalton Trumbo, who got the sack, takes up deep thinking. Take away their hobbies and they're unhappy. When they're unhappy, I'm unhappy. For God's sake, Tracy doesn't paint when he's acting. Gable doesn't shoot ducks. Trumbo doesn't think when he's writing for pictures. I say let them keep their goddam hobbies. They're all a bunch of capitalists anyway."

The order of creation in Hollywood still works backward, and not only in the matter of filming the end or middle of a picture before the beginning. A man who recently had the job of working up advance interest in a yet-to-be-made picture based on *The Robe* managed to commit the biggest Bible publisher in the country to putting out an edition of the New Testament containing color photographs from the film. "I get this plug in the Bible," he said to me. "Then I hear we need someone of the caliber of Tyrone Power to play the hero. We get Power, see? Then we put him in the Bible. *Then* we put him in the picture. Only trouble is we can't make the picture yet. Ty is too busy." Evidently, Communism is also responsible for this trouble. Power, returning from a trip abroad lately, announced that he had seen so much suffering in Europe that he had come back determined to spend his time fighting Communism. This, as interpreted by Louella Parsons, meant that he had given up Lana Turner for the cause.

Hollywood, for the most part, is waiting earnestly for the Thomas Committee to define Communism, to name at least one film it considers

Communistic, and to set down rules about what should and should not be thought about by a good American. Until the Committee offers something helpful, however, Hollywood feels it has no choice but to pay close attention to the counsel of Louella Parsons, Hedda Hopper, and Jimmy Fidler, whose guidance to date has consisted of warnings that the public will not be satisfied with the blacklisting of only ten men, that the public wants Congress to complete its investigation of Communism in the industry, and that all writers, actors, producers, directors, and agents who have ever contributed so much as a nickel to the League of Women Shoppers had better announce their political views if they know what's good for them. Those who fear the thunder on the Right say they are going to leave Hollywood. "I'm a dead duck!" one sad-eyed misanthrope exclaimed to me. "All I can do now is go someplace and raise chickens. Been thinking of doing it for nine years anyway." Some say they will go back to Broadway or write novels, projects they too have been considering for nine years, more or less. A number of actors and producers, including Charlie Chaplin, are planning to go to England, France, or Italy, where they believe that they will be free to make the kind of pictures they like. Jack L. Warner, busiest of the Brothers, is genially inclined to bolster up the courage of those who are ready to throw in the towel. "Don't worry!" he roars, slapping the backs of the lesser men around him. "Congress can't last forever!"

Some people in Hollywood like to think of it as still a place for pioneers. "We're the modern covered-wagon folks," I was told by Ruth Hussey, the actress, who returned here not long ago from an appearance on Broadway. "We are, we're the modern covered-wagon folks. Pioneers come out here broke, and within a few years they're earning fifty thousand a year." In a way, Miss Hussey is exceptional. Everybody else seems eager to complain about the difficulty of making or keeping money. Studios complain about their telephone bills. Drivers of studio cars complain that they are now being paid by the trip instead of by the week. Santa Anita racetrack officials complain that betting has fallen off. Informal statisticians complain that only seventy-five million people a week went to the movies in 1947 and that maybe only sixty million will go in 1948. Producers complain about bankers' reluctance to lend them money. Bankers complain that the revenue from American films shown overseas in 1947 was only $100,000,000, which is $38,000,000 less than the revenue from American films shown overseas in 1946, and that the revenue in 1948 may be as low as $50,000,000. Both Anglophiles and Anglophobes complain about the British import tax, imposed last August, which would confiscate seventy-five per cent of the English earnings of any American film imported since then. Studio executives complain about production costs and overhead, and studio workers complain about being laid off to cut down on production costs and overhead. The employment of actors and writers is said to be the lowest in twenty years. As of the first of the year, twenty-three feature pictures were in production, as against twice that number in January of last year. "Hollywood is girding its loins," a representative of the Motion Picture Association of America said to me. "Hollywood is pulling in its belt. Hollywood is pinching its pennies, taking stock of its cupboards, buckling down, putting its shoulder to the wheel and its nose to the grindstone, and looking deep within itself. Hollywood is *worrying about the box office.*"

Almost the only motion-picture star who is taking conditions in his stride is Lassie, a reddish-haired male collie, who is probably too mixed up emotionally over being called by a girl's name to worry about the box office. Lassie is working more steadily, not only in films but on the radio, than anyone else in Hollywood. He is a star at M-G-M, the leading studio in Hollywood, which is fondly referred to out here as the Rock of Gibraltar. Visitors there are politely and desperately requested not to discuss politics or any other controversial matters with anyone on the lot. Louis B. Mayer, production chief of M-G-M, recently took personal command of the making of all pictures, of the purchase of all scripts, and of the writing of all scripts and commissary menus. The luncheon menu starts off with the announcement that meat will not be served on Tuesdays. "President Truman has appealed to Americans to conserve food, an appeal all of us will gladly heed, of course," it says. Patrons are politely and desperately encouraged to eat apple pancakes or broiled sweetbreads for lunch. Lassie eats apple pancakes for lunch. Visitors are politely and desperately introduced to Lassie, who ignores them. "We'd be in a hole if we didn't have Lassie," I heard an M-G-M man say. "We like Lassie. We're sure of Lassie. Lassie can't go out and embarrass the studio. Katharine Hepburn goes out and makes a speech for Henry Wallace. Bang! We're in trouble. Lassie doesn't make speeches. Not Lassie, thank God." At the moment, Lassie is making a picture with Edmund Gwenn about a country doctor in Scotland. Originally, the script called for a country doctor in Scotland who hated dogs, but a part has been written in for Lassie, the plot has been changed, and the picture is to be called *Master of Lassie*. "It will help at the box office," Lassie's director says. Only three other pictures are in production at M-G-M, the biggest of them being a musical comedy called *Easter Parade*, starring Fred Astaire and having to do with Easter on Fifth Avenue at the beginning of the century. One of Lassie's many champions at M-G-M told me that he had favored writing in a part for Lassie in *Easter Parade* but that he had dropped the idea. "I couldn't find a good Lassie angle," he explained.

The most noticeable effect on Hollywood of the Thomas Committee investigation is, perhaps, an atmosphere of uncertainty. A man I know named Luther Greene, who belongs to what he calls the C.I.S. ("the cheap international set," he says. "I just get passed around from party to party"), took me one evening to a small gathering at the Beverly Hills home of N. Peter Rathvon, a former New York attorney and investment banker who is now president of R.K.O. Greene and Rathvon, it seemed, thought that I might find an evening in the Rathvon household instructive. Rathvon is a mannerly, mild, yet stubborn little man, with the unwavering enthusiasm of a film-magazine fan for the movies. He has been converted, he says, to Hollywood's suburban family life. "People enjoy having babies out here," he says. "They enjoy inviting each other to dinner and sitting in the sunshine. That's life." Rathvon has two daughters and a son, rarely dines in a restaurant, and takes a sun bath at least once a week. Two of the ten men who were cited with contempt by Congress—Adrian Scott and Edward Dmytryk—worked at his studio, and it was he who had to inform them that they had brought disgrace upon R.K.O. and to dismiss them, a task he did not relish. After dinner, there was, as there is every evening the Rathvons are at home, a movie. That evening it was *Good News*, which deals with college life. After the showing, one of Rathvon's daughters, who goes to the Westlake School for Girls, denounced it as positively silly. Rathvon posted himself behind a small bar and made drinks for everybody. Then he offered to show Greene and me around his house. "Charles Boyer used to live here," he said. "It's an odd sensation, very odd, to live in a house Charles Boyer used to live in." He led us up a narrow spiral staircase, like those in lighthouses, to a bedroom with blond, primavera-paneled walls and another small bar. "This was Charles Boyer's bedroom," he said. "It's my bedroom now." Greene told Rathvon that I had heard a lot about the movable glass roof over the patio of the house, and asked him to show me how it worked. Our host took us downstairs, pushed a button in the patio, and then seemed to stop breathing. The glass roof overhead slid back, exposing the heavens. He pushed another button and watched anxiously as the roof moved back into place. "I used to be fond of playing with this," he said. "These days, I never know whether it's going to come back."

Later, after a prolonged discussion of Charles Boyer's acting, Charles Boyer's reading habits, and Charles Boyer's intelligence, someone said that Charles Boyer, together with several hundred other stars, had signed a statement protesting that the Thomas Committee investigation was unfair and prejudiced.

"What about that, Peter?" Greene asked. "A lot of people in your business feel that a man's politics has nothing to do with his work in pictures. Why, Scott and Dmytryk made *Crossfire* for you on a shoestring—five hundred and ninety-five thousand dollars. Took them twenty-two days. You'll gross three million on that picture. For heaven's sakes, why *fire* the men?"

"I sure hated to lose those boys," Rathvon said miserably. "Brilliant craftsmen, both of them. It's just that their usefulness to the studio is at an end. Would you like to go out on the terrace and look down on the lights of Hollywood?" Everyone said yes, and we all went out on the terrace to look down on the lights of Hollywood.

On our way home, Greene said that his social evenings were becoming more and more of a strain. "Everyone spends the night looking at those goddamn lights," he said unhappily. "I think I'll go to Lady Mendl's tomorrow."

The Screen Writers Guild a while back voted to intervene as *amicus curiae* in the civil suits that five of the ten blacklisted men have brought against their studios for breaking their contracts. It also decided to decline an invitation of the Association of Motion Picture Producers to cooperate in eliminating subversives from the studios. The Guild agreed, in addition, to oppose the blacklisting of writers because of their political views, as long as those views do not violate the law. On the other hand, the Guild turned down a proposal by some of its members to give financial and public-relations support to the ten men in their trials for contempt. The Motion Picture Association of America, which voted with the Producers' Association to blacklist the ten men and not to employ or re-employ any one of them until he is acquitted of contempt of Congress or swears that he is not a Communist, not long ago addressed a communication to Adrian Scott, one of the ten. From it, Scott, who had then been out of work about two weeks, learned that the 1947 Humanitarian Award of the Golden Slipper Square Club, a philanthropic organization in Philadelphia, had been given to Dore Schary, R.K.O.'s executive vice-president in charge of production, for having made, among other pictures, *Crossfire*, which Scott produced and Dmytryk directed. According to an inscription on the award, it was made for Schary's "contribution to good citizenship and understanding among men of all religions, races, creeds, and national origins." The award was accepted for Schary by Eric Johnston, president of the Motion Picture Association, who told the Philadelphians, "In Hollywood, it's ability that counts.... Hollywood has held open the door of opportunity to every man and woman who could meet its technical and artistic standards, regardless of racial background or religious belief." "We're not supposed to be useful any more because they say the public has lost confidence in us," one of the ten blacklisted men said to me. "But they're not withdrawing any of the pictures we worked on. Ring Lardner's name is thrown on the screen in front of the public seeing *Forever Amber*. Lester Cole's name is up there on *High Wall*. If the public has confidence in these pictures, the public still has confidence in us."

An exceedingly active Hollywood agent, a woman, claims that since the start of the Congressional investigation the studios have been calling for light domestic comedies and have been turning down scripts with serious themes. "You might say the popular phrase out here now is 'Nothing on the downbeat,'" she said. "Up until a few months ago, it was 'Nothing sordid.'" The difference between "Nothing sordid" and "Nothing on the downbeat," she explained, is like the difference between light domestic comedy and *lighter* domestic comedy. After the investigation got under way, the industry called in Dr. George Gallup to take a public poll for the studios. Dr. Gallup has now submitted figures showing that seventy-one per cent of the nation's moviegoers have heard of the Congressional investigation, and that of this number fifty-one percent think it was a good idea, twenty-seven per cent think not, and twenty-two per cent have no opinion. Three percent of the fifty-one percent approving of the investigation feel that Hollywood is overrun with Communism. The studio executives are now preparing a campaign to convince this splinter three per cent, and the almost as bothersome ninety-seven per cent of the fifty-one percent, that there is no Communism in the industry. There is some disagreement about whether the industry should tackle the unopinionated twenty-two per cent or leave it alone.

In the midst of the current preoccupation with public opinion, many stars are afraid that the public may have got a very wrong impression about them because of having seen them portray, say, a legendary hero who stole from the rich to give to the poor, or an honest, crusading district attorney, or a lonely, poetic, antisocial gangster. "We've got to resolve any conflicts between what we are and what the public has been led to believe we are," one actor told me. "We can't afford to have people think we're a bunch of strong men or crusaders." At the Warner Brothers studio, some time ago, I accepted a publicity representative's invitation to watch the shooting of a scene in *Don Juan*, a Technicolor reworking of the *Don Juan* made in 1926 with John Barrymore. Filming of the production has since been called off, owing to the illness of the star, Errol Flynn, but he was still in good health the day I was there. "I want you to meet Errol," said the publicity representative. "Just don't discuss anything serious with him—politics, I mean." Being a publicity man out here seems to have taken on some of the aspects of a lawyer's and an intelligence agent's duties and responsibilities. Studio visitors who are suspected of having ways of communicating with the public are always accompanied by a publicity man, or even two publicity men. The present-day importance of the publicity man is indicated by the fact that a member of the trade at M-G-M now occupies the office of the late Irving Thalberg, Thalberg still being to Hollywood what Peter the Great still is to Russia. I asked Flynn, who stood glittering in royal-blue tights and jerkin, golden boots, and a golden sword, how his version of *Don Juan* compared with Barrymore's. "That's like comparing two grades of cheese," he said moodily. "The older is probably the better. But I'm trying to make my Don Juan as human as possible. Jack's was a tough Don Juan. Mine is human. The script calls for one of the Spanish nobles to tell me that Spain is going to war. 'You're not afraid?' he asks me. 'Yes, I am afraid!' I reply. I added that line to the script myself. I don't want to be heroic. This picture is definitely non-subversive."

A Paramount man informed me that he had the perfect solution for both the split-personality problem and the Thomas Committee problem. "Make your pictures more of a mish-mosh than ever!" he said, glowing all over with health, well-being, and the resolution of a man who has at last found inner calmness. "*Confuse* the enemy—that's my technique. Confuse them all!" He has apparently confided his formula to Ray Milland, a Paramount actor whom I came across while he was working on *Sealed Verdict*. "My picture is politically significant," Mr. Milland said to me. (Paramount publicity men, like the Warner men, warn visitors not to discuss politics with stars, but Mr. Milland brought up the subject himself.) "This is a picture about political justice," Milland went on. "I play Major Robert Lawson, a brilliant young American prosecutor in the American-occupied zone of Germany, where I am closing my case against six Nazi war criminals, including General Otto Steigmann, whose war crimes against humanity were most revolting. I get Steigmann condemned to death by hanging, and then I am visited by a beautiful French model named Themis Delisle, and I fall in love with her. No, first Themis Delisle tells me that Steigmann is innocent, *then* I fall in love with her. My young aide, Private Clay Hockland, has been having an affair with a seventeen-year-old German girl, who is pregnant and shoots Private Hockland and then becomes seriously ill, although Private Hockland is also seriously ill after the *Fräulein* shoots him." Milland was interrupted by a man who wanted to comb his hair. "Later," Milland said to him, and firmly continued telling me about Private Hockland's death, the assorted difficulties of the ladies in the cast, and the problem of getting penicillin in the black market for the *Fräulein*. He was interrupted periodically by the man who wanted to comb his hair, but he proceeded unswervingly to a castle, for the hanging of General Steigmann. "I tell the General his mother has snitched on him," Milland said, "but he boasts that Hitlerite Germany will rise again. I knock him to the floor and take a vial of poison from a scar on his cheek, for Themis Delisle has revealed his last and most dramatic secret. Steigmann confesses his guilt, and Themis returns to France to defend herself, but she leaves with the promise that a certain brilliant young American lawyer—me—will be fighting on her team." Milland beckoned to the man with the comb. "Now," he concluded belligerently, "I'd like to see the Thomas Committee find anything in *that*."

Walter Wanger, head of Walter Wanger Pictures, Inc., maintains that the public has an unjustifiably poor opinion of Hollywood, and one day, trailing the inevitable publicity man, he took me to his studio commissary to tell me about the progress the industry has made since he got into it, twenty-five years ago. "In those days, we couldn't even have an unhappy ending," he said. "Today, pictures are different. Pictures have made great and wonderful contributions to the country and to the world." Wanger ordered coffee. Then he said that pictures had helped raise our standard of living, had encouraged understanding among men, and had, because of their merit and integrity, contributed to social progress. Wanger drank his coffee. I mentioned the last two Wanger pictures I had seen—*Arabian Nights* (love in a Baghdad harem) and *Canyon Passage* (Technicolor on the prairie). "I made those pictures because I wanted to be a success," Wanger replied. "If you want to stay in this business, if you want to make pictures that contribute to the country's welfare, you've got to make pictures that make money."

Some producers express the interesting point of view that there are no Communistic pictures, that there are only good pictures and bad pictures, and that most bad pictures are bad because writers write bad stories. "Writers don't apply themselves," I was informed by Jerry Wald, a thirty-six-year-old Warner Brothers producer, customarily described as a dynamo, who boasts that he makes twelve times as many pictures as the average producer in Hollywood. "Anatole France never sat down and said, 'Now, what did a guy write last year that I can copy this year?'" Wald assured me. "The trouble with pictures is they're cold. Pictures got to have emotion. You get emotion by doing stories on the temper of the times." The Congressional investigation, he said, would have no effect on his plans for this year's pictures on the temper of the times. These will include one on good government (with Ronald

Reagan), another about underpaid school teachers (with Joan Crawford), and an adaptation and modernization of Maxwell Anderson's *Key Largo* (with Humphrey Bogart, Lauren Bacall, Edward G. Robinson, and Lionel Barrymore). "Bogart plays an ejected liberal," Wald said, "a disillusioned soldier who says nothing is worth fighting for, until he learns there's a point where every guy must fight against evil." Bogart, who two or three months before had announced that his trip to Washington to protest against the methods of the Thomas Committee hearings had been a mistake, was very eager, Wald said, to play the part of an ejected liberal.

At Wald's suggestion, I had lunch one day with several members of the *Key Largo* cast, its director, John Huston, and a publicity representative at the Lakeside Golf Club, a favorite buffet-style eating place of stars on the nearby Warner lot. The actors were in a gay mood. They had just finished rehearsing a scene (one of the new economies at Warner is to have a week of rehearsals before starting to film a picture) in which Bogart is taunted by Robinson, a gangster representing evil, for his cowardice, but is comforted by the gangster's moll, who tells Bogart, "Never mind. It's better to be a live coward than a dead hero." Bogart had not yet reached the point where a guy learns he must fight against evil. Huston was feeling particularly good, because he had just won a battle with the studio to keep in the film some lines from Franklin Roosevelt's message to the Seventy-seventh Congress on January 6, 1942: "But we of the United Nations are not making all this sacrifice of human effort and human lives to return to the kind of world we had after the last world war."

"The big shots wanted Bogie to say this in his own words," Huston explained, "but I insisted that Roosevelt's words were better."

Bogart nodded. "Roosevelt was a good politician," he said. "He could handle those babies in Washington, but they're too smart for guys like me. Hell, I'm no politician. That's what I meant when I said our Washington trip was a mistake."

"Bogie has succeeded in not being a politician," said Huston, who went to Washington with him. "Bogie owns a fifty-four-foot yawl. When you own a fifty-four-foot yawl, you've got to provide for her upkeep."

"The Great Chief died and everybody's guts died with him," Robinson said, looking stern.

"How would you like to see *your* picture on the front page of the Communist paper of Italy?" asked Bogart.

"Nyah," Robinson said, sneering.

"The *Daily Worker* runs Bogie's picture and right away he's a dangerous Communist," said Miss Bacall, who is, as everybody must know, Bogart's wife. "What will happen if the American Legion and the Legion of Decency boycott all his pictures?"

"It's just that my picture in the *Daily Worker* offends me, Baby," said Bogart.

"Nyah," said Robinson. "Let's eat," said Huston.

After a while, Bogart began to complain about the iron curtain that separates the stars from the public. "There's only four rips," he said glumly, "four outlets through the iron curtain—Louella, Hedda, Jimmy, and Sheilah Graham. What can a guy do with only four rips?"

"Nyah," said Robinson.

Hollywood has various ideas about what the iron curtain is and where it is. Twentieth Century-Fox is making a picture called *The Iron Curtain*—about Communist spies' stealing atomic-bomb secrets in Canada—around which there is an iron curtain keeping visitors from everyone and everything connected with the picture. A Los Angeles newspaperman tried, unsuccessfully, to penetrate it. He was investigated by a man from Twentieth Century-Fox. A lady named Margaret Ettinger, who is generally credited with being "everybody's press agent" and who handles vaseline, diamonds, and Atwater Kent as well as many movie and radio stars, says there is an iron curtain around Louella Parsons. "Louella is my cousin, but I have a tougher time breaking into her column than into Hedda's," she says. Sheilah Graham, whose syndicated column appears locally in the Hollywood *Citizen-News*, in writing a few weeks ago about a certain star's red sweater and a certain singer's flashy red car, remarked that the color was still popular in Hollywood. The newspaper received a lot of letters calling Miss Graham a Communist. One of them suggested that an iron curtain be set up around *her*.

A few weeks ago, many people in Hollywood received through the mails a booklet called "Screen Guide for Americans," published by the Motion Picture Alliance for the Preservation of American Ideals and containing a list of "Do"s and "Don't"s. "This is the raw iron from which a new curtain around Hollywood will be fashioned," one man assured me solemnly. "This is the first step—not to fire people, not to get publicity, not to clean Communism out of motion pictures but to rigidly control all the contents of all pictures for Right Wing political purposes." The Motion Picture Association of America has not yet publicly adopted the "Screen Guide for Americans" in place of its own "A Code to Govern the Making of Motion and Talking Pictures," which advances such tenets as "The just rights, history, and feelings of any nation are entitled to consideration and respectful treatment" and "The treatment of bedrooms must be governed by good taste and delicacy." Although it is by no means certain that the industry has got around to following these old rules, either to the letter or in the spirit, there is a suspicion that it may have already begun at least to paraphrase some of the "Screen Guide's" pronouncements, which appear under such headings as "Don't Smear the Free Enterprise System," "Don't Deify the Common Man," "Don't Glorify the Collective," "Don't Glorify Failure," "Don't Smear Success," and "Don't Smear Industrialists." "All too often, industrialists, bankers, and businessmen are presented on the screen as villains, crooks, chiselers, or exploiters," the "Guide" observes. "It is the *moral* (no, not just political but *moral*) duty of every decent man in the motion picture industry to throw into the ashcan, where it belongs, every story that smears industrialists as such." Another admonition reads, "Don't give to your characters—as a sign of villainy, as a damning characteristic—a desire to make money." And another, "Don't permit any disparagement or defamation of personal success. It is the Communists' intention to make people think that personal success is somehow achieved at the expense of others and that every successful man has hurt somebody by becoming successful." The booklet warns, "Don't tell people that man is a helpless, twisted, drooling, sniveling, neurotic weakling. Show the world an *American* kind of man, for a change." The "Guide" instructs people in the industry, "Don't let yourself be fooled when the Reds tell you that what they want to destroy are men like Hitler and Mussolini. What they want to destroy are men like Shakespeare, Chopin, and Edison." Still another of the "Don't"s says, "Don't ever use any lines about 'the common man' or 'the little people.' It is not the American idea to be either 'common' or 'little.'" This despite the fact that Eric Johnston, testifying before the Thomas Committee, said, "Most of us in America are just little people, and loose charges can hurt little people." And one powerful man here has said to me, "We're not going to pay any attention to the Motion Picture Alliance for the Preservation of American Ideals. We *like* to talk about 'the little people' in this business."

I was given a copy of "Screen Guide for Americans" by Mrs. Lela Rogers, one of the founders of the Motion Picture Alliance for the Preservation of American Ideals. Mrs. Rogers, the mother of Ginger, is a pretty, blond-haired lady with a vibrant, birdlike manner. "A lot of people who work in pictures wouldn't know Communism if they saw it," she said to me. "You think that a Communist is a man with a bushy beard. He's not. He's an American, and he's pretty, too." The Congressional investigation of Hollywood, Mrs. Rogers thinks, will result in better pictures and the victory of the Republican Party in the next election. "Last month, I spoke about Communism at a ten-dollar-a-plate dinner given by the Republican Party," she said. "My goodness, I amassed a lot of money for the campaign. Now I have more speaking engagements than I can possibly fulfill." Mrs. Rogers is also writing screenplays. I wanted to know if she was following the "Do"s and "Don't"s of the "Screen Guide for Americans." "You just bet I am," she said. "My friend Ayn Rand wrote it, and sticking to it is easy as pie. I've just finished a shooting script about a man who learns how to live after he is dead."

Other people in the industry admit that they are following the "Guide" in scripts about the living. One man who is doing that assured me that he nevertheless doesn't need it, that it offers him nothing he didn't already know. "This is new only to the youngsters out here," he said. "They haven't had their profound intentions knocked out of them yet, or else they're still earning under five hundred a week. As soon as you become adjusted in this business, you don't need the 'Screen Guide' to tell you what to do." A studio executive in charge of reading scripts believes that Hollywood has a new kind of self-censorship. "It's automatic, like shifting gears," he explained. "I now read scripts through the eyes of the D.A.R., whereas formerly I read them through the eyes of my boss. Why, I suddenly find myself beating my breast and proclaiming my patriotism and exclaiming that I love my wife and kids, of which I have four, with a fifth on the way. I'm all loused up. I'm scared to death, and nobody can tell me it isn't because I'm afraid of being investigated."

William Wyler, who directed the Academy Award picture *The Best Years of Our Lives*, told me he is convinced that he could not make that picture today and that Hollywood will produce no more films like *The Grapes of Wrath* and *Crossfire*. "In a few months, we won't be able to have a heavy who is an American," he said. The scarcity of roles for villains has become a serious problem, particularly at studios specializing in Western pictures, where writers are being harried for not thinking up any new ones. "Can I help it if we're running out of villains?" a writer at one of these studios asked me. "For years I've been writing scripts about a Boy Scout-type cowboy in love with a girl. Their fortune and happiness are threatened by a banker holding a mortgage over their heads, or by a big landowner, or by a crooked sheriff. Now they tell me that bankers are out. Anyone holding a mortgage is out. Crooked public officials are out. All I've got left is a cattle rustler. What the hell am I going to do with a cattle rustler?"

Hollywood's current hypersensitivity has created problems more subtle than the shortage of heavies. *Treasure of Sierra Madre*, a film about prospecting for gold, was to have begun and ended with the subtitle "Gold, Mister, is worth what it is because of the human labor that goes into the finding and getting of it." The line is spoken by Walter Huston in the course of the picture. John Huston, who directed it, says that he couldn't persuade the studio to let the line appear on the screen. "It was all on account of the word 'labor,'" he told me. "That word looks dangerous in print, I guess." He paused, then added thoughtfully, "You can sneak it onto the soundtrack now and then, though." At a preview, in Hartford, Connecticut, of *Arch of Triumph*, attended by its director, Lewis Milestone, and by Charles Einfield, president of Enterprise Productions, which brought it out, the manager of the theater asked Einfield whether it was necessary to use the word "refugees" so often in the picture. "All the way back to New York," says Milestone, "Charlie kept muttering, 'Maybe we mention the word "refugees" too many times?' 'But the picture is *about* refugees,' I told him. 'What can we do now? Make a new picture?'"

A Msgr. Devlin, the Western representative of the Legion of Decency, has been on the set of *Joan of Arc*, which is being produced by Walter Wanger and stars Ingrid Bergman, since production started, and the services of a Father Doncoeur, of France, were enlisted shortly afterward. The director, Victor Fleming, who directed *Gone with the Wind*, said to me, "We've worked very closely with the Catholic Church, doing it the way they want it done. We want to be sure all these artists don't get a bum steer." I watched the shooting of a scene in which Miss Bergman, supposedly dying, lay on a prison bed of straw. The Bishop and the Earl of Warwick, her captors, leaned over her, and the Earl said, "She must not be allowed to die. Our King has paid too much for this sorceress to allow her to slip through our fingers." "Cut!" Fleming shouted. "Say that as if you *mean* it," he went on frantically. "She's *valuable property!* She must not be allowed to *die!* We have to finish the picture with her! This picture is costing three million dollars! Put more *feeling* into it! She must not be allowed to *die*, goddammit!" Just before the cameras were started up again, Fleming remarked, "*Gone with the Wind* was more fun than this. It cost about a million and a half more than *Joan*." Everything, apparently, used to be more fun.

Most producers stick firmly to the line that there is no Communism whatever in the industry and that there are no Communistic pictures. "We're going to make any kind of pictures we like, and nobody is going to tell us what to do," I was informed by Dore Schary, the R.K.O. vice-president and winner of the Golden Slipper Square Club's Humanitarian Award. He is a soft-spoken, unpretentious, troubled-looking man in his early forties, who might be regarded as one of Miss Hussey's "modern covered-wagon folks." In sixteen years, Schary pioneered from a $100-a-week job as a junior writer to his present position, which brings him around $500,000 a year. When he testified before the Thomas Committee, he said that R.K.O. would hire anyone it chose, solely on the basis of his talent, who had not been proved to be subversive. The R.K.O. Board of Directors met soon afterward and voted not to hire any known Communists. Schary then voted, like the other producers, to blacklist the ten men because they had been cited for contempt. He is talked about a good deal in Hollywood. Many of his colleagues are frequently critical of the course he has taken, and yet they understand why he has done what he's done. "I was faced with the alternative of supporting the stand taken by my company or of quitting my job," Schary told me. "I don't believe you should quit under fire. Anyway, I like making pictures. I want to stay in the industry. I like it." Schary is one of the few Hollywood executives who will talk to visitors without having a publicity man sit in on the conversation. "The great issue would have been joined if the ten men had only stood up and said whether or not they were Communists," he continued. "That's all they had to do. As it is, ten men have been hurt and nobody can be happy. We haven't done any work in weeks. Now is the time for all of us to go back to the business of making pictures, good pictures, in favor of anything we please." I asked Schary what he was planning to make this year. "I will assemble a list," he said. He assembled the following out of his memory, and I wrote them down: *Honored Glory* (in favor of honoring nine unknown soldiers), *Weep No More* (in favor of law and order), *Evening in Modesto* (also in favor of law and order), *The Boy with Green Hair* (in favor of peace), *Education of a Heart* (in favor of professional football), *Mr. Blandings Builds His Dream House* (in favor of Cary Grant), *The Captain Was a Lady* (in favor of Yankee clipper ships), *Baltimore Escapade* (in favor of a Protestant minister and his family having fun).

"Committee or no Committee," Schary said, "we're going to make all these pictures exactly the way we made pictures before."

Rush

May 28, 1949

ON THE TOWN, a forthcoming picture based on the recent musical about three sailors on twenty-four-hour liberty in New York, will have a smattering of local shots, and there's a chance we may turn up in some of them, thanks to our having spent a couple of hours one morning last week trailing after Gene Kelly, Jules Munshin, and Frank Sinatra, who play the three sailors. Kelly is not only acting and dancing in the picture but directing it, and it was at his suggestion that we joined Munshin and him at his suite in Hampshire House. They were both dressed in sailors white uniforms and had on a glowing sunburn makeup. Munshin sat gazing gloomily at a battered Navy white hat while Kelly stood at a window, apparently trying to stare down two small pink clouds. "We can't get started yet," Kelly said. "There won't be enough light for fifteen minutes." "I hope it rains," Munshin said. "Then I might get to see something of this town." "You went to the fights last night," Kelly said. "You don't care *how* you look in the morning." "Sinatra looks worse," Munshin said, with dour satisfaction. "The fans got hold of him outside Toots Shor's."

Kelly told us that his plan for that morning was to have the three sailors shot taking a ride on a Fifth Avenue bus and then looking around down at the Sub-Treasury Building. "I've already seen the Sub-Treasury Building," Munshin said. "I want to go see a ball game." Kelly sighed and went on to say that all the local scenes he was shooting would take up about three and a half minutes at the opening and closing of the picture. "But we're really covering the place," he said. "George Washington Bridge, Brooklyn Bridge, Mulberry Street, the R.C.A. Building, Grant's Tomb, Carnegie Hall, the Museum of Natural History, and Third Avenue. The other day, we took a walk through Central Park and saw some people riding horses, and we decided to get a shot of the three of us riding horses, instead of that old rowboat corn. Munshin did some fine acting on his horse." "I was not acting," Munshin said. "I am deathly afraid of horses." "We're doing a hell of a lot of work for three and a half minutes," Kelly said, "but I figure it's worth it."

We have to plan our shots like a Commando raid to get a good natural setting without crowds. We mask our camera in a station wagon and we hide in a car. Then we run out, take the shot, hop back in the car, and beat it." He stared once more at the sky and said, "O.K. The light's in. Let's go."

The three of us repaired by car to the corner of Fifth and Fifty-ninth, where we found a truck on which the top of an old open-top bus had been set up. A camera crew was stationed at the front end, where about half the seats were occupied by extras. A patrol car appeared, and a group of onlookers quickly gathered around us on the sidewalk. "Where's Sinatra?" Kelly asked. "Hiding in the Park," said a young man, taking a small metronome from his pocket. "The time on this is a hundred and sixteen beats to the minute," he added. "The song we're singing goes 'New York, New York, it's a wonderful town,'" Kelly told us. "We've got a horn up there to play the song for us. The real soundtrack is back in Hollywood. The song used to go 'New York, New York, it's a Hell-uv-a town,' but of course we had to change it." He looked at the crowd. "I'll die, standing up there yelling in front of all those people," he said. One of the onlookers stepped up to him and said, "I'm sorry to worry you, Mr. Kelly, but Fifth Avenue doesn't have open-top buses any more." "This picture is timeless," Kelly told him. Sinatra suddenly appeared and hustled to the top of the bus, followed by Kelly and Munshin. Off went the truck-bus down the Avenue, preceded by the patrol car and followed by us, in a car with a makeup man, who said to us, "When I get home, I'm going prospecting in the desert for uranium."

After several trips up and down stretches of Fifth Avenue, the strange motorcade returned to Fifty-ninth Street. Sinatra ran for a car, shouting, "Into the Park, quick!" We joined Kelly and Munshin in another car. "We sneak down to Broad and Wall Streets now," Kelly said. "Get this, Munshin. We run up the steps of the Sub-Treasury Building and look at the statue of George Washington. Please try to act interested." "I am interested," Munshin said. "These sailors' uniforms are wonderful," Kelly said. "They're cut absolutely right. They're perfect to dance in." Down at the Sub-Treasury Building, we were met by a red-faced cameraman, who complained, "Look! I got all sunburned waiting for you." Sinatra soon turned up, and the three sailors ran up and down the steps of the Sub-Treasury Building until Kelly was satisfied with the shots. By that time, a crowd the size of a bond rally had gathered. Kelly regarded it benignly. "This is like dancing in a theater," he said, "I like it. There's nothing to equal the impetus you get from a couple of thousand eyes watching you, instead of a bunch of electricians. It makes you feel like a round actor again." "Maybe we could see a show tonight," Munshin said. "Nothing doing," Kelly told him. "We've got to get up early tomorrow morning and go down and look at the Statue of Liberty."

# Feeling Lost

February 17, 1950

Charlie Chaplin has been spending a few days at the Plaza, and we found him in his suite there, handing soiled laundry to a maid. The first words we heard him speak were "*Here's* a very dirty shirt." He looked in fine shape—pink-cheeked, with pure-white hair, bristling white eyebrows, and freckled hands. The problem of the laundry left him slightly distraught, and as soon as the maid departed, he turned around once or twice, in a sort of dance, then motioned us to a chair and lighted on the edge of a couch. Mrs. Chaplin came in from the next room to say that she was going shopping, and Chaplin asked her to pick up a couple of hundred dollars for him. "I don't like to cash checks at the desk in the lobby," he told us, after Mrs. Chaplin left. "At the same time, I hate to slash into a place with no money at all. It makes me feel lost." He gazed thoughtfully at a toy on a nearby table. "There's something I got for the kids," he said. "I have three from the age of four down, besides the two grown boys, Charles, Jr., and Sydney. They're both actors. Sydney is a good comedian, whimsical, with an excellent lilt, and he has size and stature. For one thing, he's over six feet. But I'm not sending *him* the toy. You put in the penny..." Chaplin searched his pockets. "There's me—haven't a cent," he said. "Anyhow, you put in a penny and out comes a colored ball of chewing gum. My kids love chewing gum. This toy will be wonderful for them. I found it yesterday, along Forty-Second Street. There was this little squashed-in place, with the toy in the window. There was a toy for chocolates, too, but I wasn't sure about giving the children chocolate."

Chaplin told us he has been walking around town a lot, to take the place of tennis, which is how he gets his exercise at home. "The other day, I walked all up and down Tenth Avenue, and I loved it," he said. "But, oh, the dirt and the ash cans!" He sat silent a moment, and then suggested that we go downstairs and have lunch. The two of us adjourned to the restaurant, where, walking just like Charlie Chaplin, Chaplin led the way to a table by a window. He sat down and looked at Central Park. It was snowing. "What beautiful snow!" Chaplin said. "I remember sitting here in this room, just like this, in the winter of 1916, after my first success. I registered as Charles Spencer—Spencer's my middle name—and I stayed here because I didn't know any other place where you could dine. The police had sent me word on the train that I wasn't to go in to Grand Central, because of the crowds waiting to see me there, so I had to get off at 125th Street—and all I was coming here for was to look for a job."

Chaplin said that he hoped in the course of his current visit to find a leading lady for a movie he's planning to make, but that he didn't know how to go about finding her. "I see shows and interview a certain number of people, out of a sense of duty, but all the people I've found I've always found by luck," he said. "This new role is a very difficult one. The girl will have to be able to act *and* dance ballet. I said something about the role a while ago, jokingly, and it came out in one of the gossip columns that I was looking for a person who could act like Duse and dance like Pavlova, and some agent called me up and said, 'I've got her!'—really quite humorlessly. I'm going to see the poor dear after lunch."

Chaplin said, over lunch, that it had taken him two years to prepare the script of his new movie, that he had composed the music for it, and that he will, as usual, direct it, produce it, and act the leading role. He's anxious to get it under way as quickly as possible. "I can't afford to wait too long on it, because I use my own money," he said. "I don't want to say much about it, but I've poured my guts into the script and I mean it to be the best thing I've ever done." His role will be different from the roles he played in his early films and from his role in *Monsieur Verdoux*, which he considers his best work. "I lost money on that one," he said. "The people who came to see me came to see the funny man. They were shocked. They couldn't adjust. They wanted to know where the big shoes were." Though *Monsieur Verdoux* was a failure in this country, it won several prizes elsewhere, including the Danish equivalent of an Oscar.

Chaplin recalled that when he entered the movies, in 1913, his contract called for three pictures a week. They used to make a picture in half a day then. Chaplin told us that he acts without any conscious intellectual activity. "All you feel while you're acting is ebullience," he said. "You intellectualize when you go into the projection room and say, 'Now, why isn't that funny?' When you get older, you know how to approach humor. The best definition of humor I ever heard is that it's getting people in and out of trouble. That's what I try to do. I'm emotional about most things but objective about my work. I don't get satisfaction out of it, I get relief." Chaplin said he doesn't have time for much of anything besides his work and his family. "I live in my very secure house of cards," he said. "I'm a self-educated man and don't get everything I'd like to get out of reading. Oh, maybe I browse through my Burton's *Anatomy of Melancholy*, but I leave most of the reading to my wife. Besides, I've an odd quirk in my sight. I see only the first word and the last in a line on a page. Must be something psychological in that, don't you think?" A man hurried up, whispered something in Chaplin's ear, and hurried away. "That's the girl's agent," he said, as we got up to go. "This will be very embarrassing. I never know what to say to them. Usually, you know, I just look at them from a distance."

## Mr. Hulot

July 17, 1954

THE FRENCH COMEDIAN Jacques Tati, whom we make no bones about calling one of the funniest men alive, was in town briefly for the opening of his movie, *Mr. Hulot's Holiday*. As was the case with his previous movie success, *Jour de Fête*, M. Tati is not only the star of the picture but also its author and director. We called on this great benefactor of humanity one warm afternoon recently and found him perplexed in the extreme by the air-conditioning of his hotel suite. He had on a blue-and-white striped sports shirt and a heavy topcoat. "My first experience of your winter-in-summer machines," he said in admirable English, fingering his topcoat and shivering. "I do not yet understand the principle. You take off your coat when you go outside and you put on your coat when you come inside. *Bien!* But where is the gain?" M. Tati is well over two yards tall and looks taller. He has broad shoulders, long arms, and big hands, and wears an expression of perpetual pleased surprise. No sooner had we sat down than he volunteered to show us a snapshot of his two children—Sophie, who is seven, and Pierre, who is five. "They are simple and honest," he said with a father's pride.

While Tati and his wife were in New York, their children stayed at Tati's father's house in Saint-Germain-en-Laye, a suburb of Paris. Tati was born a few miles from there, in Le Pecq, in 1908. His real name is Jacques Tatischeff, and if he liked, he could call himself a count. His grandfather, Count Dimitri Tatischeff, an attaché of the Russian Embassy in Paris, married a Frenchwoman. On Tati's maternal side, his grandmother was Italian and his grandfather was Dutch. This man, van Hoof by name, ran a picture-framing shop in Paris and numbered among his customers Toulouse-Lautrec and van Gogh. On more than one occasion, van Gogh offered to pay his bill with some of his paintings, but canny old van Hoof held out for cash. Tati's father took over the business, and Tati, at sixteen, was sent to a college of arts and engineering to prepare him for a prosperous picture-framing future. After a year's fumbling with more mathematics than he knew what to do with, Tati gave up college, and his father bundled him off to London, to serve as an apprentice to an English framer. He boarded with a family whose son, also seventeen, had a passion for rugby, and in six months Tati learned much English, much Rugby, and very little picture framing. "Rugby is not a gentle game," he told us. "Sometimes the players hurt each other quite badly, and afterward they wish to be friendly again, so they have dinner together and try to make one another laugh. I used to imitate the way Rugby players look during a game. Everyone would laugh at me, and I was encouraged to start imitating people playing tennis and other sports. My friends said, 'Why not go into the music halls?' I went back to Paris and told my father I wanted to quit picture framing and do imitations. You can imagine his anger. He said at last that I could do as I pleased but he wouldn't give me a sou."

Young Tati's specialty was so peculiar that not an impresario in Paris would look at him. "For years, I was broke," Tati said. "I slept every night in a different place. I sat in cafés and talked with friends, and when I needed to eat, I would go to a certain cabaret and imitate a drunken waiter who is constantly making mistakes. For an evening of supposedly drunken waiting, I would be given my dinner and fifty francs. It was the happiest and most free time I have ever known." Tati got his big break in 1934, when a friend arranged for him to appear on a program at the Ritz with Chevalier and Mistinguett. "I was so frightened that though I was supposed to go on first, I couldn't stand or talk," Tati said. "I hid in a corner backstage and the show started without me. When it was over and the people were leaving, the manager of the show saw me hiding in the corner. He ran out on the stage and shouted that one of the entertainers had been forgotten. Then he introduced me. The people returned to their seats and I had to go on. The next thing I knew, I heard them laughing. I could not imagine that they were laughing at me. I looked around for the entertainer they were laughing at. No one else was onstage. It had to be me. Soon they were applauding and shouting, and the manager was shaking my hand. Then came the impresarios, and I was playing in music halls and circuses all over Europe."

This was Tati's first visit to the United States. He was scheduled to play at the Radio City Music Hall in 1939 but wound up in the French infantry instead. He attended several baseball games in the course of his visit and plans to add a baseball pantomime to his sports act. It took him a year and a half to make *Jour de Fête* and as long to make *Mr. Hulot's Holiday*, and he is only just beginning to think about a new movie. His favorite comedian is an English music-hall performer named Little Tich, whom he saw when he was seven. The comedian who makes him laugh most is the late W. C. Fields.

He admires Chaplin, but for the most part Chaplin doesn't make him laugh. "Chaplin is full of ideas," Tati said. "I am so busy watching the working out of his beautiful ideas that I never find time to laugh."

In Charge

March 30, 1963

WE HAD A pleasant lunch the other day with that master maker of movie thrillers, Alfred Hitchcock, who had come to town for the opening of his latest picture, *The Birds*. A dapper, roly-poly little man of sixty-three who when he walks appears to be on casters and when seated holds himself plumply erect, like a benign Cockney Buddha, Mr. Hitchcock has a rosy dome, rosy cheeks and dewlaps, small, merry brown eyes, and a pursed, protuberant mouth, out of which proceeds, in a gravelly, urgent, mocking voice, an effortless flow of polished reminiscence. For Mr. Hitchcock isn't only a great director; he is also a performer, vocal as well as visible on TV and at least fugitively visible in each of his pictures. "I even turned up in *Last Year at Marienbad*," he told us. "The director, Alain Resnais, is an old friend of mine, and he was eager to provide a glimpse of me in his charming nightmare. I was a blurred profile in one of the corridor scenes, but I daresay most people were far too busy admiring the baroque moldings along the ceiling to notice me."

A famous trencherman and wine lover (at lunch, we freshened our palates with Dom Pérignon, then advanced with deliberation to melon, a well-done outside cut of roast pork loin, asparagus, and black coffee), Mr. Hitchcock told us he has an adequate cellar at his place in California. "My wife and I had a bottle of Cheval Blanc '45 one evening last week," he said. "It has reached an excellent point in its career. I like wines that last, that keep their bloom, *I* mean to keep blooming for decades. We live very quietly, a long way up the coast from Hollywood. We have two hundred acres overlooking Monterey Bay. No swimming pool. No parties. We see as much as we can of our daughter, our son-in-law, and three grandchildren. François Truffaut spent some time with us recently. He's taking a year off from his movie work to write a book about me. Claude Chabrol wrote a book about me several years ago. I'm what one might call the *doyen* of the *nouvelle vague*. Oh dear! I hate to be the *doyen* of anything; it makes me sound much older than I feel. I think they admire the way I manage to express an idea by putting two little bits of film next to each other. Most movies are just pictures of people telling stories. My movies are the pictures telling stories. Truffaut is a most remarkable director, but I keep warning him to be careful; he isn't making pictures for a single street, by which I mean the Champs-Elysées, but for the world. The movies are the only art form that is truly global. I like to think of my pictures' being able to convey the same thing to different audiences in cities and towns and villages all over the earth. Extraordinary, to have the power to make those millions of unseen people laugh or cry out of fear! I must say I enjoy being in charge of people's emotions."

Mr. Hitchcock directed his first picture in 1925, in London, after serving a couple of years' apprenticeship with UFA in Berlin. He gained fame the following year with a movie version of Mrs. Belloc Lowndes' novel *The Lodger*. "That picture created a sensation," he told us. "It was something absolutely new. Intellectuals in England have always been fascinated by crime; they love thrillers. Wells, Galsworthy, and all that sort of people became fans of mine. Shaw was very keen about my work. My first success in this country was *The 39 Steps*. Then, I suppose, *The Lady Vanishes*. Among my biggest hits have been *Notorious*, *Rope*, *Rear Window*, and *Psycho*. I've made only fifty pictures all told, which isn't so many over a period of thirty-eight years. My favorite picture is *Shadow of a Doubt*, with Joseph Cotten and Teresa Wright. The screenplay was by Thornton Wilder. As far as I know, it's the only screenplay he ever wrote. We weren't quite sure how to start the picture, and Thornton said, 'Well, there's this short story by Hemingway where a man is lying in bed in the dark, waiting to be killed.' I, who fear being influenced by anyone in my work, was astonished that a great writer should not be afraid of another writer's influence. We didn't use that beginning, but we were very relaxed. I believe in keeping calm as I believe in blooming. Do have another drop of champagne."

# Reasons of the Eye

February 13, 1965

OUR MAN STANLEY rushed into the office, a sixteen-millimeter Arriflex on one shoulder and a Nagra synchronized sound recorder under his left arm, and declared that he had just finished shooting a movie—fifteen thousand feet of film—featuring his typewriter, uncovered and motionless, without him at it. He informed us that it was a highly charged portrait of The Writer, 1965, and assured us that although he would have to stay with his Moviola for a while, he had no intention of abandoning the written word. To prove it, he presented us with the following notes:

"Enrolled in course called 'The Visual Nature of the Film Medium,' given by Slavko Vorkapich, Mondays at 8 p.m. at Museum of Modern Art. Forty dollars for ten lecture-seminars. Real bargain. About same price as twelve hundred feet of black-and-white raw stock. Getting Vorkapich as teacher almost like getting Eisenstein. With-It people know Vorkapich born in Yugoslavia, March 17, 1895; studied painting in Paris; emigrated to New York in 1920; emigrated to Hollywood in 1921; made experimental film *The Life and Death of a Hollywood Extra*, with miniatures, on kitchen table, in 1928; created montage sequences for *Crime Without Passion* (1934), *Viva Villa!* (1934), *David Copperfield* (1935), *A Tale of Two Cities* (1935), *The Good Earth* (1937), *Test Pilot* (1938), etc. First lecture listed in syllabus as 'Introduction: The Eye Has Its Reasons.' At Museum, few minutes before eight, found big mob of fellow-students pushing into auditorium in basement. Latched onto seat in rear, practically last of four hundred eighty seats in auditorium, beside eager, studious-looking young man wearing steel-rimmed spectacles. Young man introduced himself as Hamilton. 'Over-subscribed!' he said, and pursed lips. Heard crowd outside clamoring to get in.

"Next to Hamilton, attractive young woman with big eyes, hair wound around head in braid, said, 'Andy Warhol got in. Herman Weinberg got in. His daughter *Gretchen* Weinberg got in.'

"'Meet Miss Ataner,' Hamilton said, nodding at young lady. 'Miss Ataner played in *Scorpio Rising*.'

"'A bit part.' Miss Ataner said. 'I sat on a hot stove?'

"'Meet Mr. Rozam,' Hamilton said, indicating dark, brooding young man on other side of Miss Ataner. 'And let me study the syllabus.'

"'I'm probably the only one here who doesn't even *want* to make a movie,'

Mr. Rozam said.

"'E. G. Marshall is sitting in the front row,' Miss Ataner said.

"Looked audience over. Very young. Average age of members somewhere in twenties. Most dressed same way they dressed in college. Many girls wearing black boots, black stockings. Many young men wearing pullover sweaters over white shirts open at collar. A few stony-faced, bearded disciples of Jonas Mekas, cinematic avant-avant-gardist. Looked over Hamilton's shoulder at syllabus. Read, under heading 'Lecture 1,' 'Unawareness of the visual-dynamic forces at work within every shot and every sequence of shots often leads to undesirable effects, unintentional ambiguities, absurdities.... Knowledge and mastery of visual-dynamic principles lends to greater clarity and force of presentation, and eventually to the development of the film as a truly independent form of art.'

"Up front, as screen was adjusted, Richard Griffith, curator of Museum's film library, came forward, looking distraught. Outsiders still protesting. Griffith introduced Vorkapich quickly (said Vorkapich would reexamine visual nature of film in this first lecture), then disappeared. Vorkapich looked like Mr. Chips. Nice. Mild, un-dramatic voice. Like good movie, lost no time getting going. Said he would start by telling anecdote about himself at beginning of film career—around time sound came in. Told how producer of film about chorus girl asked him to shoot scene of her walking and dreaming of seeing her name in bright lights. Shot took long time to set up, lot of work, lot of money. Had to build track for dolly, so that camera could follow girl walking. 'And the cameraman wanted good lighting on her face, because she was a star in *real* life,' Vorkapich said. Lot of laughs in audience. Laughs knowledgeable. Vorkapich told how shot was failure. 'That beautifully lighted face was bobbing up and down, swaying from side to side, but the way the shot came out, the girl did not seem to be *walking*,' he said. 'My shot was a failure. When I think of all that work, all that time for the dolly! But I did not understand the principle of induced motion: If a stationary object is shown against a moving background, the object appears to be moving and the background seems to be stationary. In most dolly shots, the distance between the moving camera and a moving object is kept constant; if the object moves against a homogeneous background, the movement of the object is canceled by the movement of the camera.'

"Overheard shaggy-mustached fellow in row behind me say, 'About time somebody gave it to them!' Asked Hamilton, Miss Ataner, Mr. Rozam for explanation. In row in front of ours, young girl in Mod getup turned around, said sternly, 'Rift between underground know-nothings and people who want to make *movies!*' Hamilton admonished Miss Ataner, Mr. Rozam, me to take notes.

"Onstage, Vorkapich took drink of water, said he would now show examples of canceled motions, including some weak spots in work of masters. 'Don't think I'm condemning the whole film, though,' he said. 'I just want to show you some things about the film language. It's like learning the English language the right and wrong ways to construct a sentence. Our language is a *recent* language, whereas the English language has been around for a long time.' Examples of lack of complete mastery of visual language then shown on screen: Gary Cooper in *High Noon*, filmed against a clear sky; Gary Cooper supposed to be walking, but only bobbing up and down. Then he showed scene of Gary Cooper walking on street, passing houses close by. Not bobbing. *Walking.* Then scene of Paul Muni walking in fields, frame showing ground under Paul Muni's feet. Not bobbing. *Walking.* Then same shot blown up so that only enlarged closeup of Paul Muni shown, without ground, against distant hill. 'Distant background will not help,' Vorkapich said. Now Paul Muni bobbing, *not* walking. 'See how we get the essence of a thing,' Vorkapich said. 'The essence of walking is progression. Now watch carefully.' On screen, enlarged Paul Muni without ground seen bobbing up and down, same as previous bobbing. Shot was then zoomed away, revealing Muni walking backward, film running backward. Audience applauded. 'Applause!' Mr. Rozam said. 'I thought these people were supposed to be *cool!*' Miss Ataner said, 'My God, he's making Andy Warhol sit still!'

"Vorkapich now saying he would take up most elementary level of filmmaking—treatment of static shots. Said he would read from Wolfgang Köhler's book *Gestalt Psychology.* Read, 'Under appropriate conditions successive presentation of two lights at two points not too distant from each other results in an experience of movement.' Assistant hung rope down middle of screen, marked areas it divided A and B. On mobile blackboard, Vorkapich wrote 'PHI.' Then he explained that perceptual phenomenon known as Phi phenomenon creates illusion of motion. Said, 'When you deal with a film, you deal with a world of illusion of reality and illusion of magic reality.' On screen, projected roll of paper toweling, first in Area A, then in Area B. Ran A-B-A-B quickly, giving illusion of roll jumping hack and forth. Hamilton, Miss Ataner, Mr. Rozam, and Mod girl looked impressed. Vorkapich read from another book, *Principles of Gestalt Psychology*, by K. Koffka: 'In stroboscopic motion, one process fuses with another process, and that even when the two processes are different in respect of color, size, and shape.' Then he showed more examples from movies: Monica Vitti and another girl in *L'Avventura* shown talking from front. Monica Vitti in Area B, looking to her left. Cut to shot from back. Monica Vitti in wrong place, looking to her right. 'Disorienting,' Vorkapich said. 'The perception to the innocent eye is a moment of confusion. The lesson is don't try to make beautiful compositions alone without thinking how they will combine with the preceding and succeeding shots. It's like using a word in a poem. We have taken the liberty of reversing the shot so that the girl would remain in the proper place and facing in the proper direction. Watch.' Showed reversal. 'Is it convincing, do you think?' he asked. More applause from audience. Miss Ataner said, 'Andy Warhol is leaving. The Weinbergs are staying.' Vorkapich showed example—this one from *Breathless*—of people getting out of position because of angle change. Then scene cut to Belmondo laughing, as if laughing at Godard's mistake. Audience dug joke. Laughed. 'When in this kind of an angle-change trouble, use the Western principle,' Vorkapich said. 'Cut away to the horse.' Hamilton, Miss Ataner, Mr. Rozam, Mod girl taking notes.

"Griffith reappeared onstage, said now there would be a question period. 'We did not expect so large a group,' he added. 'Any questions?' Girl rose. Asked if showing movie examples of faults out of context distorted film. Vorkapich said no—faults were still there. 'It's like getting the language wrong,' he said. 'It's like constructing a sentence that reads, "Walking briskly, she stood in the middle of the road."'

"Lecture-seminar continued with more scenes from famous movies—faulty scenes, also great scenes, illustrating how to put Phi phenomenon to creative use. Vorkapich showed a sequence from *High Noon*—series of shots, all stationary, all same length: Cooper watching clock, bad men waiting, Grace Kelly worrying. Series of cuts effectively created feeling of waiting, of tension. Clarity helps a film to become art, Vorkapich explained. 'We're just at the beginning,' he said. 'There's much to be done.'

"At end of session, conferred with fellow-students. Formed film company called HARS—for Hamilton, Ataner, Rozam & Stanley. Much to be done."

# Godard Est Godard

October 9, 1965

EXTÉRIEUR: Philharmonic Hall. End-of-summer twilight. Long shot reveals people hurrying toward Hall, across open plaza with fountain—singles and couples. Closeup of poster near fountain reading, "3rd New York Film Festival." Closeups of singles and couples hanging around fountain, eying each other carefully, nervously, grimly. Many girls alone, wearing tight-fitting pants. Many young men alone, wearing tight-fitting pants. Some sloppy, intellectual-looking types regarding everybody else with hatred. Some Festivalgoers greeting each other with exaggerated exuberance, false friendliness, and making references to Cannes, Berlin, and Venice. Twilight deepens. Taxi draws up to curb. Slightly built man in his mid-thirties gets out of taxi in leisurely way and pays driver, taking a loose bill from his pocket. He is wearing a dark suit, white shirt, knit tie, moccasins, and horn-rimmed glasses with slightly tinted lenses. His face is completely immobile as he calmly takes his time about examining change he gets from taxi-driver. His face in closeup reveals eyes, behind glasses, likewise devoid of expression. Hand-held camera follows young man as he moves away from curb, walking toward Philharmonic Hall, paying no attention to other Festivalgoers, many of whom stare at him and start talking, in an effort to be overheard by him: "Jean-Luc Godard... Jean-Luc Godard... Jean-Luc Godard... *Breathless*... Brilliant technique... *Vivre Sa Vie*... Genius... Golden Bear Award... Innovator... Sexual liberation... *A Woman Is a Woman*... Anna Karina... Jean-Paul Belmondo... *Cahiers du Cinéma*... *The Married Woman*... Jean-Luc Godard... Jean-Luc Godard... Jean-Luc Godard."

INTÉRIEUR: The lobby of Philharmonic Hall. Hand-held camera goes through revolving door with young man. We see his image multiplied by glass in revolving door. Camera plays for a while with other images seen in glass of revolving door, then reveals distorted image, in glass of revolving door, that emerges as a derby-hatted dwarf clutching copy of *Cahiers du Cinéma*. Camera plays a while longer with revolving door, now seen upside down. Festivalgoers seen upside down. Finally, hand-held camera hurries to catch up to young man, showing him from rear. Camera somewhat shaky, but no matter. All part of technique. Camera shows Festivalgoers pawing over movie-literature table set up in lobby. Copies of *Films in Review*, *Films*

*& Filming*, *Film Quarterly*. Derby-hatted dwarf reading *Films in Review*. Ready now for inside jokes. Closeup of montage of scenes from films *Breathless*, *Vivre Sa Vie*, *The Married Woman*, and *Contempt*. Cut to closeup of the married woman's nude back from *The Married Woman*. Cut to closeup of a woman's hand, rings on fingers, paging through *Films in Review* on lobby table. Closeup of woman's forefinger and thumb turning page showing sexy scene from *Vivre Sa Vie* to reveal page showing sexy scene from *Breathless*. Camera shows literature-examiners quickly turning from literature and following young man. Dwarf runs after him, his face immobile, too. Hand-held camera accompanies young man up escalator, focusses on his face, still immobile, his eyes showing nothing, nothing at all, in the way of reaction to what is around him. Camera shoots young man on escalator from a few steps above him, showing faces of young men and women below him regarding him with adoration. Then camera shoots from a few steps below him on escalator, showing heads turned down toward him, regarding him with what looks from this angle like even more profound adoration. Camera zooms in on metal steps of escalator, showing feet of Festivalgoers. Lots of sandals. Black boots. Courrèges-type white boots. Space shoes. A woman's bare feet. The young man's moccasins. The woman's bare feet move in on the moccasins. One bare foot brushes one moccasin. Cut to young man's face. Immobile. Still cool. Sound now gets louder and louder. The click-click-click of the escalator, which had started as barely audible, now becomes louder and more insistent. Very metallic.

INTÉRIEUR: The seats in the Hall. Young man is not to be seen. Camera, still hand-held, moves jumpily along rows of seats. Faces upturned. Very little buzzing. Several middle-aged and elderly ladies in each row, among grim-faced pants-wearers. Some obvious celebrities in audience. One young woman wearing transparent black lace tights and matching top, escorted by foppish young man. All they do is look, look, look. Many young men in audience wearing sweaters instead of shirts and jackets.

INTÉRIEUR: The stage. The Hall becomes dark. Long shot from rear of Hall shows darkness blacking out backs of heads of audience. Now shown as black silhouettes—all the same—looking up at stage, at rectangular white screen. Then total blackness. Spotlight on stage. Man walks into spotlight, announces the opening of the Third New York Film Festival, says he is happy that the Festival will open with the showing of *Alphaville*, directed by Jean-Luc Godard. Man says that Jean-Luc Godard is with them tonight in person. "Jean-Luc... Godard!" he announces. Young man whom hand-held camera has been following steps into spotlight. Big ovation from audience. Prolonged. Devoted. Strong.

Godard's *Alphaville* is projected on screen, and as it starts, camera zooms back from stage. Over blurring heads of audience, still applauding enthusiastically, we at last see title of *this* movie:

GODARD EST GODARD

Now, after credits, movie finally gets going.


INTÉRIEUR: Godard's hotel room. The young director, wearing same suit and tie but this time a shirt with stripes, is sitting on sofa, sipping tea with cream and eating buttered toast. He is wearing the moccasins. He is wearing the tinted glasses. He is watching a television set, which is turned on with picture but without sound. The picture is of one of those afternoon game shows ceremoniously conducted by an overly cheerful m.c. Closeup of Godard's face; the upper half, over the rim of the teacup, reveals absolutely no expression in the eyes behind the glasses as he watches the m.c. Seated on a straight-backed chair, her back to the window, and facing Godard, is a very serious-looking woman, a French Film Office aide, dressed seriously in a black dress. She converses with Godard in English.

WOMAN: This evening you are scheduled to participate in a panel discussion at the Film Festival.

GODARD (*without changing his expression or looking away from the television screen*): Yes. (*He speaks in a soft voice, without expression.*)

WOMAN: The panel discussions are called "Film '65." Some of the topics are "Do We Need a New Film Criticism?," "Style, Content, and the Plotless Film," "Film and the Good Society." They are being held in a new auditorium near Philharmonic Hall, at Lincoln Center. There will be film critics seated with you on the panel. Perhaps you have heard of these film critics? Parker Tyler? Pauline Kael? Andrew Sarris? Hollis Alpert? (*She pauses after each name, and after each pause Godard nods affirmatively at the television set.*) There will be a young American director, James Ivory, on the panel, and the moderator will be Arthur Knight. He used to be a full-time film critic, but now he has graduated to a job as a kind of professor in California.

GODARD: I have heard there are many such professors of films in California now. Why do they not make Adolfas Mekas a professor of films in California? I saw his picture *Hallelujah the Hills*. It is a marvellous picture.

WOMAN: Yes, it would be nice if they made Adolfas Mekas a professor, the way Arthur Knight is a professor. (*Her face goes as blank as Godard's.*) You do not mind appearing in a panel discussion with our film critics?

GODARD: I am used to doing it. There is a television program in France called *The Mask and the Pen*. It is taped, in the afternoon, in a theater. Mostly old ladies are in the audience. We discuss Eisenstein. Or they ask me questions about my movies. On the panel are the French critics: Georges Sadoul; Claude Mauriac, of *Figaro Littéraire*; Pierre Marcabru and Jean-Louis Bory, of *Arts*. The critics like to talk about the meaning of my movies. I go each time I make a movie. The more I'm getting older, the more I'm getting interested in what people have to say about my movies. Also, it makes publicity for each new movie. Of the ten movies I have made these past seven years, only three made money—*Breathless*, *Vivre Sa Vie*, and *The Married Woman*.

WOMAN: Yesterday, at the Festival, do you remember the young man who was wearing blue jeans who asked you for your autograph? I forgot to tell you he is a student at the University of Minnesota. He told me your autograph brings ten dollars there.

GODARD: Yes. I have heard the kids in America say about *Breathless* that it was for the first time they are seeing their own life in a picture. It is of their own kind.

WOMAN: But do you really want to know what people in the audiences say about your pictures?

GODARD (*coolly and tonelessly, after taking a sip of tea*): In my pictures now, I am more and more improvising, and so I don't always know what I have done in the picture. But if I shot a tree, and if people are telling me it's a tree, then I know it's a tree. My new picture, *Pierrot le Fou*, got rather bad reviews at the Venice Film Festival. Afterward, I showed the picture to François Truffaut.

WOMAN: Your closest friend from your *Cahiers du Cinéma* days.

GODARD (*with a small smile*): I don't know if we're friends, but we're very close. He said it's a startling film, and he said, "I hope everybody doesn't start to make movies like this, because then I'll have to give up making movies."

WOMAN: But Truffaut wrote *me* that the picture was superb. He said it reaches new heights of improvisation.

GODARD: I'm not sure. I might have gone too far in working by instinct. I'm happy I'm still a critic. I still write for *Cahiers du Cinéma*. I will always be a critic. I will never stop being a critic. Next month, I go to Sweden to prepare my next picture, based on two de Maupassant short stories—"Paul's Mistress" and "The Signal." I'm doing the adaptations myself. The picture will be produced by the Svensk Film Industri, which has produced all the Ingmar Bergman pictures since 1957. While I am in Sweden, I will interview Ingmar Bergman for *Cahiers du Cinéma*.

WOMAN: How do you feel about making a new picture?

GODARD: I feel in danger each time when I am going to make a picture. I never feel safe while making the picture. When I get into the editing room to edit my picture, then I feel safe at last. I always feel safe there.

WOMAN: Do you see many movies?

GODARD: I go to the movies at least ten times a week. I like to go to movies. I like to see people move. (*Camera has been cutting back and forth in closeup from Godard's face to the woman's. Now it pans briefly to the television screen, which is still silent. Over the picture of contestants on the television screen we hear Godard's voice continuing.*) I saw *Darling* last night. It is a very bad picture. It is a Vicki Baum story, a Daphne du Maurier story, a very bad picture. If a picture is a bad picture, I go to sleep watching it. There are three types of bad pictures: one, pictures like *Darling*, which don't affect me at all; two, like *Zorba the Greek*, which exasperate me; and, three, like many French films that depress me so much I don't feel like making films anymore. These are mostly French films, because I still go to see American films like a tourist. Although I must include *What's New Pussycat?* among the films in the third category. It is a bad picture. It is like such a bad picture that one wonders if it is not good.

WOMAN: How many categories do you have for good pictures? (*Camera zooms in for closeup of Godard.*)

GODARD: Each good picture has its own category. (*He puts down his teacup, takes a box of cigars from the table, puts a cigar in his mouth, and lights it. The cigar is small and has a pale-yellow paper covering. He puffs at the cigar and then takes it from his mouth. He blows out the smoke without putting effort into it.*)

INTÉRIEUR: The auditorium. Godard is seated onstage, behind a table. To his right are Pauline Kael and Parker Tyler. To his left are Arthur Knight, James Ivory, Andrew Sarris, and Hollis Alpert. The atmosphere of a college talkfest. No sound at all. We see the mouths moving in what looks like serious, grim, pedantic discussion. Mouths in closeup. Pan from one mouth to the next. Get all the mouths confused with each other. A couple of tongues. A few sets of teeth. There is a burst of sound suddenly—Donald Duck, playing-the-tape-backward gabble. Then silence again. Fast cuts—closeup of Godard looking coolly to his right, of a mouth moving in gabble, of Godard looking coolly to his left, of another mouth, looking just like first mouth, moving in gabble. Cut to closeup of dwarf sitting in front row. His mouth moves in time, silently, with other mouths. Cut to woman in black, in audience. Her mouth looks just like first mouth. She has her head held high. She looks at Godard with shining pride. Cut to closeup of Godard's face looking down at audience. His face shows no expression at all.

INTÉRIEUR: The rear of the auditorium. Last row. Two seats in near corner occupied by young couple, kissing coolly. They are seen from rear, profiles of heads in full-screen closeup. Young man's hair is long, straggly. He wears black turtleneck sweater. Girl's hair is cut in what used to be called Buster Brown style back in Carl Laemmle days. She wears black turtleneck sweater.

GIRL (*withdrawing mouth from boy's mouth and speaking in a monotone*): If Arthur Knight can be a California movie professor, then Andrew Sarris should be a California movie professor.

BOY (*studying her face and putting both of his hands over her Buster Brown bangs*): That is true. Andrew Sarris is as much a professor as Arthur Knight is a professor. (*He puts his mouth on hers.*)


INTÉRIEUR: The lobby of the auditorium. Panel discussion has ended. Audience is filing out of auditorium. Woman in black waits for Godard. He joins her.

WOMAN: Well, was it like *The Mask and the Pen*?

GODARD (*in the soft, expressionless voice*): The same. Quite the same.


FIN

# Anatomy of a Commercial Interruption

February 19, 1966

# ANATOMY OF A COMMERCIAL INTERRUPTION
## A FILM 70MM. ULTRA PANAVISION TECHNICOLOR

### FILMED ENTIRELY ON LOCATION

Starring Otto Preminger, producer and director of twenty-eight films, including *Laura* (1944), *Fallen Angel* (1945), *Daisy Kenyon* (1948), *Whirlpool* (1949), *Angel Face* (1952), *The Moon Is Blue* (1953), *The Man with the Golden Arm* (1955), *Saint Joan* (1957), *Bonjour Tristesse* (1958), *Anatomy of a Murder* (1959), *Exodus* (1960), *Advise and Consent* (1962), *The Cardinal* (1963), *In Harm's Way* (1964), and *Bunny Lake Is Missing* (1965); director of seven films, including *A Royal Scandal* (1944), *Forever Amber* (1947), and *Porgy and Bess* (1959); and actor—always playing the part of a Nazi—in the four films *The Pied Piper* (1942), *Margin for Error* (1943), *They Got Me Covered* (1943), and *Stalag 17* (1953).

With Hope Bryce Preminger, Mark Preminger, Victoria (Missie) Preminger, Bill Barnes, Bob Romaner, Marvin Schwartz, Lester L. Cooper, Jr., Myles J. Lane, Justice Arthur G. Klein, Joseph Villante, Archer Winsten, Elia Kazan, Gilbert Lloyd, and others.

EXTERIOR. New York City. Early on a cold, sunny morning around Thanksgiving, 1965. Manhattan's Upper East Side. A Panavision view of East Sixty-fourth Street from a helicopter, taking in, roughly, thirty blocks to the north of Sixty-fourth, thirty blocks to the south, between the East River and Central Park. While the camera pans slowly across this section of Manhattan, sound of traffic is heard. No music. Then, as the camera zooms in on Otto Preminger's townhouse, between Park and Lexington Avenues, there is a surge of city music—brassy and percussive, and with a few references to "Take the 'A' Train." A skinny, urban tree, now bare and limp, stands at the curb in front of the townhouse, which is a remodeled brownstone. The house, standing among clean-looking and sleek-looking townhouses and apartment buildings, is the cleanest-looking and sleekest-looking house on the block. It has been painted light gray, and two and a half stories have been built on at the top, making it five and a half stories high. The new top floors contain, in addition to a nursery and servant quarters, a gymnasium—complete with sun lamp, motorized bicycle exercise machine, and sauna—and a film-projection room. The projection room has a tremendous picture window, facing the street, and during film-viewing hours this is covered with a Panavision-size screen. The front of the first floor of the house has three large, long French doors. Between them and the picture window at the top there are two windows to a floor, all of them just as large as the French doors. Most of the windows have vertical white Venetian blinds. The door of the house, like the doors leading to all Preminger domiciles and all Preminger offices, is painted black, and there is a legend on it, in glinting brushed-aluminum Saul Bass modern type, reading, "129 East 64." The door is opened from the inside. Holding it is a white-jacketed butler. The Premingers' nanny, a gaunt, wispy-haired, friendly-looking woman, emerges, looks up and down the street, and turns to look inside the house. She watches as Preminger's two children march outside. They are five-year-old twins, Mark and Victoria, wearing matching brother-sister outfits of navy-blue raincoats, leggings, navy wool caps, and matching gloves. Victoria's hair falls loosely from under the cap to her shoulders. The children look very wide awake and watchful. Preminger comes out of the house, a somewhat puzzled but benign expression on his face, and the butler closes the door behind him. Preminger, a well-built man six feet tall and with sad eyes and a pink, clean-shaven head, looks fit; his complexion is a deeper pink, attesting to use of the gymnasium's sun lamp. He wears a navy-blue wool topcoat, a gray, worsted suit, black, shapely London-made loafers, and no hat. His head gleams in the sunlight. He glances at the house directly across the street, and the camera pans to it. It is the town house of the architect Edward Durell Stone, and the facade is masked by one of the concrete grilles that are Stone's trademark. The camera pans back to Preminger, who is grimacing in disapproval at the other house. He looks at his wristwatch, which is platinum, square, and very thin; the time, in closeup, is eight-forty. His face assumes its former expression of puzzlement as he looks at his children, and he stretches out his hands to them. Holding their hands, Preminger paces back and forth in front of his house, looking toward Park Avenue. The children, imitating him, peer up the street impatiently. Then a blue-and-white taxi with obtrusively large dents in its front and sides is seen turning onto the street from Park Avenue. Preminger has been looking at his wristwatch, and now he gives the taxi a reluctant, tight smile. The driver of the taxi is a young man in his late twenties, a part-time actor named Bob Romaner, who is wearing a shapeless red wool sweater torn and unraveling at both elbows. He has long, shaggy hair and a three-day growth of beard. On his face is an adamant look of high expectation. MARK (*holding his mouth in precisely the same manner as his father holds his, and then opening it slightly to speak*): Here is Mr. Romaner!

VICTORIA: Here is Mr. Romaner!

PREMINGER (*who has a Viennese accent and speaks with dry emphasis and resigned indulgence*): Here is Mr. Romaner!

(*He opens the door of the taxi. The children jump in. Preminger heaves himself in after them. He puts his head out for a last glance at his house, and, with a sigh, closes the taxi door. The taxi lurches toward Lexington Avenue.*)

INTERIOR. Taxi. Mark and Victoria are sitting back properly in their seats, both giggling and swinging their legs rhythmically up and down. Victoria has her hands folded in her lap. Preminger, sitting at their left, is smiling at them, but his expression as he regards them is still one of bewilderment, mixed with a touch of amazement. Bob Romaner turns his head at intervals to look at the three of them. Attached to the top of his dashboard is a small color snapshot of his own two children—a boy and a girl, both under five.

MARK AND VICTORIA (*chanting in unison*): Late for school! Late for school! Late for school!

PREMINGER: I do not *like* to be late. I believe in being on time. It is very important not to be late. I believe very strongly in this.

ROMANER (*jauntily*): This traffic! It was murder this morning getting to your house, Mr. Preminger! Your case starts today, huh? (*He turns around and gives Preminger a knowing look.*)

PREMINGER (*good-naturedly*): I am not supposed to discuss my case before the judge gives his decision. So I obey the rules. I do not talk.

ROMANER (*looking back at Preminger again, with an even more knowing look*): Keeps you out of the office, huh? Keeps you from getting your work done?

MARK: Daddy works all the time.

VICTORIA: Daddy is always working.

PREMINGER (*to Romaner, with dry interest*): How is your career? (*He goes on without waiting for an answer.*) I saw your film about the bum on the Bowery. You were very good. You were very convincing.

MARK AND VICTORIA (*chanting*): Working, working, always working, always working! (*They giggle.*)

ROMANER (*as camera picks up his face, wearing an expression of pleasure, in closeup, in his rearview mirror*): Then you've got a part for me in your next picture—right? (*He turns and winks at the children.*) Right, Mr. Preminger?

PREMINGER: I will do my best to find a part for you. If I can, I will.

ROMANER: I hope you win your case with Columbia Pictures, Mr. Preminger. I'd like to see you casting your next picture. (*He laughs.*)

PREMINGER (*with a wry smile*): I told Columbia I will fight this case as long as I have to, to keep them from mutilating my picture on television with cuts and commercial interruptions. I told them it is nothing personal. It is the principle of the thing. But right now they are mad at me. They refuse even to give me prints of their pictures, which they always did, so that I could show them at home. But the trial will not interfere with my work. I am preparing my next picture now. For you, I will do my best. Because I *like* you, Mr. Romaner.

ROMANER (*with great confidence*): You won't be sorry, Mr. Preminger, I promise you.

PREMINGER: I do not intend to be sorry, Mr. Romaner. And all I will ask of you is that perhaps you may want to get a shave soon.

ROMANER: Tomorrow. Yesterday I worked two shifts. I didn't even have time to see my kids.

MARK (*imitating his father's tone*): You may want to get a shave, Mr. Romaner. (*Preminger is regarding his son with admiration and near-astonishment as the taxi draws up in front of Lycée Français, a private school on East Seventy-second Street, near Fifth Avenue.*)

PREMINGER (*with satisfaction*): We are not late.

EXTERIOR. Street. The children hop out of the taxi, and Preminger follows, taking each by the hand.

MARK (*calling back*): I hope you have a nice day, Mr. Romaner.

VICTORIA (*very politely*): *I* hope you have a nice day, Mr. Romaner, and I hope you get a shave tomorrow.

MARK: And *I* hope you get a shave tomorrow.

(*Preminger quickly escorts the children into the school, their figures merging with those of several other children and their mothers or nannies, all intent upon being on time. The taxi, by prearrangement, waits for him. He returns in a few minutes and reenters the taxi.*)


INTERIOR. Taxi. Preminger is now sitting in the middle of the rear seat.

PREMINGER: We go now to court—60 Centre Street. I am not to be called immediately. However, it would be more polite if I am there.

ROMANER (*nodding joyously and heading for the East River Drive*): I wish I could attend the trial. But I'm not exactly dressed for the occasion. Anyway, I've got to keep working. Until I get that part, Mr. Preminger—right? (*He turns around and winks.*) But can you at least give me an explanation of the trial? What it's all about? A brief summary? I'm really very interested, Mr. Preminger. Especially since it concerns the business I hope to be in full time. (*He grins.*)

PREMINGER: It is all very simple. (*He sighs wearily and looks out the window blankly, not seeming to respond to any one particular sight.*) I am trying to get an injunction against Columbia Pictures and their subsidiary, Screen Gems, to restrain them from showing my picture *Anatomy of a Murder* on the hundred and one television stations to which they sold the picture. We have a temporary injunction now to keep them from cutting the picture on television until the case is decided. They have the right to release the picture, in theaters and on television. But my contract with them gives me the right to determine the final form and content of my film. So I am charging violation of my contract. Also, they sold my film in a bunch, with fifty-nine other films, to all these television stations for ten million dollars. It is known as block booking, which I do not think is permitted by the law. There were two other good films in the bunch—*Picnic* and *Pal Joey*—but most of the others were tenth-rate. It is to me an unbelievable thing. All they care about is the money. I believe it is bad business to worry about the immediate buck. I am not like that myself. I do not want a fortune. I do not want to leave a fortune to my children, because I do not think it is good for children to inherit a lot of money.

ROMANER: That's my own attitude exactly! I can afford to have that attitude! (*He laughs.*) So about the trial. Anything else?

PREMINGER: In New York, over Channel 7, *Anatomy of a Murder*—the film is a hundred and sixty-one minutes long—was shown and it was interrupted for commercials thirteen times, and in Los Angeles the showing was interrupted twelve times. Each interruption had at least two commercials, sometimes three or four commercials. On Channel 7, there were thirty-six commercials during the showing of the picture.

ROMANER: Thirty-*six!*

PREMINGER: I believe the commercial interruptions destroy the value of the picture. Why should the picture be shown in mutilated form just because it is shown at home? It is to me an intolerable thing. (*Preminger sounds very calm and very sure of his ground. He maintains the tone of a completely reasonable man.*) It is grotesque. I really think it is uncivilized.

ROMANER (*agreeably, while appearing to have more important worries on his own mind*): That's the whole thing? (*They are now driving quite fast down the East River Drive, and Romaner keeps his eyes on the heavy traffic.*) So how old is that picture? When was it made?

PREMINGER: I cannot remember dates and years. About 1959, I think. There are only three dates I am sure of. On the twenty-first of October, 1935, I arrived in this country from Vienna. On the third of October, 1960, my children were born. And on the fifth of December, 1906, *I* was born.

(*They draw up in front of the New York County courthouse. Preminger pays Romaner and gives him a tip in bills. Then he opens the door and steps out.*)

EXTERIOR. Taxi. Near long, broad expanse of steps leading up to entrance of the pillared New York County courthouse.

ROMANER (*rolling down his far window and leaning out*): Thanks, Mr. Preminger! Good luck! Maybe I'll come back for you later!

(*The camera pans from the taxi, as it speeds away, to Preminger's back. He holds his hands, one in the other, behind his back as he hurries up the steps. Then we see Preminger from the front. He takes the steps easily, without puffing, but his movements are those of a child—disjointed and overactive. The stairway is shown as gray, stony, formal, legalistic. Some legal music is heard—mostly oboes and bassoons, playing staccato in a sardonically strict rhythm, with references to "Who's Sorry Now?" Then we have a closeup of Preminger entering the building. His head now looks pinker than his face. There is a puffiness under his eyes, which continue to show sadness.*)

INTERIOR. Corridor leading to the courtroom where Preminger's case is being tried. The camera dollies along beside Preminger as he walks toward the courtroom, revealing faces of typical court-corridor loungers: a surly, hostile young man being harangued by a surly, hostile older man; worried-looking litigants from nearby courtrooms; a tall, thin, white-haired court buff of about seventy-five wearing a pince-nez and a checked suit, wing collar, and flowing purple necktie; a lot of bustling attorneys. They all seem to come to attention and watch Preminger advance toward the courtroom.

INTERIOR. Swinging double doors. There is a little rectangle of glass near the top of each door. A closeup of the doors and a black-and-white rectangular sign beside them. The sign reads, "Trial Term. Part II. Mr. Justice Klein." A view from the rear as Preminger pushes the doors open and enters the courtroom. The legal music comes up strong, with a vague but good-natured reference to the signature theme of the *Perry Mason* show.

INTERIOR. Courtroom. The words "IN GOD WE TRUST" appear in raised brass letters on paneling behind judge's bench. The judge has not come in, and the attorneys for both sides are conferring informally at a large table in the area between the judge's bench and the spectators' benches. An American flag stands on the floor to the right of the judge's bench, and a witness chair and an empty jury box to the left. A court officer, with a brush mustache, sits, frowning, at a table to the right of the judge's bench. He wears a dark-blue uniform, with brass buttons and a gilt badge. There are large windows on either side of the room, and on the wall behind the spectators' benches there is a large clock. The attorneys are sorting papers, then taking more papers out of briefcases and suitcases. Marvin Schwartz, of the law firm of Sullivan & Cromwell, is Preminger's trial counsel. A stocky, rather heavy-breathing man wearing charcoal-rimmed glasses, he is assisted by Lester L. Cooper, Jr., who looks very young and unmarked, with a round, small face, reddish hair, a Southern accent, and predictable yes-sir-and-yes-ma'am manners. Myles J. Lane, of the firm of Schwartz & Frohlich (a different Schwartz), is trial counsel for the defendant, the Columbia Pictures Corporation and Screen Gems, Inc., and he is assisted by Irving Moross, a man in his fifties, and Stuart Schwartz (also unrelated to Marvin Schwartz). Mr. Lane is sturdy-looking but pale. He is wearing a light-brown suit, with a tan-and-brown figured necktie and a matching pocket handkerchief. Stuart Schwartz looks a little more experienced, a little older, and a little less eager to please than young Lester Cooper, Jr. Several other assistants are puttering around with papers, all of them looking serious, even gloomy. The camera picks up Preminger as he walks into the courtroom, taking off his topcoat as he walks. He folds his coat and lays it on a rear bench. Then he takes a seat in the front row of the spectators' section. He looks relaxed and expectant. The puzzled expression has vanished. Marvin Schwartz comes over and shakes Preminger's hand, and Cooper does the same. Then Preminger is joined by Bill Barnes, his assistant-of-all-trades, who is an even-featured, good-looking young man, shining and clean, and who has a mild Southern accent, like Cooper's, and London-made shoes, like Preminger's. Barnes looks faintly harassed. After speaking to Preminger, he takes off his coat, folds it, and lays it next to Preminger's.

PREMINGER (*counting the defendants' lawyers and apparently enjoying himself*): One, two, three, four. They have four lawyers. I have only two on my side. But I need only two lawyers. I have *good* lawyers.

SCHWARTZ (*with a short, uneasy laugh*): Wait until we get the decision.

PREMINGER (*immediately*): My esteem for you will not be determined by whether you win or lose. I judge only effort, not results.

SCHWARTZ: I admire your objectivity.

COOPER (*looking admiring*): That's sure kind of you, sir.

BARNES (*to Preminger*): We discovered (*he indicates Cooper*) that we went to school together. Episcopal High School in Alexandria, Virginia.

PREMINGER: I am impressed. Did you men know that I am a lawyer myself?

COOPER: Is that a fact, sir? My, I'd never have guessed you were a lawyer!

PREMINGER: Why not? I am a passable lawyer. When they were trying to censor *The Moon Is Blue*, I was able to use what I knew to fight the censorship. The present fight is like the fight I put up to keep *The Moon Is Blue* exactly the way I made it, without censorship, without cuts. It is not that a few cuts here and there in the picture would have changed that picture. In themselves, they wouldn't have mattered. But the right of free expression is important to me. My luxury is to have certain principles, and this is one of them.

(*Closeup of court officer's mouth. Wide mouth, red lips, big teeth under the brush mustache.*)

COURT OFFICER: All rise! (*A long shot. Everybody stands. Judge Arthur C. Klein enters, wearing a black robe, with a white shirt and a black tie. He has a gray brush mustache and is rather bald, and he has on horn-rimmed glasses. He and the court officer look like brothers.*)

COURT OFFICER (*closeup of mouth again*): Hear ye! Hear ye! All persons having business at this Trial Term, Supreme Court, Part II, held in and for the County of New York, will draw near, give your attendance, and ye shall be heard!

(*A closeup of Judge Klein looking around the courtroom, noticing the presence of Preminger. Cut to Preminger, in closeup, looking back at the judge, and smiling, with mouth closed. Dissolve.*)

INTERIOR. Courtroom. A somber-faced, slightly built gentleman enters the room carrying a portable stenotype machine and takes a seat at right angles to the witness box. Marvin Schwartz is about to make his opening statement. The camera starts with him, then pans slowly, as he speaks, to the faces of the key figures—Lane, Preminger, Barnes, the judge—and back to

Schwartz. From time to time, the camera cuts to the court reporter tapping on his machine.

MARVIN SCHARTZ: (*swaying back and forth as he speaks, and projecting a deep, resonant voice, which immediately makes him sound authoritative*): May it please the Court, the complainants in this action [Preminger and Carlyle Productions, Inc.] seek an injunction as well as an accounting for damages. But, as I am sure Mr. Lane has advised the Court, in his preliminary memorandum on their motion for severance, Judge Murphy severed all issues relating to damages, and so the only issue which is involved in the trial which begins this morning is the plaintiffs' demand for an injunction—an injunction to compel the withdrawal by the defendants from television exhibition of the motion picture *Anatomy of a Murder*. The grounds upon which we rely for an injunction are essentially four, and I will come to those in a moment. (*As Marvin Schwartz speaks, cut to the clock on the rear wall. The time shown is 10:08. The large black minute hand is seen ticking off a minute, to 10:09.*) At the heart of the matter—at the heart of the matter—it is our position, Your Honor, as a matter of contract and as a matter of common law, that the creator of a work of entertainment, whether or not it be a work of art, but the creator of a work of entertainment, has in this case by contract and has in general at common law the right to an injunction to prevent the mutilation, if not the destruction, of his work. Now, the work here is a motion picture, as Your Honor knows, entitled *Anatomy of a Murder*. Apart from the fact that it was widely acclaimed as a serious dramatic study of the administration of justice—in addition to that, it met *instant commercial success*. The evidence will show that, by and large, a picture which has grossed, domestically, in excess of four million dollars acquired a listing in *Variety* as an all-time grosser. This picture grossed five million. (*Cut to Preminger. His face is motionless. Barnes turns to him and whispers in his ear. Preminger nods, his face still motionless. Cut back to Schwartz.*) We are here not only because the plaintiffs seek to prevent the mutilation of something which is theirs, which they did; we are here as well because there is a lot—a very lot—of money involved here. Under the contract under which this picture was made by the plaintiffs and sold for theater distribution by the defendants, the plaintiffs are entitled to forty-five per cent of the net proceeds—as we shall see, this is a far different thing from net profits—but forty-five per cent of the net proceeds. Whereas the defendant, Columbia, is entitled to thirty per cent of the net proceeds. (*Cut to court reporter tapping on his machine as Schwartz speaks. He lifts his eyebrows at the words "million," "proceeds," and "profits."*) Since this has been a successful picture, first released in 1959, it has ahead of it not only years of exhibition on television but, we believe, years of theatrical reissue. These should, we hope, be profitable, all considered. So we are concerned with protecting a commercial value as well as the integrity of a work created by these plaintiffs. Now, I think it appropriate, in view of the issue of cutting and editing, to note at the outset what kind of a picture this is. I do not mean to deprecate comedy. I do not mean by *any* means to deprecate musical comedy. (*Cut to the key faces, all serious, except that of Judge Klein, who looks entertained.*) But this is a serious dramatic study of the trial of a criminal case. Much of the picture takes place in a courtroom, in a real courtroom in the peninsula country of Michigan. The author of the book was Judge John Voelker of the Michigan Supreme Court. The picture has been acclaimed as a faithful depiction of the way a criminal case is tried, and, if I may add at this point, the trial justice was played by a lawyer who in his lifetime was almost as beloved here by his fellows at the bar as he was in his native Boston, Joseph N. Welch. Now, this case, I think, is governed by a contract, and I think Your Honor will conclude when the evidence is in that it will be the contract which will govern and determine this issue here. Now, that contract, I think the evidence will show, also is a most unusual, if not unique, contract in the motion-picture industry. It is unique, Your Honor, in the sense that in order to induce Mr. Preminger (*cut to closeup of the faces of Preminger and Barnes, both listening grimly*) a widely known and successful producer of motion pictures, to make a series of motion pictures for Columbia, these defendants, by contract, gave to him what I think the evidence will show is almost unparalleled control of the pictures he was to make. (*Barnes glances sidewise, significantly, at Preminger, but Preminger does not acknowledge the look.*) His control extended from the selection of the script, in which these defendants had no voice (*cut to Lane and his assistants, all looking grimmer than Preminger and his group*); the selection of the cast, in which they had no voice; the selection of the cameramen, the electricians—indeed, of anyone who had any role in the production of the pictures—and extended, finally, to the right by contract to determine the final form (*cut back to Martin Schwartz, whose voice has now taken on a tone of legal righteousness*), the one form in which this (*brief pause*) picture (*brief pause*) could be exhibited, and we say that that right (*brief pause*) to determine the form of the picture, given by contract, extends not only to theaters in the United States but to theaters throughout the world, in every language (*brief pause*), on ships at sea (*another*), in airplanes (*again*), and even (*word emphasized before brief pause*), we say, on *television!* (*Cut to Preminger, who appears to be on the verge of a smile.*) On the cutting-and-editing clause, which is at the heart of this controversy, we think the evidence will show, and the evidence including the defendants' own contract file (*cut back to Marvin Schwartz*), that the words "final cutting and editing" are words of everyday parlance in the motion-picture industry. They mean that the person who has the right to make the final cutting and editing has the right to determine, at least for purposes of theatrical exhibition, the final form, the final content of the picture, and that once the person who has the right to make the final cutting and editing has delivered that picture to the distributor, not a scene may be cut, not a word may be cut. Now, before turning specifically to the contract and the provisions which we say were breached… (*Schwartz's voice gradually fades out. Dissolve.*)

INTERIOR. Courtroom. Closeup of Judge Klein, who seems to be enjoying himself very much.

JUDGE KLEIN (*nodding to Myles Lane*): All right, Mr. Lane.

(*Pan to Lane as he rises and starts to speak. He does not sway, like Marvin Schwartz, but hunches forward, looking a bit fierce.*)

LANE: Your Honor, my opening remarks will be brief, because I think we have set forth in our brief to Your Honor our position fairly, clearly. However, I want to emphasize the fact now that we are—when I say "we," Columbia Pictures and Screen Gems—have licensed this picture in about a hundred different situations for television exhibition on the basis of the contract right which was included in the original contract which was entered into between Carlyle Productions, Incorporated, and Columbia Pictures. So we claim that we do this, as we have had the right to do this ever since that contract was signed. We have the right to distribute this picture, both for theatrical exhibition and also for television exhibition. Mr. Preminger, who is a plaintiff in this case, we take the position he has no standing at all in this case, because the contract that was made with Columbia Pictures—

JUDGE KLEIN: Excuse me. (*Lane looks a little cross.*) Mr. Schwartz, I was going to suggest that you might go into that, so will you just make a note, and then I will hear you on these affirmative defenses.

(*Schwartz looks pleased and nods, and then makes a note.*)

LANE: In 1958, the contract that was entered into between Carlyle Productions and Columbia was, as I say, just between those two corporations. As I understand it, Mr. Preminger was an employee of Carlyle Productions, Incorporated, at that time, and therefore, because he has, in effect, no contractual right insofar as this picture is concerned, we maintain that he has no standing in an action for an injunction. This is *not* his picture, although he did direct it. (*Cut to Barnes, who is giving Preminger a look of exaggerated amused indignation. Preminger's noncommittal expression remains fixed.*) This was the picture of Carlyle Productions, Incorporated. It is true that Mr. Preminger was the major stockholder of Carlyle Productions, Incorporated, but by the same token, irrespective of that, he was only an employee at the time. (*Cut back to Lane.*) He was working for Carlyle, and he was not a party to the contract, as such. (*Cut to court reporter, who is frowning at his machine.*) Now, in listening to Mr. Schwartz, and what he says he intends to prove (*cut to Schwartz, whose mouth is pursed*), there is no issue in this case of mutilation of film *at all!* It is not a question of mutilation. (*Cut to Preminger, who at last reacts with amused derision, expressed in a glance at Bill Barnes, and who then, at a movement behind him, looks over his shoulder at the elderly court buff with the pince-nez and the flowing purple tie, who has just come in. The buff is very attentive. Preminger gives him a double take, and then turns around again.*) The only issue in this case (*cut back to Lane, who is raising his voice*), as I see it, and I think as Judge Murphy decided when he severed the action, is whether or not we have a right to distribute this picture on TV with minor cuts, and with the insertion of commercials. There is nothing in the case about a mutilation. (*Lane is looking belligerent, and he pauses rather lengthily to consult some papers on the table before him. As he starts talking again, we cut to the clock and watch it advance another minute, then back to Lane again.*) What the plaintiff is contending, that if we show this picture on TV with cuts, minor cuts—and I might say that the paragraph in the various contracts with the various stations modifies this to a situation where the minor cut will not interfere with the artistic or dramatic presentation of the picture—but what they are contending is that if we do permit stations to exhibit this picture with minor cuts, and with commercials, that it will result in a condition that cannot be compensated by money. In other words, the damage is irreparable, so they say, if we use these cuts and commercials. (*Cut to Preminger in closeup, leaning toward Barnes.*)

PREMINGER (*whispering in Barnes' ear*): Go outside and call up the agent and find out if they want to sell that book at the price I offered. (*Barnes nods, and tiptoes out through the swinging doors.*)

LANE: There is a clause in the contract which gives us the exclusive right to show this picture on television. If what the plaintiff contends were true, that the plaintiff has the right to determine whether or not we can market this picture for television without minor cuts and without the right of the television stations to insert commercials, that would, in effect, give the plaintiff the veto power over this particular exclusive right to television exhibition. In other words, the television clause would be meaningless.... We will also show that, at the time that Mr. Preminger, or his company that he was working for at the time, which he had a stock interest in, we will show at that time that he was well aware of what transpires in the motion-picture industry, and well aware of the custom in the trade both in the motion-picture industry and in the television industry, and that he knew, as a matter of fact, that the only way you could market a picture for television was by giving the television stations these rights that I have referred to already. And as a matter of fact, we will show Your Honor that there are other pictures that he had something to do with the production and direction of, that he himself had an interest in those pictures, and yet they were sold for television, and in those very pictures they had cuts and commercials.... Cutting and editing is what is done just before the picture is released for the motion-picture exhibition in theaters. We maintain that that is a great deal different from cutting and editing as it pertains to television!

JUDGE KLEIN: In other words, your position is that the cutting and editing referred to in this contract applies only to the production of the picture itself, and has nothing to do with the television showing?

LANE: That is right. Because if it had something to do with television, they would have that clause in the television clause in the contract.

JUDGE KLEIN: We can go into that during the course of the trial. (*He addresses himself to Marvin Schwartz.*) Do you want to comment just briefly on these other points? I don't know whether defendants' counsel is seriously pressing the three points that he made: One, that Mr. Preminger is merely an employee of Carlyle, and therefore has no place in this suit. That becomes serious, if he is sustained on that. And then, if he is sustained on the other one with regard to Carlyle, that will leave you without a plaintiff at all. So I want you to just comment briefly.

SCHWARTZ (*rises to his feet and starts swaying*): Surely, Your Honor. In the first place, this contract provides that this picture may not be exhibited anywhere without carrying with it a credit, a credit to Mr. Preminger. The picture is produced by him and directed by him. Wholly apart from the contract, and even if there were no contract here at all, it seems to me clear, on the cases we have cited in our brief, that if they threaten to show a different version of the picture from the one which he produced and directed, that he not only has standing to bring suit but he is entitled to an injunction. Secondly, this contract very specifically contemplates that the picture will be produced, will be directed by Preminger... (*Voice fades out. Dissolve.*)


INTERIOR. Phone booth in the corridor. Barnes, within, is seen through the glass door. He is looking very much in charge. He talks with great animation, studying a pencil in his hand as though it were extremely important. (*Dissolve.*)


INTERIOR. Courtroom. Barnes is back in his seat next to Preminger.

JUDGE KLEIN: The Court cannot close its eyes to the fact that there are television showings such as the *Schaefer Award Theatre* that shows a movie with only four cuts in it, I think. And this, in my opinion, makes it more attractive. (*The judge suddenly looks a little bit like Bosley Crowther.*) I might say that this has no legal force and effect, but I think you are before the right judge in one sense. (*Quick cut to Preminger, looking wise.*) That is, I am a great moviegoer; I love the movies. And I find, also, that almost the only thing that is any good on television today is the showing of some of these movies, and I have seen some horrible examples of what television stations, if they do it, or whoever does it, do in cutting these pictures. How they can destroy not only the artistic value but the entire story value. You can't even follow the story (*the judge looks pained*), for the number of cuts and the way they are made. So that I am sure we can all agree here that while some cuts should have been made to permit this advertising, certainly it can't be too many, nor can it have the effect, as Mr. Schwartz puts it, of mutilating the picture. (*Dissolve.*)

EXTERIOR. Centre Street, outside the courthouse. A long shot of Preminger coming down the steps of the courthouse, holding his hands behind his back and taking the steps down in the same childlike manner he took them going up. Following him in single file are Bill Barnes, Marvin Schwartz, and Lester Cooper, Jr. They are shown walking quickly, dodging traffic as they cross Centre Street, and talking and gesticulating. Then a camera in a helicopter picks them up and trails them for three blocks, until they reach Gasner's Restaurant, a hangout of lawyers, judges, etc. It has a glass front and an old, established, solid, homey appearance. Preminger leads the way inside.

EXTERIOR. Side exit from the courthouse. The camera picks up Judge Klein coming out, his judicial robe off, his topcoat on, accompanied by a man who looks like still another version of the judge. The legal music starts up again, very softly and controversially; the oboes are arguing with the bassoons. The two men are shown from the rear as they walk, nodding judiciously at each other. The camera follows them as they make their way to and into Gasner's. Next, the camera picks up the court buff with the wing collar, and shows him going to the same restaurant. Last, the camera picks up a familiar-looking figure, who turns out to be (in a cameo part) Roy Cohn playing himself. He happens, on this occasion, to look very angry. He is alone, and is also on his way to Gasner's. Then the camera picks up Myles

Lane, with his entourage—first from the rear, then from the front—coming down the courthouse steps, and follows them to a nearby Schrafft's.

INTERIOR. Gasner's Restaurant. A large place, with a checkroom at the entrance, which is a bottleneck. We have a shot from overhead, of a crowd of customers, all men, bunched up and trying to check their coats. Preminger hands his coat to an attendant, a young woman, who does a quick double take at seeing him.

PREMINGER (*addressing the young woman*): They told me when I'd come here you would play for me the theme song from *Exodus*. So. I do not hear it.

YOUNG WOMAN: Today our machine is broken.

PREMINGER: All right, darling. (*He rubs his hands together like a winner.*) I come here anyway. For your blintzes.

INTERIOR. Gasner's Restaurant. A large table. Preminger and his party. Waiters are serving everyone cheese blintzes.

PREMINGER (*to a waiter*): Bring some extra cherry preserves, please. As long as I eat blintzes, I like them with a *lot* of cherry preserves. (*He turns to Barnes, Cooper, and Schwartz.*) This restaurant has the best cheese blintzes in the world.

SCHWARTZ: Do you have a Viennese cook, Mr. Preminger?

PREMINGER: No. We have a Finnish couple, and our cook speaks little English, but it does not matter, because we eat very simply at home. And here is my only chance to eat blintzes. We like this Finnish couple we have very much. They never did this kind of work before. I sent the man to my tailor, and he learned how to press a suit. Now he is very good at it. (*The others look mildly impressed. The waiter brings a saucer heaped with cherry preserves, and Preminger takes it eagerly and serves himself a large helping, then urges it on his fellow-lunchers. We hear the strains of blintz music—a balalaika against the background of a large string section.*) This is the best part of the whole trial, eating cheese blintzes.

SCHWARTZ: I admire your point of view.

PREMINGER (*looking flattered*): The blintzes make it all worthwhile—even listening to Columbia's lawyers! (*Everybody laughs.*)
COOPER: Don't you think that's going *too* far, sir?
PREMINGER: No. (*Takes a large bite, and chews and swallows cheerfully.*) I would be willing to live on Centre Street in order to have a lunch every day of these blintzes! (*Everybody laughs again. The camera pans around from one table to another. Judge Klein is sitting with his companion, and both are eating blintzes. The court buff is eating blintzes. Roy Cohn is shown standing outside the checkroom, waiting to hand over his coat. He seems to be thinking of blintzes.*)

INTERIOR. Schrafft's. Myles Lane is sitting with his colleagues. They are having light lunches.
LANE (*to his companions*): Heavy lunches aren't good when you're working. I'm a kind of a soup man myself. (*They nod in agreement.*) But let's go to Gasner's on the last day of the trial. (*The others nod again, looking comforted.*)

EXTERIOR. Steps of the courthouse. Preminger, going up, is seen from the front. He holds his hands behind his back. Bill Barnes is quickly briefing him about a writer under consideration for a screenplay job.
BARNES: He's supposed to be good on novels, but he did one screenplay and it was supposed to be a bad screenplay.
PREMINGER (*quickly*): That he wrote a bad screenplay doesn't mean anything. (*Laughs. Barnes looks at him in wonder.*) That someone writes a *good* screenplay doesn't mean anything, either!

INTERIOR. Courtroom. The judge has not arrived yet. Preminger is sitting on the front bench, reading some typewritten letters. The attorneys are getting their papers ready. Barnes stands off to one side, chatting with Cooper, who is gazing in admiration at Barnes's shoes.
BARNES: I like these shoes, because they're comfortable. Traveling a lot, the way I have to do with Mr. Preminger, I find with these shoes

you don't bust laces, and you can wear these shoes with anything—sports clothes, dinner jacket, anything at all.

COOPER: What do you say if people say you're imitating Mr. Preminger?

BARNES: One thing I've learned from Mr. Preminger is you don't worry about what people say. You don't worry about things like that at all. (*Dissolve.*)


EXTERIOR. Air view of the courthouse, starting low over the steps, then going up and up, until the courthouse is a pinpoint in lower Manhattan. Shot from a helicopter, which travels uptown, over the Empire State Building, Central Park, and the Harlem River, to the Bronx, descending, as though arbitrarily, at the junction of Fordham Road and Jerome Avenue. The camera zooms to the marquee of the Lido Theater, where the double-feature billing reads, "Frank Sinatra Dean Martin Deborah Kerr *Marriage on the Rocks* and *Bunny Lake Is Missing*." Closeup of cashier's cage, inside which sits a middle-aged lady with exceptionally golden and blown-up hair, heavy blue eye shadow, an orange satin dress, and an orchid pinned to one shoulder. The camera goes up to her as though buying a ticket, then goes inside.


INTERIOR. The Lido. The camera dollies up to the ticket-taker, an irritable-looking elderly gentleman who is sitting on a stool at the entrance and smoking a newly lit large cigar. He does not remove the cigar as the camera dollies past him and to his right, past a candy and ice-cream counter laden with Baby Ruth bars, Oh Henry! bars, Almond Joy bars, Planters Peanuts, Frozen Ice Cream Puffs, and Chuckles. The camera advances inside, past a row of dispensing machines—orange-soda, cream-soda, cigarette, and candy machines. A closeup of sign at one aisle reading, "Smokers Seated on Right Only." The camera heads for the left aisle, following a male patron who is taking off his topcoat as he goes in. He is wearing a Hawaiian-print sports shirt, with no jacket and no tie, and his outline looks seedy and bowed against the screen, which shows Frank Sinatra and Deborah Kerr winding up *Marriage on the Rocks* with their heads together, looking synthetically joyful for the end of their film. A front shot of the other patrons in the theater: a few defeated-looking men, but mostly careworn women, eating Chuckles or peanuts or ice cream, wearing frowzy hats, seated singly or in pairs or in trios. They are afternoon customers who have paid ninety-nine cents for their out-of-the-house double feature. The camera pans from their stupefied faces to the screen, which shows the opening title of the next picture: "Otto Preminger Presents *Bunny Lake Is Missing.*" (*Dissolve.*)

INTERIOR. Courtroom. All the members of the cast are present and in their places—Judge Klein, Marvin Schwartz, Myles Lane, Preminger, Barnes, and the various spectators. Rising to swear in a witness is the court clerk, who is a gray-haired man with a gray, cropped mustache; he wears a regular business suit, and he somewhat resembles Judge Klein, too. Approaching the witness box is the witness for the plaintiff. He is an affable-looking, neatly dressed middle-aged man.

COURT CLERK: Raise your right hand. (*The court officer holds a Bible for the witness, who puts his left hand on it.*) You do solemnly swear that the evidence you will give the Court in the cause on trial shall be the truth and nothing but the truth, so help you God? (*The court clerk is projecting beautifully, and as he winds up, he glances at Preminger, who is looking admiring and amused.*)

MAN: I do.

COURT OFFICER (*projecting as nicely as the court clerk*): Be seated. Give your name and residence.

MAN: Carmelo Joseph Villante, 245 East Sixty-third Street, New York City. (*Closeup of the court reporter tapping on his machine, looking bored. Cut to Marvin Schwartz, who stands and addresses the witness.*)

SCHWARTZ: Mr. Villante, what is your occupation?

VILLANTE: Vice-President, Batten, Barton, Durstine & Osborne advertising agency.

SCHWARTZ: And is Batten, Barton, Durstine & Osborne one of the leading advertising agencies in the United States?

VILLANTE: Yes, it is.

SCHWARTZ: Will you tell the Court what your connection is with the television program known as the *Schaefer Award Theatre*?

VILLANTE: Schaefer Beer, one of our clients, sponsors the *Schaefer Award Theatre* in its entirety.

SCHWARTZ: And what is your personal connection with that program?

VILLANTE: As account supervisor of the Schaefer Beer account, I personally am responsible for the *Schaefer Award Theatre* as a television property.

SCHWARTZ: Will you describe that program to the Court, for the record?

VILLANTE: The basic concept of the *Schaefer Award Theatre* is, we take the best available first-run motion pictures, unedited, and we put them on in place of the *Late Show* on WCBS-TV in New York, here, with a great deal of promotion and with only four commercial intermissions.

SCHWARTZ: Are any of the pictures ever shown with deletions or eliminations of any kind?

VILLANTE: Not to my knowledge.

SCHWARTZ: Is any picture ever shown with more than four interruptions for commercials?

VILLANTE: No.

(*Cut to the clock. The time shown is 10:12. Dissolve. The clock again. The time is now 10:38.*)

LANE (*cross-examining Villante*): Can you answer this question: When the public, or you yourself, part of the public, look at a picture and you see a number of commercials on it, do you have any resentment against the station, or is your resentment, if you do have any resentment, against the producer of the picture?

SCHWARTZ (*jumping to his feet*): I object to that question, Your Honor. I will withdraw my objection if the witness will tell me that he understands that he is unhappy at being invited to make disparaging remarks about competitors.

JUDGE KLEIN: Before you put him on the spot, I will overrule your objection. So whether he is unhappy or not, if he can answer the question, he should.

VILLANTE: As a viewer, naturally I resent them.

LANE: Is your resentment against the station?

VILLANTE: I do not pinpoint it. It is just a general, over-all resentment.

LANE: Well, is your resentment against the producer or director of the picture?

VILLANTE: No, I doubt if it would be against the director of the picture. (*Cut briefly to Preminger, who looks glum. Then cut to the judge, who looks lively.*)

JUDGE KLEIN: *My* resentment would be against the advertiser!

LANE: In fact, isn't one reason why you have four commercials the fact that Schaefer has determined that the public ire at too many commercials is directed to the sponsor?

VILLANTE: That is true. I think—Let me just qualify that for a moment. I think we take a more positive viewpoint on the thing. We do not say: Here is a negative that we are going to turn into a positive. What we are doing here is making a very positive statement by saying that we are taking the public interest, and we are only going to show four commercials, because we, as television viewers, this is how we would like to see a movie. Basically, this has been the concept.

JUDGE KLEIN: Is there anybody else in other advertising that does that?

VILLANTE: Unbelievably, no, to my knowledge. (*He looks a trifle smug.*)

LANE: I believe you said that you had the right to select the places where these commercials are put in. (*Cut to the clock, and then cut back to Lane.*) And do you have a background yourself in motion pictures?

VILLANTE (*chuckles and looks proud*): I am the greatest movie fan in the United States.

JUDGE KLEIN: Next to *me!* (*He looks prouder than Villante. Dissolve.*)

INTERIOR. Corridor of the courthouse. A telephone booth. Barnes, inside, is seen through the glass door. He has a stack of dimes on the shelf under the telephone. Looking preoccupied, he makes one call after another.

INTERIOR. Courtroom. Villante is being excused by the judge, and, as he steps down, Barnes returns from making telephone calls and begins reporting the results to Preminger. Villante stops to shake Preminger's hand.

VILLANTE (*with tremendous enthusiasm*): Mr. Preminger, isn't it wonderful the way the judge is a fan of the *Schaefer Award Theatre?*

PREMINGER (*dryly*): Wonderful. (*He turns back to Barnes.*)

BARNES: The contract is in the office, on your desk, all signed, sealed, and delivered.

PREMINGER: Have someone bring it down to me here. I want to get the project started. I do not want to waste time. (*Pan to Marvin Schwartz, who is calling the next witness.*)

SCHWARTZ: Mr. Archer Winsten! (*Winsten comes forward. He is a tall, somewhat bohemian-looking fellow, with a "Front Page" newspaperman's forthright manner. He wears a dark-blue shirt, a maroon tie, and a dark suit.*)

COURT CLERK (*again projecting*): You do solemnly swear that the evidence you will give the court in the cause on trial shall be the truth and nothing but the truth, so help you God?

WINSTEN: I do. (*He sits down in the witness chair.*)

COURT OFFICER: Be seated. Give your name and residence.

WINSTEN: Archer Winsten, 425 West Broadway, New York City.

SCHWARTZ: Mr. Winsten, will you tell the Court what your occupation is?

WINSTEN: I am the movie critic and the ski editor of the New York *Post.*

JUDGE KLEIN: And the *what* editor?

WINSTEN (*calmly*): Ski editor.

JUDGE KLEIN: Ski? S-k-i?

WINSTEN (*just as calmly*): That is right. (*The judge and most of the other people in the room laugh. Preminger is shown with a straight face. Winsten smiles calmly.*)

JUDGE KLEIN: Is there any connection between the two?

WINSTEN: No connection, except that I like to do both.

SCHWARTZ: For how long have you been a movie critic, Mr. Winsten?

WINSTEN: Twenty-nine and a half years.

SCHWARTZ: All of that time with the New York *Post?*

WINSTEN: Right.

SCHWARTZ: Have you seen the motion picture *Anatomy of a Murder*?

WINSTEN: Yes.

SCHWARTZ: What, Mr. Winsten, in your opinion, would be the effect upon the quality of *Anatomy of a Murder*—

LANE (*jumping to his feet*): I object to any questions along that line to this witness. I don't think he is qualified to give any opinion.

JUDGE KLEIN (*to Schwartz*): You haven't finished your question, have you?

SCHWARTZ: No, Your Honor.

JUDGE KLEIN: Let him finish the question first and then make your objection, and I will rule.

SCHWARTZ (*trying not to look put upon*): Let me begin it again. It will probably be easier. What, in your opinion, Mr. Winsten, would be the effect upon the quality of *Anatomy of a Murder* if during the course of its exhibition, either in a theater or on television, it was interrupted on twelve separate occasions and during each interruption two or more commercial announcements were shown?

LANE: Now my objection, Your Honor. I don't think that this man is qualified to give an opinion, and I don't think his opinion would be relevant to the issues in this case.

JUDGE KLEIN: Well, let me understand the question. Do you mean what is his opinion with regard to the effect on the *picture*?

SCHWARTZ: Yes.

JUDGE KLEIN: Or the effect on the viewer?

SCHWARTZ: Effect on the picture, which I believe necessarily, has an effect on the viewer.

JUDGE KLEIN: It does seem to me, gentlemen, that more important than this witness's opinion with regard to whether these deletions or commercials, or whatever you call them, would have any effect on the picture is what the effect on the viewer would be. After all, I am certain that these movies shown on television are shown to get business, and certainly they don't intend to just have movie critics enjoy the picture. I am going to permit it, but I might say that I doubt it will have a great deal of probative value. However, I will permit it. Objection overruled.

LANE: I point out Mr. Winsten is a *movie* critic but not a *television* critic.

JUDGE KLEIN: That is true.

LANE (*petulantly*): They are diffcrent.

JUDGE KLEIN (*pointedly patient*): We are talking about the picture itself. (*He turns to Schwartz.*) You want to know what effect it would have?

SCHWARTZ: Yes—whether in theaters or in television.

LANE: May I point out the effect in the theater is of no consequence as far as this case is concerned. We are talking about motion pictures on television, not in the theater. This is free television.

JUDGE KLEIN: I think at the heart of this whole case, the crux of this, is Mr. Preminger's contention that the artistic value of this picture is destroyed by these deletions or interruptions, or whatever you might call them. I will take it for whatever it may be worth. The objection is overruled.

SCHWARTZ: Do you have the question in mind, Mr. Winsten?

WINSTEN: Yes, I have, and I have a couple of answers, going back to the medium itself, the sequence of pictures, the fact that a motion picture is made as an illusion. (*Takes a deep breath.*) It is an art based on cutting and sequence of cutting. The person who makes the picture makes the picture in terms of the effect of these cuts on an audience, and [how] the entire sequence mounts to climax is a matter of his art and his way of cutting this thing. Now, if you interrupt this somewhere along the line, obviously you are going to destroy—or damage, at least—his original effect, his intended effect. I would say this from a critical point of view. (*Takes another deep breath.*) I can also say that I have seen interruptions in a theater and they are very damaging. (*Cut to the clock. The camera watches the clock advance twelve minutes in one actual second. Then cut back to Judge Klein, Winsten, and the lawyers.*)

JUDGE KLEIN: Let me ask you one question, Mr. Winsten. Do you watch movies on television?

WINSTEN (*with subdued passion*): Not if I can help it!

JUDGE KLEIN: Well, those that you see, they all do have interruptions, do they not, for commercials?

WINSTEN: As far as I know, almost everything has interruptions for commercials, including football games, and I must say I resent them—the interruptions.

JUDGE KLEIN: Football games aren't so bad; they usually do it during the time out. Go ahead. (*Nods to Schwartz.*)

SCHWARTZ: Players welcome it. (*Laughs, alone.*) Now (*clears throat*), what, Mr. Winsten, in your opinion, would be the effect upon the quality of *Anatomy of a Murder* of deletions from the picture of scenes or sequences by a person other than the director?

WINSTEN: I can't say positively what the effect would be, because the contention is always made that things can be improved by a person of greater artistry. Well, now, if you could get someone of greater artistry coming along and making cuts, there might be an improvement. The assumption, however, is that the person who made the picture knew what he was doing, was going to make his points, and put in there only what was necessary. So that if it is a perfect work of art anything taken out will be a loss.

SCHWARTZ: Thank you. I have no further questions. (*Schwartz sits down, and Lane rises.*)

LANE: Mr. Winsten, have you seen *Anatomy of a Murder* on television?

WINSTEN: No, sir.

LANE: Have you seen the picture itself?

WINSTEN: Yes, sir.

LANE: Would you say that your opinion as to whether a picture could be cut with minor cuts is a subjective one?

WINSTEN: Well, in stating that it can be improved or worsened, I don't say it is a subjective opinion. Obviously it is true, or it can remain exactly the same, in effect, but it depends in every case what the picture is, what the cuts are. In general, that it changes the picture yes, I would say generally it does, and this is not a subjective opinion. I would say, that this is a critical opinion that would be generally held.

LANE: Would you say that some other person, some other expert, some other director or producer might disagree with your opinion?

WINSTEN: I doubt it. (*Cut to Preminger, who is listening attentively.*)

LANE: Now, do you consider commercials as being part of the picture?

WINSTEN: I have been watching a picture, been watching TV—oh, perhaps not too closely, but sometimes one doesn't watch TV too closely—and I have been confused to the point of thinking I was still looking at the story. This is particularly true of those noon-time soap operas, and I would go from an event where two women, a mother and daughter, were having a hard time to two women having another hard time, and find out that I was listening to their trouble with soap. (*Cut to our old friend the clock, and watch it advance ten minutes in one actual second.*)

LANE: In your opinion, do the commercials themselves, the commercials, affect the quality of the picture?

WINSTEN: Perhaps, in contrast, they would make the picture seem better. I can imagine that that would be so, although it never happened to me.

LANE: So are you in a position now to make a statement as to whether or not certain parts of that picture, *Anatomy of a Murder*, could be deleted without great damage to the picture?

WINSTEN: I am not in a position to say that. The only thing I could say is that it is a murder-and-suspense picture, so that if you take out any vital part or any contributing factor, you have lessened the effect, I would guess. (*Dissolve.*)

INTERIOR. Gymnasium in Preminger's house. Rise-and-shine time. A wall clock with second hand near the entrance to the sauna reads exactly seven o'clock. Preminger enters wearing dark-blue swimming trunks and rubber-soled slippers, and gets on the bicycle exercise machine. He reaches forward and turns on a tiny portable Sony television set on a shelf under the sun lamp. Then he turns on the sun lamp, which is trained on his face and chest. He starts pumping, simultaneously watching a news program on television. The second hand goes around the clock face fifteen times, speeded up. Then Preminger dismounts and goes into the sauna. (*Dissolve.*)

INTERIOR. Taxi. Bob Romaner is heading south on the East River Drive. Romaner's passengers are Preminger and Bill Barnes. Romaner is talking, very cheerfully, and Preminger and Barnes are listening, both with half smiles. Romaner manages to look alert as a driver, even though he is keeping an eye, by way of the rearview mirror, on his passengers' reactions.

ROMANER (*winking, in the mirror, at Barnes*): I guess you heard what

Mr. Preminger said when he saw the film I made about the Bowery, with myself playing the bum on the Bowery.

BARNES: He said you were very good.

ROMANER: He said, "You were so good I'm surprised you didn't get arrested!"

PREMINGER: I *am* surprised.

ROMANER: He liked the way I photographed—isn't that what you said, Mr. Preminger?

PREMINGER: I like you, Mr. Romaner. I admire you.

ROMANER (*as though addressing Barnes*): He was going to lend me his sixteen-millimeter to make the film. But I said, "Look, forget it. I'm going to shoot this film on my own eight millimeter, and I want you to look at it." So I shot it on my own. It's all mine. I brought it to him in his office. I was impatient for him to see it. He wanted to see it later, but I was so impatient he sat right down on the floor in his office, and we showed it in the corridor, where it was dark. (*Preminger laughs, looking interested as Romaner talks about him.*)

BARNES: I understand you played in a film with Peter Sellers.

ROMANER: In that television film *A Carol for Another Christmas*. I played a football player. I carried him in, with three other football players. And I also played in *The Reporter* on television, with Harry Guardino. I played a policeman. And I guess you know I'm in *As the World Turns*, the leading soap opera on television. I work a lot with that show. I play an intern.

PREMINGER: And when you do not act, you don't mind doing this work?

ROMANER: I don't like to be idle. As soon as I've finished an acting job, I jump right back in the cab.

PREMINGER: It is admirable. It is very amusing. (*Dissolve.*)


INTERIOR. Courtroom. Elia Kazan gives his name and residence and prepares to testify. He wears a gray business suit, a white shirt, and black tie. His hair is thick and gray, and is combed neatly back and parted on the side. He shifts around in the witness chair, making himself comfortable, and smooths a hand over the front of his jacket, which is buttoned.

SCHWARTZ: And for how many years have you produced or directed motion pictures?

KAZAN: Since 1945. It is twenty years.

SCHWARTZ: Can you tell the Court the names of some of the pictures you have produced or directed?

KAZAN: Well, I produced and directed *America America, On the Waterfront, East of Eden, Viva Zapata!, Gentleman's Agreement, Baby Doll, A Face in the Crowd, A Tree Grows in Brooklyn, Boomerang*, and some others.

SCHWARTZ: And have any of your pictures won Academy Awards?

KAZAN: Two did, yes.

SCHWARTZ: Does the term "cutting and editing" have an accepted meaning in the motion-picture industry?

KAZAN: Yes, it is one of the functions of a director-producer that are most essential. It is the thing that in many cases makes the picture what it is. It is one of the three most important functions that a director or producer has, and it does have an accepted meaning. (*He unbuttons his jacket and puts his hands in his pants pockets.*) It is one of the pillars on which our craft is built.

SCHWARTZ: Can you relate it in terms of more important or less important to such things?

KAZAN: There are three important things in making a film. One is the preparation of the script and the casting. I would say [that] would be roughly a third; and a third would be the actual shooting of the picture, the photography of the principal scenes; and then the final third would have to do with this process of cutting or editing and the scoring and the final putting together of the picture. A good job of editing can make a crucial difference in the effect of a picture. A sloppy or bad job of editing can reduce the value of a picture a great deal. It is a very crucial and ticklish and sensitive part of our work.

SCHWARTZ: As distinguished from "cutting and editing," does the term "final cutting and editing" have an accepted meaning in the motion-picture industry?

KAZAN: Yes, it does. There are certain directors and producers in our industry who have worked a long time and worked very hard and had some success and they get a right, finally, known as the final cutting. The final cutting means that the film is the way the artistic director of the film meant it and wants it to be. He thinks that the various values are correctly exposed in the way he leaves the picture. It is a long and sensitive process, and when you say "Final cut" and you have that right contractually, you say, in effect, to the distributor of the picture or the financial producers of the picture, "That is the way I meant the picture to be. That is the way it is."

SCHWARTZ: If a producer has by contract the right to make the final cutting of a picture, as you have defined it, may, as that term is understood in the industry, may thereafter the distributor make any change in the picture?

KAZAN: None whatever—not if he has that right contractually. That is what the right means.

SCHWARTZ (*rather dramatically*): Can he make any eliminations from the picture?

KAZAN (*just as dramatically*): None! (*Cut to Judge Klein, who looks quite fascinated.*)

SCHWARTZ: May he show the picture with intermissions or interruptions?

KAZAN: Not unless it has been in the plan originally and not unless it was in the contract, in the understanding, in the basic understanding. (*Cut to the court buff, who looks much concerned, and is taking notes on a legal-size lined yellow pad. The court buff uses a wooden pencil, the point of which he wets rather often with the tip of his tongue as he takes his notes.*)

SCHWARTZ (*putting his hands in his pants pockets and turning to his left, and then, as he phrases his question, slowly turning his body to face the witness*): What, in your opinion, would be the effect upon a picture, a serious picture, if when the picture was shown on television it was interrupted at twelve separate places, and if during each interruption there were screened two or more commercial announcements?

KAZAN (*keeping his hands in his pockets and crossing his legs*): Well, I have never been in a courtroom before in this position (*looks at the judge, who gives him a compassionate nod*), and I don't know about legalisms, but this is not a—I mean, it is something we have all seen a thousand times or a hundred times. We have TV sets and we see what the effect is. I have seen pictures I liked very much hurt very badly by the interruptions. I find, inevitably, the flow of a picture is severely damaged. The continuity of thought is lost, and, what is worse than that, the buildup, the feeling that the director works so hard to get, that there be a mounting feeling of some kind or other, is dissipated, leaks out. The interruptions are, furthermore, often put where they shouldn't be. They are the kind that are callow and stupid and insulting to the intelligence of the viewer, and I don't know how to restrain myself about it. (*He's all worked up and looks again at the judge, who looks even more sympathetic than before.*) It is absurd and it is insulting to the original maker of the picture, but aside from that it hurts the audience's appreciation of what could have been a wonderful experience. It is chopped up. Diverted. Diffused. Is that sufficient? Does that answer your question?

JUDGE KLEIN (*gently sympathetic and knowledgeable*): Well, would your answer be the same, sir, if there were only four interruptions?

KAZAN (*still hotheaded*): Yes, it would, if the interruptions weren't placed carefully and weren't reckoned in the original plan. I would still think that the effect would be harmful unless the interruptions had been planned for, unless the film was planned to allow a break, but even at that I would say it is harmful. (*Looks at the judge.*) I can't take any attitude but this, Judge. I still think it would be harmful, because your interest has hopefully been caught up in a human drama, in the fate of certain human beings, and then you are forced to watch something about beer or brassières or soap, or something else. It can't be anything but harmful. I am against it altogether.

JUDGE KLEIN (*still gently sympathetic*): Have you had any of your pictures done on television?

KAZAN: I sure have! A picture of mine—

JUDGE KLEIN (*interrupting enthusiastically*): *East of Eden*?

KAZAN: *East of Eden* was done. *On the Waterfront* was done. There were five or six interruptions for commercials after the first reel, and somewhere—I turned the picture off about a third of the way through; I was embarrassed and humiliated by what had been done—but somewhere, before I left, there was a commercial very much like the scene that had been on just before the commercial, so for one split second, I imagined, an innocent viewer would think that is part of the picture, and I just stopped looking at the film. (*He looks hurt. Cut to the judge, who is giving a couple of sympathetic clucks. Cut to Preminger, who looks patient.*)

JUDGE KLEIN: Didn't you think that something like that might happen, sir, if you agreed to have your picture shown on television?

KAZAN (*hotly*): I never *did* agree. I never was consulted or never did agree to it.

JUDGE KLEIN (*looking rather scholarly*): All right, go ahead. (*He nods at Schwartz.*)

SCHWARTZ (*satisfied*): Your witness, Mr. Lane. (*Lane gets to his feet and takes a step forward, slowly.*)

LANE: Mr. Kazan, did you see the picture *Anatomy of a Murder* on TV?

KAZAN: No, I didn't.

LANE: Did you see it when it played in the theater?

KAZAN: Yes, I did.

LANE (*looking unimpressed by the witness*): That was when—in 1959?

KAZAN: Whenever it came out—shortly after it came out.

LANE: Would you say this film can't be cut because it is unique?

KAZAN (*seemingly just as unimpressed by Lane*): Would I say it can't be cut because it is unique? No, I wouldn't phrase it that way. I would say that the director of the picture cut it as it should be cut, and it should be left alone.

LANE: Would you say that this picture is unusually suspenseful?

KAZAN: Yes.

LANE: Would you say that it has an unusual dramatic quality?

KAZAN: Yes, I would.

LANE: Are you familiar with the novel?

KAZAN: No.

LANE (*putting his hands in his pockets, in his turn*): In your opinion, could the novel on which this picture is based—could that be cut without any material damage?

SCHWARTZ (*leaping to his feet*): I object, Your Honor! If I can't question theater interruptions, I wonder why Mr. Lane can question about novels!

LANE: This is cross-examination, Your Honor. It is a little different.

JUDGE KLEIN: Not that different, but I will permit it. (*He gives an uncovered yawn.*)

KAZAN: I don't understand the question. I didn't read the book. (*Everybody except Lane laughs.*)

LANE: I don't see anything funny about this, Your Honor.

KAZAN (*smiling broadly*): It is very funny, I think. You asked me—

JUDGE KLEIN (*motioning to Kazan to keep quiet*): All right. Please.

KAZAN (*grinning*): I am sorry.

JUDGE KLEIN: *I* am the director here! Not you, sir! (*Looks at Kazan sternly but in such a way as to indicate that he's only kidding.*) *You* answer the questions!

LANE (*angrily*): I asked if in your opinion could any of the passages of the novel be cut—

KAZAN: But I didn't read the novel!

LANE (*angrily trying to finish his question*): —without any material damage?

KAZAN (*stubbornly*): I didn't read the novel.

LANE: Your opinion is a subjective one, is it not? This is your own opinion?

KAZAN: Yes, it is mine, yes.

LANE: Could other directors or producers have a different opinion insofar as this picture is concerned?

KAZAN (*coldly*): Could they? Yes, they could.

LANE: And isn't it possible?

KAZAN: I doubt it, but they could, yes.

LANE: It is possible they could disagree with you with reference to any cuts in this picture?

KAZAN (*mechanically, and a bit in the manner of Marlon Brando*): It is possible, yes.

LANE: You say that nothing in that picture could be withdrawn, could be deleted, without materially damaging the picture?

KAZAN: Yes. The picture had a strong effect on me, and I think the effect of a picture is due, among other things, very largely to its editing. I had to feel that if it had an effect on me, without knowing the details, that the editing was right. I wouldn't like anyone to touch it. (*Dissolve.*)

INTERIOR. Courtroom. Preminger, his hands intertwined in his lap, is seated in the witness chair, hunched forward slightly, and looking happy for the first time in the course of the trial.

SCHWARTZ (*standing, holding his charcoal-rimmed eyeglasses and biting on one of the stems*): Can you tell the Court, briefly, of your educational background and your early experience in the theater?

PREMINGER (*happily*): Well, from the age of nine years old I wanted to be an actor. I became an actor in Max Reinhardt's Vienna Theater at the age of seventeen. My father was at one time the Attorney General for the Austrian Empire and later on a lawyer, and he was very unhappy about this choice, and as an accommodation—

JUDGE KLEIN (*straining to miss not a word*): About his choice or your choice?

PREMINGER: About *my* choice. And as an accommodation to him I agreed to finish some kind of studies, and because he was a lawyer, I studied law, and at the age of twenty—between twenty and twenty-one—I became a Doctor of Law of the University of Vienna, but I never practiced law. As a matter of fact (*laughing*), by that time I had given up acting and I had my own theater as a director, and eventually, before I came to the United States, in 1935, I had taken over Max Reinhardt's theater in Vienna and ran it as a manager-producer and director, and in 1935 I came to the United States, directed one stage play, and had a contract to go to Hollywood with Twentieth Century-Fox, where I started to make motion pictures.

SCHWARTZ: When you made *Anatomy of a Murder*, under the contract which you have before you as Exhibit 1, did you make it in such a way that parts could be eliminated from it without affecting its quality?

LANE (*jumping to his feet*): Well—

PREMINGER (*quickly answering, talking through Lane*): No!

LANE: I object!

JUDGE KLEIN: Just a minute!

LANE (*petulantly*): I move to strike that. I object to the question as calling for a conclusion!

JUDGE KLEIN: Overruled. The answer is no.

SCHWARTZ: Did you make *Anatomy of a Murder* in such a way that it could be interrupted—

PREMINGER (*impatiently talking through his own attorney*): No!

SCHWARTZ (*patiently finishing his question anyway*): —for commercials or for any other purpose, without affecting its quality?

PREMINGER (*loudly, assertively*): No!

LANE (*on his feet again*): Same objection, Your Honor.

JUDGE KLEIN (*quickly*): Overruled. (*Looks at Preminger with anticipation.*)

PREMINGER (*smoothly*): No.

JUDGE KLEIN (*looking as though he were trying to conceal his own amusement*): May I suggest, Mr. Preminger, that you don't answer a question if you see Mr. Lane getting up to make an objection. It takes him a long time to get up. (*Smiles at Lane.*) If you get up a little faster, you might prevent his answering.

PREMINGER (*trying to look sorry*): I will wait.

SCHWARTZ (*hands in pockets, glasses on*): Now, you have already testified, Mr. Preminger, who it was that determined the final form and content of a picture when the picture was made at a studio by a salaried producer and director. Now, turning to the pictures which you have made as an independent producer, who in each case has determined the form and the content in which the picture was released by the distributor?

LANE (*quickly on his feet*): Objection to that, Your Honor. It has nothing to do with the issues in this case—not relevant.

JUDGE KLEIN: Well—

LANE (*talking fast*): We have one contract in this case and that is the *Anatomy of a Murder* contract, and I think that any question should be directed to that.

JUDGE KLEIN (*taking off his glasses, covering up a yawn, and shaking his head*): I don't know where this is leading to or what the purpose is, but I have assured both you gentlemen that there may be much irrelevant, immaterial matter that is in evidence here, but when I review this, the testimony, as well as the exhibits, I will disregard anything along that line. I am sure you appreciate, Mr. Lane, we don't have a jury here, and therefore we don't have to be as careful about that. I am familiar with the rules, and while I will say I would be tempted to sustain your objection at this point, I do want to get in as much as possible, in the event the appellate court might want to review these proceedings. So I will permit it. (*Nods to Schwartz.*) Go ahead.

SCHWARTZ: Do you have the question in mind, Mr. Preminger?

PREMINGER: Yes. In the very first independent picture that I made, *The Moon Is Blue*, I obtained what I consider the real—only real—achievement of my career. (*He pauses, and then emphasizes each of his next words carefully.*) The final-cutting-and-editing clause—that means the right to determine the way the picture will be presented to audiences all over the world. (*Schwartz hunts around on his table among stacks of papers and folders, looking for something. In the lull, Judge Klein leans over to Preminger. In closeup, he talks very, very quietly to him.*)

JUDGE KLEIN (*confidingly*): You know, I once was an actor, too. I was an extra in Max Reinhardt's production of *The Miracle* in New York, in 1924. I carried a spear.

PREMINGER (*in the same confiding manner*): And I was a nun in Max Reinhardt's Salzburg Festival production of *The Miracle*. I was really the assistant director, but I played a nun besides.

SCHWARTZ (*consulting notes*): When, Mr. Preminger, was the first time you learned that Columbia and Screen Gems were planning to distribute *Anatomy of a Murder* on television?

PREMINGER: In June, 1964.

SCHWARTZ: And where were you at the time?

PREMINGER: I was in Honolulu, Hawaii.

SCHWARTZ: And what were you doing there?

PREMINGER: I was directing a picture called *In Harm's Way*.

SCHWARTZ: And how did you learn of this fact of Columbia's plans?

PREMINGER: I learned it from a group ad inserted by Screen Gems in the weekly *Variety*, a trade paper that appears in New York.

SCHWARTZ: After you learned of this, what did you do?

PREMINGER: I immediately called Mr. Leo Jaffe [Executive Vice-President at Columbia] in New York.

SCHWARTZ (*to Cooper*): Will you please hand Exhibit 18 to Mr. Preminger? (*Cooper hands Preminger a sheet of paper.*) Does Exhibit 18, Mr. Preminger, assist you in determining the date on which you called Mr. Jaffe?

PREMINGER (*reading the paper*): Yes. It was the day before this letter was dictated and sent by me.

SCHWARTZ: And what was that date?

PREMINGER: June 8, 1964.

SCHWARTZ: Can you tell the Court, as best you now recall it, what you said to Mr. Jaffe in this telephone conversation, and what he said to you?

PREMINGER: I said to Mr. Jaffe that I was shocked by this ad, which was in many ways a violation of my contract, because we had agreed that no ads which refer to my pictures could ever be inserted into any paper without being submitted for approval first. I finally pointed out that if they really wanted to put the picture on television, they had the duty to consult with me first, and that I strenuously objected, for several reasons, that the picture should be exhibited on television so soon after its original release, and without the benefit of a theatrical reissue. (*Cut to the court buff, who is quietly, and without taking his gaze from the witness, unwrapping a ham-on-white sandwich in his lap. He takes a surreptitious bite, chewing silently. No one seems to notice him.*)

SCHWARTZ: Now, can you tell us what Mr. Jaffe replied to you?

PREMINGER: Mr. Jaffe told me that he was not familiar with this ad or with the intentions of Screen Gems; that I would—that *he* would look into it; that if it were true that they intended to release it on television without consulting with me, I had—and I remember the word, because I never used it and he used it several times in this case, and I quote the word—I certainly had a serious grievance. He promised to immediately get in touch with the executives of Screen Gems and, if they had any plans, to stop them. I must admit that I got very excited during this conversation, and Mr. Jaffe assured me that he would do everything in the world to give me satisfaction and to let me know what happened. (*Cut to the sandwich-eater again and then back to the witness, Schwartz, and the judge.*)

SCHWARTZ: In this conversation, did Mr. Jaffe say to you, in words or substance, that *Anatomy of a Murder* had already been sold for television?

PREMINGER: No.

SCHWARTZ: Did he tell you, in words or substance, that Screen Gems had given the television stations the right to cut the picture or make eliminations from it?

PREMINGER: No.

SCHWARTZ: Did he tell you, in words or substance (*making the most of this particular legal rhythm*), that Screen Gems had given the television stations the right to interrupt the picture for commercials?

PREMINGER: No.

SCHWARTZ: Did he tell you, in words or substance... (*Voice fades. Cut to the clock, which goes ahead an hour or so. Back to Schwartz.*)

SCHWARTZ: Mr. Preminger, does the phrase "final cutting and editing" have an accepted meaning in the motion-picture industry?

PREMINGER: The phrase "final cutting and editing"...

LANE (*on his feet*): Your Honor, I will have to object.

SCHWARTZ (*quickly*): Answer that question yes or no, if you can.

PREMINGER: Yes.

SCHWARTZ: Could you tell us what is the meaning of that term "final cutting and editing," in the motion-picture industry?

LANE (*up again*): As the witness understands it, is that correct?

JUDGE KLEIN: Obviously, that is all he can tell us. His understanding.

PREMINGER (*with the air of a little boy whose honor has been defended*): The phrase "final cutting and editing" means that the person who has the right to the final cutting and editing determines the final form and content of the motion picture as it is to be exhibited by the distributor of the motion picture. Nobody can cut or add or change the sequence, or anything, in this motion picture after the right of the final cutting and editing has been executed. This applies to the showing of the picture in theaters, on television—

LANE (*standing*): Objection to that, Your Honor!

PREMINGER (*not paying any attention to Lane and continuing to talk*): —in homes, sixteen-millimeter.

LANE (*shouting*): Objection! I move to strike it! He was asked about *in the motion-picture industry*. Now Mr. Preminger is volunteering about television and everything else.

JUDGE KLEIN: This is *his* understanding of what the term *means*. He says it applies to all forms of exhibition, regardless of where.

LANE: The question was, I believe, restricted to the motion-picture industry.

JUDGE KLEIN: I don't recall that it was at all.

SCHWARTZ (*agreeably*): No, Sir.

LANE: Could we have the question, then?

SCHWARTZ: What is the meaning of the term?

PREMINGER (*impatient to talk*): May I continue?

JUDGE KLEIN: Go ahead.

PREMINGER: It is—in my opinion, there is no question that only one version of the motion picture exists, and that is the version that has been delivered or released by the person or the people who have the right to the final cutting and editing. In *my* contract, this right is qualified in one point.

SCHWARTZ (*indulgently*): You are going beyond my question.

PREMINGER: I am sorry.

SCHWARTZ: Have you finished your answer to my question of what the term "final cutting and editing" means?

PREMINGER: Yes.

JUDGE KLEIN: Excuse me a minute. Let me ask him at this point: You say this applies to showings on television as well?

PREMINGER (*vehemently*): Everywhere!

JUDGE KLEIN: Well, you know, do you not, sir, that when a movie is shown on television, there are commercials interspersed?

PREMINGER: There have also been showings in theaters for years—and they are less now—where people arbitrarily interrupted pictures and cut them. That doesn't mean that it is right.

JUDGE KLEIN: I am not interested in that.

PREMINGER: It is a malpractice on television that they do it.

JUDGE KLEIN: My question to you, since you are telling us your understanding of this term "final cut" that you say applies to any showing even if it is on television—

PREMINGER: Yes.

JUDGE KLEIN: The next question is: You know, do you not, that it is the practice to display or exhibit these films with commercials?

PREMINGER: With the permission or the tolerance of the people who have the final cutting and editing!

JUDGE KLEIN: In other words, it is your contention that that term means that even where it is shown on television, they have to come back to whomever they make the contract with—

PREMINGER (*talking through the judge with enthusiasm*): Right!

JUDGE KLEIN: —to determine where the commercials shall go. Is this your position?

PREMINGER: Either with their permission or with their tolerance. Without their objection.

JUDGE KLEIN (*looking thoughtful and yawning*): I think this might be a good point to suspend for lunch. (*Dissolve.*)

INTERIOR. Gasner's Restaurant. A closeup of a plate of golden-yellow cheese blintzes, brown along the edges, with pure-red cherry preserves dripping from the top of each of three blintzes on the plate. The camera pans up from the food to the face of the eater, Judge Klein. He looks at the plate with joyous anticipation. Cut to three more plates of cheese blintzes. Pan up to the faces of Preminger, Schwartz, and Cooper. We hear some blintz music. There is a long shot of the tables in Gasner's, all crowded. The music subsides, and we hear a lot of talking, a clatter of dishes. One closeup after another, in quick succession, of plates of cheese blintzes—one plate, three plates—being scooped up and the plates left clean. (*Dissolve.*)

INTERIOR. Courthouse. The corridor outside Judge Klein's courtroom. Preminger and Barnes are walking toward the entrance to the courtroom. They are approached by a morose-looking, chubby man with a round face and rosy cheeks. Preminger gives him a friendly nod.
  PREMINGER (*to Barnes*): Here is Mr. Jaffe.
  JAFFE (*somewhat short of breath but trying to sound casual*): I've been hearing my name being bandied about in there. (*He laughs in a forced way. Preminger laughs as though he were enjoying himself.*) How do you feel, Otto?
  PREMINGER: I feel better now, because now, when I go in there, I can *talk!*
  JAFFE (*giving another forced laugh, and looking uneasy*): No reason we can't be friendly.
  PREMINGER: I am *very* friendly. But your bosses are very personal about this trial. I ask them for prints of Columbia pictures to show in my screening room, but they refuse to give me any pictures. I think that is very silly. To refuse to give me *pictures!*
  BARNES: Well, we're getting pictures from Paramount and from Fox. We're getting a lot of good pictures.
  PREMINGER (*teasingly*): Mr. Jaffe is going to his office from here, and

he will tell them to send me pictures.
     JAFFE: Well, I don't know... (*Preminger turns abruptly and goes into the courtroom, and Barnes quickly follows.*)


INTERIOR. Courtroom. Preminger is seated in the witness chair again, and Lane is cross-examining him.
     LANE: Mr. Preminger, in your direct examination, I believe that you testified that you did not learn anything about the suggested release of *Anatomy of a Murder* for reissue purposes until sometime in September or the summer, was it, of 1965? Is that correct?
     PREMINGER (*strongly*): No. I did not learn about the picture having been reissued until after it had played in three places. We discussed the reissue of the picture constantly, from June, 1964, up to September—as long as we were on talking terms—September, 1965. Constantly, I was promised the reissue, and we did discuss it, but the plans for this particular reissue, which was done secretly and behind my back, were not divulged to me.
     LANE: I move to strike that out, Your Honor.
     JUDGE KLEIN: Strike it out. Just answer the question, *please*. (*He yawns, covering his mouth, then takes off his glasses, rubs his eyes, and puts his glasses back on.*)
     LANE: Isn't it a fact that you had agreed to release *Anatomy of a Murder* with a picture called *Who Was That Lady* in December of 1962?
     PREMINGER: No.
     LANE: You deny that?
     PREMINGER: Yes.
     LANE: Did you agree to release *Anatomy of a Murder* with a picture called *Who Was That Lady* in January of 1963?
     PREMINGER: No.
     LANE: Did you have any conversations about reissuing it at that time?
     PREMINGER: Yes.
     LANE: And wasn't it agreed at that time?
     PREMINGER: No.
     LANE: It was not?
     PREMINGER: I stopped it.

LANE: But before it was stopped, hadn't you agreed that the picture could he reissued—

PREMINGER (*impatiently interrupting the question*): No.

LANE (*looking irritated*): —with *Who Was That Lady?*

PREMINGER: No.

LANE: Now, is it not a fact that a Mr. Prinzmetal [I. H. Prinzmetal, one of Preminger's attorneys] has authority to respond to any letters received by the various corporations and companies which you have been affiliated with?

PREMINGER: Yes.

LANE: With reference to your pictures *Laura*, *Fallen Angel*, *Forever Amber*, *Bonjour Tristesse*, and *Exodus*, these were pictures that you either produced or directed, were they not?

PREMINGER: Or both.

LANE: Or both, yes. And isn't it a fact that these pictures were shown, at one time or another, on television?

PREMINGER: I didn't see them, but, to the best of my knowledge, yes.

LANE (*looking foxy*): Now, did you ever consult, or were you ever consulted by, anyone either on a network or on a local television station as to how these particular pictures that I have just referred to should be exhibited or advertised?

PREMINGER: No.

LANE: And isn't it a fact that you know of no custom in which a station or network consults with the director or producer of a feature film as to how this feature or picture should be advertised on television?

PREMINGER (*looking extremely puzzled*): I don't understand your question.

LANE (*to the court reporter*): Read the question back.

COURT REPORTER (*reading without expression*): "And isn't it a fact that you know of no custom in which a station or network consults with the director or producer of a feature film as to how this feature or picture should be advertised on television?"

PREMINGER: I still don't understand the word "custom" in this connection.

LANE (*restraining sarcasm*): You know what the word "custom" means.

PREMINGER (*now enjoying himself*): Yes, I know what the word "custom" means.

LANE: What does it mean?

PREMINGER (*looking thoughtful*): Hmm?

LANE (*repeating*): What does it mean?

PREMINGER (*indulgently*): Well, there are various meanings of the word. It is customary to have a lady walk through a door first. That is a custom. I mean, I cannot give you the exact definition as in a dictionary. I would have to look it up. But I don't know of any customs in television, or in—

LANE (*thinking*): Let me see…

PREMINGER (*gently sarcastic*): We don't live by customs. We live by *contracts.*

JUDGE KLEIN (*reading*): I didn't get the end of that.

COURT REPORTER: "We don't live by customs. We live by contracts."

PREMINGER (*talking fast and strong*): Not by customs. I have never heard anybody do anything in my profession by custom.

LANE: I move to strike the answer as not responsive.

JUDGE KLEIN: I will strike it, though the witness evidently doesn't understand what you mean when you use that term. You may go into it a little further, if you care to. (*Preminger looks at the judge, smiling. The judge glances at him, poker-faced, and looks back to Lane.*)

LANE: Mr. Preminger, I am going to read from a deposition which was taken of you on the twenty-seventh of October, 1965…. (*Voice fades. Dissolve.*)

INTERIOR. Preminger's house. Following a hard afternoon in court. Preminger's gymnasium. Preminger, wearing his blue swimming trunks, is sitting on his mechanical bicycle and pumping while the sun lamp shines on his face and chest. His children, Mark and Victoria, also wearing blue swimming trunks, are climbing around on the gym ladders along one wall. Mark seems to be very agile. Preminger occasionally glances at them, gives them a small smile, and pumps harder. Barnes comes into the gymnasium, studying some notes.

MARK (*not a bit distracted*): Hi, Billbarnes! (*First and last names are apparently one to him.*)
VICTORIA: Hi, Billbarnes!
BARNES (*going over to the children, each of whom holds on to a ladder with one hand and grabs one of his hands with the other and kisses it*): Hello, Mark. Hello, Missie. (*Turns to Preminger and speaks soberly.*) We can start looking at locations next week.
PREMINGER (*still pumping*): And I want to start seeing actors—young actors—next week. Then we will be through with the trial. We will wait only for the judge's decision. Now I will go take my Jacuzzi bath! (*He pauses while the children's nanny comes in and hustles them out, and then he goes on talking.*) You know what it is, a Jacuzzi?
BARNES: I *think* I've heard about them.
PREMINGER: The brochure that comes with it describes it as a hydromassage. It says it is like ten thousand little bubbles massaging your body. (*He laughs, dismounts, and heads for his bath. Dissolve.*)

INTERIOR. Preminger's house. The living room, on the second floor. White walls, on which hang, mostly in simple gold frames, paintings by Matisse, Braque, and Picasso. At a touch from Preminger, a Modigliani on one wall swings up, revealing a cozy little bar behind it. On another wall, over an off-white sofa that is fourteen feet long, hangs a huge Miró. It has a dark wood frame, a foot wide, made by Miró himself of wood from the roof of a Spanish peasant's house. A picture window takes up the better part of the back wall, looking out upon a Giacometti sculpture on the terrace, which, in turn, looks out upon a garden in which there is a Henry Moore "Seated Woman." The chairs in the living room are of aluminum and black leather or black wool, and are modern in design. Preminger and his wife, the former Hope Bryce, a tall, attractive, dark-haired woman wearing a simple, sleeveless black dress, are having drinks with guests, Gilbert Lloyd and a young, pretty woman named Enid Pariser. The voices of Mark and Victoria are heard babbling upstairs in their quarters. Lloyd, who is from London, represents the Marlborough Fine Art Gallery, Ltd., there, owned by his family. He is a handsome, dark-haired young man. Everybody is admiring the paintings on the walls and murmuring indistinctly. We hear faint picture music, with one brief, bitter reference, in D Minor, to Moussorgsky.

PREMINGER (*indicating the Matisse*): This Matisse is not my Matisse. This one is a replacement. Pierre Matisse sent it to me, temporarily, to take the place of *my* Matisse, which I have lent to the University of Southern California for an exhibition there.

MRS. PREMINGER: I like the replacement.

PREMINGER: It is pretty.

MISS PARISER: You have only modern paintings?

PREMINGER: Yes. I know the Renaissance paintings are beautiful. I still like them. But I have no desire to own them. It is not that I don't like old paintings. I know they are good. But they no longer do anything to *me*. I believe strongly that people must have the courage to live in their own period. (*Dissolve.*)


INTERIOR. Preminger's house. The dining room, on the first floor. Light-gray walls. Paintings, behind glass, by Chagall (two), Dufy, Klee, Bissier, and Rouault. The table, which is of light-gray marble matching the light-gray marble floor, is round and sixty-three inches in diameter. It is laid with black straw placemats, simple all-white Rosenthal china, and modern Danish silver. The centerpiece is a crystal bowl, with apricot carnations floating on water. The chairs have black leather cushions and clear-plastic backs—very modern. Through a picture window the diners—Preminger and Mrs. Preminger, Lloyd and Miss Pariser—look out at the Henry Moore sculpture in the garden. It is subtly lighted. Preminger and Lloyd are reminiscing about Vienna.

PREMINGER: Your grandfather used to sell antiques to my father in Vienna. Did you know that? (*The Finnish butler comes in from the kitchen with a platter of roast beef and passes it around. He wears a white jacket.*)

LLOYD (*nodding*): And did you know that my grandmother was in the crowd scene you shot there for *The Cardinal*? (*The two women laugh appreciatively.*)

PREMINGER (*smiling*): They did not like me in Vienna. When I asked them to sing the Horst Wessel Song for the picture, they all pretended they did not know the song. (*He looks wise.*) There was a headline in one Vienna paper saying "Otto Go Home!" (*Dissolve.*)

INTERIOR. Preminger's house. The projection room. The two couples are getting ready to see some films—non-Columbia films. White walls, with paintings by Miró (early), Manessier, Modigliani, and Dubuffet. Preminger sits down on a sofa at a long marble-topped table. The top slides back, revealing a panel of twenty-six buttons. A large painting by Ben Nicholson on the back wall goes up as Preminger pushes a button, revealing the projection booth, and at the same time a large white screen comes down over the front picture window. He pushes other buttons, showing his guests how these operate a large color-television set, a hi-fi set, and the sound for the films. He pushes still another button, and the lights dim and then go out. The film title flashes on the screen: *Alphaville*, by Jean-Luc Godard. (*Dissolve.*)

INTERIOR. Courtroom. Preminger is seated in the witness chair again. Lane is still cross-examining him. Preminger is beginning to look stubborn. Lane seems to be growing quite impatient with the witness. The judge yawns occasionally but still seems interested.

LANE: And, pursuant to this particular clause, isn't it a fact that Columbia had the right to exhibit this picture on television?

PREMINGER (*stubbornly*): Yes, but always the *same picture*.

LANE: I didn't get that last.

PREMINGER: *That* picture, the picture that *I* made.

LANE: We are talking about *Anatomy of a Murder*.

PREMINGER (*quickly*): I am talking about *Anatomy of a Murder*, the way *I* made it.

LANE: Forget that.

PREMINGER (*immediately*): I don't *want* to forget it!

LANE (*pleadingly, to the judge*): I move to strike the answer, Your Honor.

JUDGE KLEIN (*impatiently*): At any rate, the answer is yes, it gives them the right on television as well as in theaters?

PREMINGER: Yes.

LANE: Now, will you look at the second paragraph of the grant-of-rights clause…. (*Dissolve*.)

INTERIOR. Courtroom.

LANE: Well, Your Honor, you may recall that the witness said he didn't know anything about television or how things were done in television. Now I want to show that this man had complete knowledge of the fact that when you sell a picture for television you must, if you want to make money on the picture, expect commercials are going to be used.

JUDGE KLEIN: I have asked him that question myself, yesterday. Yes, Mr. Preminger?

PREMINGER: May I say that this depends—that television is not a law. This depends on how you negotiate with television. If you negotiate strongly, if you have something to sell, like one single picture of the quality and the desirability of *Anatomy of a Murder*, you can get almost all conditions in.

JUDGE KLEIN: Mr. Preminger, now, I know this has been covered, but so has everything else, I must say, in this whole trial been covered any number of times. You knew, did you not, sir, when you signed any contract, when you signed this contract, that [the picture] would at some time be shown on television?

PREMINGER: Probably. Yes.

LANE (*going on*): You mention the word "television" is in here?

PREMINGER: Yes.

LANE: You also know, do you not, sir, that these companies, the television stations that broadcast these pictures, are doing this for profit, so that they can advertise particular products?

PREMINGER (*stubbornly*): Between 1956 and today, this has been changed at least twenty times, and in the next ten years there will be no interruptions in any motion picture…. (*Dissolve*.)

INTERIOR. Courtroom. Both Preminger and Lane seem to be rather wrought up, each making no attempt to conceal disapproval of the other.

LANE: Do I understand, then, by your statement that the cutting and editing of *Exodus* and *Bonjour Tristesse* [on television] in no way damaged your reputation as a producer—

PREMINGER (*so eager to answer that he talks through Lane*): No, that is not—

LANE (*adamantly*): —and director (*he decreases the speed of his words, pronouncing each one slowly and distinctly*), because… you… had… sold… your… rights… to… these… pictures…. Is… that… correct?

PREMINGER: No! It damaged my reputation just the same—only I couldn't help it, because I couldn't stop it. This is the first picture where I have the *right* to stop it, and that is why I am in this lawsuit and that is why I am sitting here and that is why I am trying to defend my right in this contract. Up to this point (*now Preminger pronounces each word slowly and emphatically, spacing out the words*), there… is… no… picture… where… I… had… these… rights. (*Dissolve.*)

INTERIOR. Columbia Pictures Building, at 711 Fifth Avenue. The seventeenth floor, which is the top floor. A row of five elevators with green-painted doors, at right angles to the entrance to Preminger's office. The office has a large door, painted black, and a brushed-aluminum doorknob. On the upper left-hand side of the door, in Saul Bass modern letters of brushed aluminum, is the name "Otto Preminger."

One elevator door opens. Preminger hurries out, his hands clasped behind his back, and Barnes follows. Preminger opens his door and enters his office.

INTERIOR. Reception area, the secretarial office, behind glass windows, and the corridor leading to Preminger's private office, which has a walnut door. Various assistants sit at clean-looking modern walnut desks and at white Formica-topped typewriter tables on which are midnight-blue I.B.M. Executive typewriters. There are many symmetrically arranged filing cabinets, light beige. The assistants look up as Preminger rushes in, to the accompaniment of office music—crisp, neat figures on the strings and woodblocks, with oblique references to Leroy Anderson's "The Typewriter." The camera dollies with him as he nods to everybody and hurries along the corridor, which has a thick, very light-gray carpet and is hung with paintings and lithographs by Miró, Picasso, and Ben Shahn. Preminger takes off his topcoat as he walks.

INTERIOR. Preminger's private office. The same light-gray carpet. Large windows on two sides of the room, with vertical white Venetian blinds like the ones on the windows of his house. The blinds of one window have been left open, showing a view of the Fifth Avenue Presbyterian Church and a fragment of skyline. Beneath a Picasso, a long sofa upholstered in black-and-white tweed stands against another wall, and between it and the entrance are white folding doors, partly open, revealing a bar, and a dressing room nearby. Preminger's desk consists of a long, rectangular slab of white marble resting on two brushed-aluminum cylinders, and it stands with its back to a row of windows. In the middle of the room, another marble-topped table is more or less wrapped around a white pillar. At it are several laminated plastic-backed, black-leather-cushioned swivel chairs—the same kind as the chairs in Preminger's dining room. On the wall near the entrance are built-in bookshelves, the top shelves occupied by leather-bound sets of Goethe and Schiller in German; the lower shelves are occupied by modern novels, encased in their paper dust jackets. Hanging on the pillar with the wraparound table and facing the desk and illuminated by a spotlight is a delicate abstract painting by Kandinsky with a pure, clear deep-blue background. On the walls, in addition to the Picasso, are paintings by Klee, Diego Rivera, and Graham Sutherland. Spaced along the walls or on shelves in the windows are: a potted plant; a Puritron machine; a large color photograph of Mrs. Preminger with Mark and Victoria; a black suitcase, bearing the initials "O.P."; a large photograph of Franklin Delano Roosevelt inscribed in ink, "To Otto Preminger, with warmest regards, Franklin D. Roosevelt"; a half-filled box of Kleenex; a color photograph of Mark and Victoria, shown holding hands, at the age of three; and a photograph of Preminger's father, shown with his head resting against one hand. On Preminger's desk, in addition to a set consisting of a black leather ashtray, a black leather pencil holder, and a black leather memo pad, are: a photograph, in a black leather frame, of Mark and Victoria as babies; a white telephone, with a white speaker and amplifying box that permit one to talk and listen to his caller without picking up the telephone; and copies of motion-picture trade papers, including the *Hollywood Reporter* and *Film Daily*, the second with a headline reading, "Preminger Courts Attention to His *Anatomy* on Video." The chair behind Preminger's desk, which is also of black leather, is very substantial and comfortable-looking. Preminger enters, with Barnes, who closes the door. Preminger tosses his coat on the sofa and sits down at his desk. Barnes stands beside him as they talk.

PREMINGER: Fighting for this principle is costing me a fortune, but to me it is worth it. Actually, I am very detached about this trial. What amazes me is Columbia's attitude of complete disrespect for the pictures. Not that I feel that any film I make is such a great work of art. Only, I do feel you should not *do* this to anybody!

BARNES: What happens now?

PREMINGER (*with a sadly incredulous air*): Now the lawyers are busy with their post-trial briefs. We have summarized our contentions, and now they summarize their contentions, then we reply to *their* contentions, and then *they* reply to *our* contentions, and then the judge gives his decision, which will be that I am right. (*He laughs sadly.*) Meanwhile, we catch up on the work. We have two pictures to prepare. Who comes today? (*His manner changes quickly to one of businesslike efficiency.*)

BARNES: Those young actors you wanted to see. And Tim Clark. Remember him? That young high-school boy with that film workshop? And some others.

PREMINGER (*looking unimpressed by the schedule so far*): Is that all?

BARNES: That new writer started working this morning. I gave him an office across the hall. He's very particular. I never *saw* anybody that particular. I gave him some of our *Bunny Lake Is Missing* memo pads, but he said he couldn't use them. He needs *blank* memo pads!

PREMINGER: Get him what he wants. When you work with a writer, you must adjust yourself to the writer.

BARNES: And I had to go out and get him a special kind of pencil sharpener. And he had to have these special bookends; he couldn't use ordinary bookends.

PREMINGER: I like to do what *they* want.

BARNES: I understand all that. With these creative people, you've got to extend yourself. I'm ready to comply. By the way, both *Thunderball* and *A Thousand Clowns* have arrived at your house for tonight. What time do you want the projectionist for?

PREMINGER: Seven-thirty. I like to have him there as soon as we finish dinner. And tomorrow I have been promised *Life at the Top*, with Laurence Harvey.

BARNES (*surprised*): But that's a *Columbia* picture!

PREMINGER: I wanted to see it. (*Gives Barnes a Machiavellian smile.*) I also wanted to test how powerful certain people are. So I called up Larry Harvey in Palm Springs. I said, "Larry, I want to see your picture, but Columbia won't give it to me to show in my screening room." And Larry told me, "That is so silly. I will call them, and I will call you right back." But before he could call me back, Leo Jaffe called me. He sounded so sad. And he said, "The picture will be in your house tomorrow afternoon."

(*Preminger's intercom buzzer sounds, and a woman's voice is heard over the telephone speaker.*)

WOMAN'S VOICE: Roger Smith is here.

PREMINGER: Send him in.

(*The door opens, and in walks Roger Smith, a handsome young actor currently starring in the* Mister Roberts *television series. He has a California sunburn, and he is, in the latest fashion, smoking a thin cigar. He is decked out in a Glen-plaid jacket, gray flannel slacks, a red vest with silvery buttons, and a striped tie. As he strides toward Preminger, he extends a hand. Preminger stands up, shakes it, sits down, and, after Smith has shaken hands with Barnes, waves him into one of the black leather swivel chairs. Barnes sits down near Smith.*)

ROGER SMITH: Mr. Preminger, it's a pleasure to know you. (*He projects evenly.*)

PREMINGER (*quickly, without elaborate preliminaries, eager to get to the point*): You live here?

SMITH: No. In California. I'm here to see about being in a play.

PREMINGER (*wasting no time*): We wanted to see you. We are doing two films, with two good parts for a young man. But I haven't seen you in films or on television. I wanted to see you mostly on Barnes's recommendation. What have you done?

SMITH: My last picture was *Auntie Mame*. When I was still a juvenile. I've stayed out of films, because—

PREMINGER (*interrupting*): Who's your agent?

SMITH: William Morris. (*Goes on, talking fast.*) And I did about five years on *77 Sunset Strip*. Not the lead. I supported Efrem Zimbalist, Jr., who played the lead. After that, I wanted to do a play, So—

(*Intercom buzzer buzzes.*)

WOMAN'S VOICE: Joe Friedman calling.

PREMINGER (*having pushed a button, picked up the telephone, and listened awhile, smiling*): You're very sweet, and I wish the same to you. Success and health first, and then the winning of *your* lawsuit. Goodbye. (*He hangs up.*)

SMITH (*smoothly picking up again*): Anyway, when I left *Sunset Strip* I played in a West Coast production of *Bye Bye Birdie*. I found I had trouble getting the right parts in Hollywood. I turned down four series on television. I felt I had to prove I can be a leading man. When they offered me the lead in *Mister Roberts*, I took it for that reason. They offered me the title role. Actually, the shows that are popular are the bigger-than-life shows like *The Addams Family* and *The Munsters*. By comparison, *Mister Roberts* is an old-fashioned show. But I'm glad I did it, because—

PREMINGER (*apparently trying to wind up the meeting quickly*): Where can we *see* you?

SMITH: I'm going to be on *Hullabaloo* next Monday night.

PREMINGER: You *sing*?

SMITH: I'm the m.c. It's going to be—

PREMINGER (*getting up abruptly, without seeming to be rude, and dispensing with elaborate goodbyes as well as hellos*): Best way to see you would be a test. (*Indicates Barnes.*) He will make the arrangements.

SMITH (*beginning to talk as he stands up, and talking very fast as Barnes stands up, too*): I've admired you for a long time. I loved *The Moon Is Blue*, and *Laura* is the best and most effective mystery I've ever seen. I was glad to see they have finally given *The Moon Is Blue* a seal.

PREMINGER (*nodding, and speaking in a very dry manner*): Posthumously!

(*Smith leaves. Barnes sees him out and returns almost immediately. He and Preminger exchange looks signifying their interest in Roger Smith.*)
BARNES: I thought he looked very Episcopalian.
WOMAN'S VOICE (*over intercom*): Stanley Darer is here.
PREMINGER: Send him in.
(*Stanley Darer enters. Darer is dark-haired, and is wearing a dark suit and a dark Paisley necktie. He is a young man with an older-than-his-years look of the kind seen on the faces of many businessmen. Barnes says hello to him and leaves.*)
PREMINGER (*again without preliminaries*): Sit down. Let me tell you what it is about. What is the name of your company?
DARER: The Darer Corporation.
PREMINGER: All right. I bought these two pictures of mine back— *The Moon Is Blue* and *The Man with the Golden Arm*. I get these calls from agents in Germany, in England, in Japan, and they want to make deals. They say: Twelve thousand dollars for Korea. But what do I know about Korea? (*He laughs. Darer laughs.*) If you are interested in handling these films, and if agents send me letters, I would send them to you, and you take over. I know your father-in-law. He's an old friend of mine. He knows the foreign market.
DARER: Well (*clears his throat*), I'd be very happy to work with you.
PREMINGER (*quickly, in his manner of accomplishing the purpose of the meeting as directly as possible*): What would your terms be?
DARER: Well, I wasn't trying to hedge. What would you suggest? I wouldn't travel. I would work from here. It should be a percentage. And are there prints available?
PREMINGER: There are seventy prints available for each film.
DARER: Well, let me throw out a figure. Fifteen per cent.
PREMINGER (*smiling but looking taken aback*): Ten is much better. Where do you get fifteen?
DARER (*with a small laugh*): Where do you get ten? (*Laughs harder.*) O.K. Ten. I'd like to start with you. (*He stands up, extending his hand. Preminger shakes it.*)
PREMINGER: I have only one stipulation. There are to be no cuts in the films. I don't want the pictures ruined.
(*Darer leaves. Preminger picks up the* Film Daily *and begins to read* "Preminger Courts Attention to His *Anatomy* on Video." *Barnes enters carrying*

*a paperback book whose front cover bears a photograph of Preminger, wearing glasses and looking pensive, within a design featuring the bracket holes on film strips.)*

BARNES (*handing the book to Preminger*): It just came in.

PREMINGER (*examining the book*): Charming.

(*Closeup of the front cover of the book shows:* Otto Preminger par Jacques Lourcelles—Cinéma d'Aujourd'hui. Éditions Seghers. No. 34. *On the back cover is a listing of other subjects in the series, by number:* 1. Georges Méliès 2. A. Antonioni 3. Jacques Becker 4. Luis Buñuel 5. Alain Resnais 6. Orson Welles 7. Jacques Tati 8. Robert Bresson 9. Fritz Lang 10. Alexandre Astruc 11. Joseph Losey 12. Roger Vadim 13. Federico Fellini 14. Abel Gance 15. Roberto Rossellini…)

(*Intercom buzzes.*)

WOMAN'S VOICE (*over intercom*): I have your call to Nelson Gidding in California.

PREMINGER (*pressing the button that permits him to hear the caller over the speaker without lifting the telephone*): Look, I got a letter from your agent about your expenses. Can you decide what low expenses you need when you come here to work on the script?

GIDDING'S VOICE: Low?

PREMINGER (*laughing*): Low. And can you come here this Sunday?

GIDDING'S VOICE: Sunday?

PREMINGER: Yes. We must decide the mood and the structure.

GIDDING'S VOICE: Let me come Monday. It's better.

PREMINGER: Why?

GIDDING'S VOICE: I'll have to tell Hildy. And my mother-in-law is here. And the boy goes back to school. And one thing and another.

PREMINGER (*laughing again*): It doesn't matter. See you on Monday. (*He presses a button turning off the speaker.*)

BARNES: Then he'll be here Monday?

PREMINGER: Yes. (*Shrugs.*) I don't want to pressure him. I hate people who pressure me. (*Taking on the manner of a sage teaching a younger man.*) One of the secrets is to organize your life so that you can do what you want to do. Here is another example of how, when I work with a writer, I adjust myself to a writer. It is like not insisting that a writer give me a treatment first of what he is going to write. Some producers insist on a treatment. I do not

ask for a treatment. Writers do not like to do it, because it takes some of the bloom off it. I do what *they* want. (*Barnes nods, and leaves.*)
WOMAN'S VOICE (*over telephone speaker*): Mr. Romaner is calling.
PREMINGER: Yes, Mr. Romaner?
ROMANER'S VOICE: I'm at the Plaza Hotel with the taxi.
PREMINGER: I don't need the taxi now.
ROMANER'S VOICE: O.K. Take care.
(*Barnes returns with Tim Clark, the high-school student with the film workshop. Tim Clark is very serious and watchful, and a bit nervous. He wears black-rimmed spectacles, and he has a short, old-fashioned haircut, a mottled complexion, and a thin face still in the stage of being formed.*)
PREMINGER (*shaking hands with the boy and motioning him to a chair*): How is your workshop?
CLARK: We're making this film about a boy and his homework.
PREMINGER: How much has it cost?
CLARK: About a hundred dollars. And we want to make another film. We're trying to find someone to finance it, and you're the only man—
PREMINGER: How much do you need?
CLARK: Two hundred dollars.
PREMINGER: But I do not finance films. I am like you. I am a man who needs financing.
CLARK: Maybe the unions would finance it.
PREMINGER (*respectfully*): I do not think that the unions would like non-union-made films. It is only the foundations that put up money. Or very rich people whom I do not know. How old are you?
CLARK: Seventeen.
PREMINGER: You are going to go to college?
CLARK: Yes.
PREMINGER: Why, if you are going to college, do you want to raise money for the workshop? You will not be in it?
CLARK: It gave me a lot. I'd like to see it continued.
PREMINGER: How come you wear your hair so short?
CLARK: I don't know.
PREMINGER: Do the students in your high school wear their hair long? Do they take drugs? Do they take LSD?

CLARK: They take everything.

PREMINGER: I'll tell you what I will do. I will match whatever money you can raise by yourselves. If you raise fifty dollars, I will give fifty dollars for your workshop. If you raise more, I will give whatever you get. (*He stands up to say goodbye, and Clark is ushered out by Barnes, who returns as the intercom starts up.*)

WOMAN'S VOICE: Howard Felsher is here.

(*Felsher, a writer and television producer, walks in and sits down, very much at ease. He and Preminger seem to be old friends. Felsher looks to be in his late thirties, and he looks well adjusted and happy. He is wearing a tweed jacket and flannel slacks.*)

FELSHER: Well?

PREMINGER (*smiling at him and shrugging*): Well.

FELSHER (*to Barnes*): I'm trying to sell him a novel I wrote. But he's not interested. The novel is about a President of the United States. And Mr. Preminger thinks Presidents are passé.

BARNES: Is the novel finished?

FELSHER: I haven't started it yet. I wanted to wrap up this unique package, sell the screen rights to it *before* I start it.

BARNES: Isn't that what Harold Robbins did? Isn't that what—

FELSHER (*his face suddenly taking on a glow of enthusiasm*): Exactly! And that's what I—Anyway, what's new?

PREMINGER: I am suing Columbia. (*He picks up a printed copy of a posttrial memorandum drawn up by his attorneys and waves it at Felsher. It is a booklet entitled "Supreme Court of the State of New York—County of New York—Special and Trial Term, Part II—Otto Preminger and Carlyle Productions, Plaintiffs against Columbia Pictures Corporation and Screen Gems, Inc., Defendants—Plaintiff's Post-Trial Memorandum."*) Printed! I feel like a publisher! I paid for it.

FELSHER (*sympathetically*): You didn't want Columbia to sell *Anatomy of a Murder* to television?

PREMINGER: It was stupid of them to sell it so fast! Next year, television will need pictures even more than now. They are running out of pictures to show.

FELSHER (*enthusiastically*): Time is absolutely on your side! You have everything going for you. (*Dissolve.*)

\* \* \*

INTERIOR. Preminger's private office. Preminger is alone, and is looking without too much interest at the book about himself. The door opens and Barnes walks in.

BARNES: Carolyn Larson is here. You told Arthur Israel, at Paramount, you would be glad to meet her.

PREMINGER: Bring her in. (*Barnes returns with Carolyn Larson. She is young and pretty, with a lot of dark-brown hair, done up in beehive style. She wears a white wool two-piece dress that comes to just above her knees. There is a pause, during which Preminger seems to be trying to decide whether or not to stand up.*)

PREMINGER (*standing up, and, as usual, dispensing with a drawn-out hello*): How are you?

MISS LARSON: Fine, sir. (*There is another pause.*)

PREMINGER (*his face taking on a benevolent expression*): Speak!

MISS LARSON (*quickly*): My name is Carolyn Larson. I was born in Stockholm, Sweden. My father was a sea captain. As a youngster, I traveled back and forth with him between Sweden and the United States. As a matter of fact, we have something in common. I am European, and you, too, are of European background.

PREMINGER (*smiling*): There is something we do *not* have in common. (*Miss Larson looks questioning.*) I have an accent. You have *no* accent. (*Miss Larson laughs.*) What are your plans?

MISS LARSON: My plans are to break into motion pictures. I played the lead in one film. It is called *The Feel of the Thing*. It is about a very talented artist who just gives it up.

PREMINGER: Who plays the artist?

MISS LARSON: Al Muscari. It was directed by David Pokotilow. (*Preminger gives Barnes a look signifying that he has never heard of either one.*)

PREMINGER: Maybe we can see the film. We need films for my projection room. I am like television. I never have enough films. How old are you?

MISS LARSON: Twenty-three.

PREMINGER: What are you doing now?

MISS LARSON: I am studying under Lee Strasberg.

PREMINGER (*kiddingly*): Who is *he*?
MISS LARSON: Why, he is the father of The Method.
PREMINGER: He is not the *father*. The uncle, maybe. Or the cousin. But not the father.
MISS LARSON (*without a pause*): To me he's like a father.
PREMINGER (*even more benevolently*): What has he done for you?
MISS LARSON: I take private lessons—
PREMINGER (*interrupting*): Why private lessons? Why not the Studio? How much do private lessons cost?
MISS LARSON: Thirty dollars a month.
PREMINGER: What *has* he done for you?
MISS LARSON: He has dug into my mind, he has dug into my soul, he has dug into my spirit. He has helped me become a person. He has given me confidence and belief in myself as a human being.
PREMINGER (*dryly*): Interesting. Has *he* any problems?
MISS LARSON: He's a human being, too.
PREMINGER: Interesting. (*Dissolve.*)

INTERIOR. Preminger's private office. Preminger is now reading a printed booklet. A closeup shows it to be another post-trial memorandum. Barnes enters, bringing with him Scott Glenn, a handsome, dark-haired young man whose walk seems to indicate considerable independence and spirit. Preminger shakes his hand and looks at him with approval.
BARNES: Scott went to William and Mary. We come from the same part of the country.
PREMINGER: I am going to do a picture with a lot of young, good parts.
GLENN (*speaking in a soft voice somewhat suggestive of the South*): I understudied Ben Piazza in *The Zoo Story*. And now I'm playing in *The Impossible Years*.
PREMINGER: What is it?
BARNES: It's a play, a hit play, on Broadway. With Alan King.
PREMINGER: I'll come to see you in the play.
GLENN (*with a young grin*): It's a small but flashy part.
PREMINGER: All right. We will come to see you.

(*Glenn gets up and leaves, walking at a leisurely pace. Preminger and Barnes watch him go out. Then they turn to each other.*)
 PREMINGER: He's nice-looking. And he will be a good-looking man. He has a Gary Cooperish quality. I *like* him. (*Dissolve.*)


EXTERIOR. Sidewalk. In front of Preminger's house. Early morning, in the middle of the third week in January, 1966. Preminger stands in front of his door, holding each of his children by the hand. All three are wearing navy-blue raincoats. All three look clean, shining, impeccable. The children are wearing their navy-blue knitted caps. Preminger grimaces at Edward Durell Stone's house across the street, then toward Park Avenue. Romaner's taxicab comes toward them, moving fast, and draws up at the curb. Romaner's hair is shaggier than before. Preminger opens the door of the taxi, ushers the children in, and climbs in after them. Then the door of his house opens, and the butler, in his white jacket, comes out carrying the large Picasso painting that ordinarily, hangs over the sofa in Preminger's office, and hands it to Preminger. The taxi heads for the children's school.


INTERIOR. Taxi. Rear seat. Preminger keeps one hand balancing the painting against his legs and the other hand on Mark's shoulder.
 MARK: Daddy took me to the St. Regis barbershop, Mr. Romaner, and we got a haircut.
 PREMINGER: Only Mark got a haircut. (*Laughs.*) I do not have much hair to cut. I shave my head. Myself. But I got a manicure.
 VICTORIA: We want *you* to get a haircut, Mr. Romaner.
 ROMANER (*looking at her in the rearview mirror*): I can't. I've got to look this way for your daddy's next picture. I think he's writing me in.
 PREMINGER: I may have news for you soon. About your part, Mr. Romaner. (*Romaner is so startled that he almost runs the taxi into the car ahead of him.*) But in the meantime, Mr. Romaner, it really would be all right for you to get a haircut. The picture does not start for two months yet.
 ROMANER: O.K., O.K. (*He seems dazed.*)
 MARK: I got *my* hair cut. At the St. Regis.

VICTORIA: The hairdresser comes to the house and does Mommy's hair, and then he does Nanny's hair, and then he gives *me* a little trim.

ROMANER (*regaining his calm and throwing Preminger a significant look in the mirror*): Whatever will be will be.

(*He draws up in front of the school. Preminger and the children get out and start toward the door of the school. The painting is left in the back seat of the taxi. The camera follows Preminger, over the painting, through the taxi window.*)

INTERIOR. Taxi. Preminger returns and gets back into the rear seat. He places the Picasso on his lap as the taxi heads for Preminger's office.

PREMINGER (*thoughtfully*): At my age, when I look at my children and listen to them talk, they seem like a miracle. (*He casually adjusts the Picasso on his lap.*) The painting I took home from the office for one day, because we needed to put it where the Matisse was, for background, for a color photograph for an R.C.A. color-television ad.

ROMANER: You really meant it—what you said about the part in your picture?

PREMINGER: Yes. You will be very good for a part I have in mind.

ROMANER: (*looking euphoric*): What will be will be.

INTERIOR. Columbia Pictures Building. An automatic elevator, at ground-floor level. The elevator is packed. Preminger is the last one in before the door closes. He is carrying the Picasso under one arm. He nods at one of the other occupants, a short man wearing horn-rimmed glasses.

PREMINGER: Good morning, Mr. Jackter. I hear you have a new job at Columbia, and are no longer the sales manager.

RUBE JACKTER (*who seems to be sucking a cough drop*): How are you feeling?

PREMINGER: Fine. You didn't know that I am really ruling Columbia now? That I am responsible for your new job?

JACKTER (*smoothly*): I told you long ago you should have taken over.

PREMINGER (*laughing*): And sue *myself*?

JACKTER (*as the door opens on a lower floor and he starts moving out of the elevator*): Take care of yourself. Everything will be all right. (*He glances at the Picasso as the door closes. Dissolve.*)

INTERIOR. Preminger's private office. He is standing on his sofa, re-hanging his Picasso. He gets down, steps back, and looks at it, and appears satisfied. His secretary, an attractive young woman, brings in a large cup of black coffee in white Rosenthal china and sets it on his desk. As she leaves, he sits down at his desk, takes a sip of coffee, and starts reading the film trade papers. His buzzer buzzes.

MAN'S VOICE (*over telephone speaker*): Otto? Nat.

PREMINGER: Where are you?

MAN'S VOICE: At your house, putting in a new screen. The old screen had a wrinkle in it.

PREMINGER: Nat, this will be an important day. Today we get the judge's decision in the case. This morning. (*He finishes with Nat and talks to his secretary over the speaker.*) Get me Dr. Seligman. (*Nelson Gidding, a rather heavy man with a large, fluffy mustache, and a friendly manner, comes into the office, in shirtsleeves, and walking in his socks. He takes a chair across the desk from Preminger. Intercom buzzes.*)

SECRETARY'S VOICE (*over the intercom*): Dr. Seligman is tied up, giving a physical.

PREMINGER: Let me talk, please, to someone in his office. Anyone.

WOMAN'S VOICE: This is Dr. Seligman's secretary, Mr. Preminger. Dr. Seligman is tied up, giving a physical.

PREMINGER: Look. Just find out. Please. Does Dr. Seligman want me to continue with the antibiotics? It's due in half an hour. (*To Gidding*) I've been fighting a virus.

WOMAN'S VOICE: I'll do the best I can, Mr. Preminger.

PREMINGER: Thank you. (*Presses button for his own secretary.*) See if you can get Mr. Schwartz or Mr. Cooper for me. (*Turns to Gidding.*) Did you know that you don't say "square" anymore? It is now square to say "square." You now say "straight."

GIDDING: That so? (*The phone buzzes.*)

SECRETARY'S VOICE: Dr. Seligman is on the line.

PREMINGER: Hello.

DR. ARTHUR SELIGMAN'S VOICE: How are you doing?

PREMINGER: Shall I continue with the antibiotics?

DR. SELIGMAN'S VOICE: I think you can knock it off. Let me know if there's any problem about it.

PREMINGER: Thank you. (*Tunes out Dr. Seligman. Buzzer sounds again immediately.*)

SECRETARY'S VOICE: Mr. Schwartz is not in. Mr. Cooper is not in. Mr. Schwartz's secretary would like to speak with you.

PREMINGER: Put her.... Yes?

VOICE OF SCHWARTZ'S SECRETARY: Mr. Preminger, Judge Klein's assistant called and left word that the judge is disposing of the case this morning. The judge is dismissing it without prejudice to a renewal.

PREMINGER (*almost without pause or reaction*): Does that mean we have lost it?

VOICE OF SCHWARTZ'S SECRETARY: I don't know.

PREMINGER (*still not changing his tone*): Please. Ask Mr. Schwartz to call me. (*Turns to Gidding, with no change in expression.*) We will live.

GIDDING: You lost a round, that's all.

PREMINGER: I really didn't feel we could lose. I felt we were so right.

GIDDING: You'll appeal, of course.

PREMINGER (*maintaining his calm without apparent effort*): We will live. It is good for the character of people to lose from time to time.

GIDDING: It isn't *you* who have lost. It's all of us—everybody in films. Every writer, every actor, every director. (*He looks militant.*)

PREMINGER: A few years from now, the whole thing will look ridiculous. There will be *no* interruptions for commercials. It seems so simple. (*Barnes enters.*) Bill, sit down. We lost the case.

BARNES: I don't believe it. How? (*The telephone buzzes.*)

MARVIN SCHWARTZ'S VOICE: The news is bad. (*He sounds depressed.*) The judge decided it's the custom in television to make minor cuts and interrupt for commercials when a picture is shown, and that you were aware of that practice when you granted the television rights.

PREMINGER: And what is a *minor* cut? They might cut one word or one minute and change the whole meaning of the picture. There is only *one* picture, and it is the picture I made, the way I cut it.

SCHWARTZ'S VOICE: I know.

PREMINGER: What can we do now?

SCHWARTZ'S VOICE: Let me read the decision. Let me think about it overnight.

PREMINGER: Don't feel so depressed. You can only have a certain percentage of success.

SCHWARTZ'S VOICE: I'm very sorry.

PREMINGER: *You* did the best you could. But if we can appeal, we should appeal. And can we extend the injunction to continue keeping them from cutting the film on television? Until the appeal is decided?

SCHWARTZ'S VOICE: Let me think.

PREMINGER (*decisively*): If we can extend it, we should extend it. I do not like to give up if I feel I am right. (*Presses button to turn off speaker.*)

BARNES: It's the principle of the thing.

PREMINGER: I must now console my wife and children. What will Mark say?

GIDDING: A lot of people and a lot of films of a lot of people are affected.

PREMINGER: I think we *must* appeal. (*Sounds puzzled.*) The very fact that a custom goes unchallenged doesn't make it law. I think the judge is wrong. This judge *acted* like a movie fan, but he decided against me.

BARNES: But it's a violation of your contract! It's the principle of the thing.

GIDDING (*still militant*): It's everybody's fight.

PREMINGER: It could be worse. Don't forget, when you go into court, there are only two possibilities: One, you win. Two, you lose. I thought I would win, because I felt I was right. I still feel I am right. But losing is not so important. It's more important to get the wrinkle out of the screen.

(*As the camera pans from Preminger's face to Barnes's face and then to Gidding's face and then to the Picasso and then to the view from Preminger's window, we again hear—now played by a full symphony orchestra—the city music, starting pianissimo and building up, with mingled references to "There's No Business Like Show Business," "The Blue Danube," and "The Stars and Stripes Forever," to a deafening fortissimo.*)

## THE END

Producer

January 4, 1969

The other day, we met Mag Bodard, the producer of *The Umbrellas of Cherbourg*, *The Young Girls of Rochefort*, *Le Bonheur*, *La Chinoise*, and *Benjamin*, all of which have comforted us in recent years in the art house around town. Mag Bodard is a woman—the only successful female producer of movies in France, or, probably, anywhere else. She doesn't look a bit like L. B. Mayer. She is a petite, wistful-appearing, red-haired woman of about fifty, and she has a small, thin face with wide eyes.

"Please outline for us, from the very beginning, how you managed to become a producer of movies," we said after shaking hands with Mme. Bodard at her digs, in the Hotel Regency.

"I am actually Italian," she began. "I was born in Turin, where my father had a vineyard."

"Red wine or white wine?" we asked.

"Red wine," Mme. Bodard said. "In the north of Italy, there is mostly red wine. I had no sugar as a child. I had meat and wine, and this is what I still like to eat—meat and wine. My name was Margherita Perato. When I was five years old, my aunt, whose husband was French, and who had no children of her own, took me to live in Paris. I learned to read and write in French, and I took all my schooling in Paris, at the Institution Maintenon. I have a younger brother and sister, and they, too, went to France to school, because my parents thought we would find better educational opportunities in France. We went home to Turin during the summer months."

"Didn't your parents miss you when you were away?" we asked.

"Not really," Mme. Bodard said, and gave a kind of detached laugh.

"After school?" we asked.

"I began to paint. Portraits," she said.

"Do you still paint?" we asked.

"Never," she replied. "I painted for about a year, and then I stopped. Once I say goodbye to one part of my life, I do not like to go back. I go on to something new." She gave us that laugh again.

"After painting?" we asked.

"I attended a private atelier to study interior decorating," she said. "Then I met my husband—Lucien Ballard, the journalist. We were married for about twenty-five years, and then we became divorced, but we are still very good friends. When the Second World War started, my husband went to

England. I stayed in Paris throughout the war. I designed fashions, mostly for small houses. The only big house I designed was for Lucien Lelong."

"Did you work for the underground during the Occupation?" we asked.

"I did what was normal in my circle," Mme. Bodard said.

"What was that?" we asked.

"Hid people who had to be hidden, passed letters that had to be passed," she said.

"And after the war?" we asked.

"My husband worked for the Agence France-Presse," she said. "He had been born in China, because his father was in the diplomatic service there, and he speaks Chinese as well as he speaks French. Eventually, he went to Indo-China for *France-Soir*, and I traveled with him. We had a small apartment in Saigon, in the center of the city. We were the only married journalistic couple in Saigon in those years—1948 to 1955—and so we received all the other journalists at home. Then I started writing articles for *France-Soir* and, later, for *Elle*. About everyday life in Saigon—how the women lived, how life went on. The articles were collected, and they made a book. The book was published in France at the time of Dien Bien Phu, the final battle. So the book was very successful."

"What was the title of the book?" we asked.

"*C'est Aussi Comme Ça*," Mme. Bodard replied.

"After Saigon?" we asked.

"We lived for one year in Hong Kong," she said. "Then I became sick, as a result of Indo-China. With malaria. With amoebic infections. With everything that was normal for people who lived in Indo-China. I returned to Paris. I wanted to do something new. Something that would be closest to my sensibility."

"Why didn't you go back to decorating or designing?"

"I don't know why. My life changes continuously. I finish with one thing, I go on to another. I don't know how to go back."

"Well, what was the something new?" we asked.

"Television," Mme. Bodard said, and she gave us another of her laughs. "I felt we were in a new world now, and I felt that it would be easier to reach this new world through pictures than through words. In Hong Kong, all the foreign newspapers had what *France-Soir* had and still has: the *bandes dessinées*—stories, mostly historical stories, told in long captions under cartoons. The stories were told in such a way that anybody could follow them. So I had the idea of bringing a kind of *bandes dessinées* to television, in the form of a special movie."

"What happened to the idea?" we asked.

"Nothing," Mme. Bodard said. I didn't do it, because it was impossible. In France, we had only one channel, and it was government-owned. There were very few hours of programs."

"Well, what did you *try* to do with the idea?" we asked.

"As always, when I have an idea, I start telling it to everybody. To everybody. *À tout le monde.* And I don't abandon it until everybody says no."

"And everybody said no?"

"Correct. So I have never made anything for television. *Now*, perhaps, *now* I may finally do something for television."

"But what did you do when you were turned down by television?"

"I decided to make movies," Mme. Bodard replied. "I formed my own company—Parc Film. Because I live near the Parc Monceau." Again, that laugh. "I had a very good script, which had been written by two friends. I felt it would make a very good, a very strong movie."

"What made you think that you could simply go right out and be a producer of movies with just a script?" we asked.

"Because if somebody wants to do something it is always possible to do it," Mme. Bodard.

"Well," we said, "what happened?"

"I brought the script to all the major French companies, and they all said no," Mme. Bodard continued. "I brought it to Pathé, and they told me my idea was an excellent idea, and that I must find a good director. So I found a good young director, Jacques Deray, who had made two movies. But Pathé said he was not well known enough, and they told me I must take a director of their choosing—one who had just had a commercial success. I was inexperienced, and so I did what they said. And it was horrible. The director they chose changed everything in the script. I was so ashamed of this film. It was so far from what I had wanted. From then on, I decided to do only what I liked and only what I wanted, and to do it alone."

"And how in the world did you get financing for a movie, with an attitude like that?" we asked.

"The work of a producer is the work of a promoter," Mme. Bodard said. "It is very hard work. And you have to believe in what you are doing. My attitude is: I want to do this film. I will guarantee the budget. I do not ask to be paid anything, because I want to keep the budget low. I ask only for my royalties. I choose what I want to do without thinking of whether it will make money. I think only of whether it is of interest to me."

"Yes, but how did you *do* it?" we asked.

"In 1962, Jacques Demy, the director, showed me the script for *The Umbrellas of Cherbourg*," she replied. "I liked it so much! I went to all the companies and tried to find the money. My faith grew stronger as I worked and as I heard Michel Legrand sing and play his music for the film. But everybody said, 'Mag Bodard is very crazy.' Everybody in the business told me I could not win with this film. Finally, André Hakim, at Twentieth Century-Fox, said he would help me. He agreed to put up one-fourth of the money—thirty million francs, or about sixty thousand dollars. In Germany, from Beta, distributors of films, I got another sixty thousand. From the Cinema Center, I obtained still another sixty thousand. The Cinema Center is something we have only in France. Everybody who makes films belongs to it, and producers give the Center a prorated percentage of the profits from their films. The Cinema Center then gives advances to filmmakers who meet their requirements."

"And the last sixty thousand?" we asked.

"From me," Mme. Bodard replied. "I put my own money in, and money borrowed from friends. Then I decided if I did not win, I would go to the U.S.A. and become a governess for children. I found out all about how to place an advertisement for a position of governess and how to come to the United States to do such work."

"Why a governess?" we asked.

"Because it seemed to be the simplest kind of job for which you need no special training," she said.

"But you didn't have to take such a job," we said.

"No. *The Umbrellas of Cherbourg* won. It was a very big success in France, in the United States, in Spain, in Japan, in South Africa—all over the world. Even the Soviet Union paid about twenty thousand dollars for this film to show it. Only in Italy, in Germany, and in the Scandinavian countries it was not a success."

"What was your second film?"

"The next year, 1964, it was *Le Bonheur* by Agnès Varda, who is the wife of Jacques Demy. For me, this film was very, very important. It was a film made by a woman, and it is exactly what goes on inside the head of every woman, except that she doesn't realize it."

"How many movies have you made altogether?"

"Eighteen—in the past six years. I know everybody now. And I have many of the good young new directors. I like working with the artistic directors—Robert Bresson, Jean-Luc Godard, Alain Resnais, Christian-Paul Arrighi. I have just finished three films for Paramount. It was very difficult to produce three films at once, but I wanted to do it, so that I would have greater freedom now to do exactly what I want. For me, producing movies is something I will not say goodbye to. I like it because the work is artistic. I like finding new talent and encouraging young people. Also, the work permits me to be independent. Also, I like it because it is dangerous. Now I have confidence in myself, but each time I start a new film, it is like taking an examination in school."

"Any other reason you like being a producer of movies?" we asked.

"It allows me to have a lot of people around me. Parc Film employs about thirty people. I like to give those people the certainty that they will always have work."

"Do you have that certainty now?"

"Yes, but to have it and to do it you must be strong. Strong."

## The Faces of the Husbands

March 15, 1969

Joe Lustig, a very nice, very serious, very hard-working publicity agent representing John Cassavetes, the movie actor and director, called us up and said, "You ought to meet John. He's making his third movie, *Husbands*, all over New York. A real New York movie. A real Schrafft's. Mickey Walker's bar on Eighth Avenue. Kennedy Airport. Port Washington. Real Port Washington houses. A real Port Washington cemetery. John is very real. You probably saw his movie *Faces* which he wrote and directed."

"Yes," we said. "Seemed real. All those people hacking away at each other and laughing wildly."

"Very real," Lustig said. "John is working the same way with *Husbands*, which he also wrote and is directing. And he's playing one of three husbands. The other husbands are Ben Gazzara and Peter Falk. And he's got *complete artistic control. Real freedom.*"

"How did he manage to get *that*?" we asked.

"By insisting on it—but he'll tell you all about it," Lustig said. "John won't work any other way. And he's given Ben and Peter a percentage of the movie instead of big salaries. You ought to see and *listen* to John, Ben, and Peter together, actually. Why don't you come and watch the dailies with us at Fox and then go on from there?"

"Fine," we said.

A few hours later, we were sitting in a Fox projection room with John, Ben, Peter, Joe, and a few other people associated with *Husbands*.

"Roll it, please!" Cassavetes commanded, in a real directorial tone, and we had a fine time watching the results of the previous day's filming, which happened to have taken place in the interior of a real Pan American transatlantic plane. According to the story of the movie, Cassavetes, Gazzara, and Falk were leaving their real, conventional Port Washington families and were heading for some real fun in London. The 5-4-3-2-1-and-action shots—like all daily film rushes, as far as we are concerned—were exciting, and interesting to watch: the repeats of the same takes, the different shots over the same dialogue. The movie was in real color.

The lights went on. We blinked at our nearest neighbor, Ben Gazzara, and thanked him for letting us watch his dailies.

"We're gambling on our own talent," Gazzara said, in his growly, sad way. "I feel young again."

"Now let's go and eat and talk," Lustig said.

"I can't," Gazzara said. "My wife has a sore throat, the girls have sore throats, and I promised to be home."

We were soon sitting at a table in a nearby Italian restaurant with Lustig, Cassavetes, Falk and the *Husbands* producer, a stocky young man named Al Ruban, who had worked with Cassavetes on *Faces*, as a producer and also as co-editor.

"We shot seven hundred thousand feet of film for *Faces*, and we edited the whole thing down to ten thousand feet in John's garage in California," Ruban said. "It took us three years. John believes in *Faces*. He waits outside the theater and asks people to go in and see the picture. Then he waits and wants to know what they thought of the picture."

Cassavetes spoke. "You want people to love what you do, right?" he said to us, somewhat belligerently.

"Yes," we said.

"If somebody tells you you're fantastic, that isn't enough!" he shouted. "They have to *mean* it!"

"O.K.," we said, feeling vaguely that we were being pushed back into *Faces*.

"You should have seen us working in his garage on *Faces*," Ruban said. "John remembers every frame—not every frame in the picture but every frame we ever *shot*."

Cassavetes gave us an intense look.

"Fantastic," we said quickly, and meaning it.

"What John believes in on the screen is life and spontaneity," Falk said to us, in his cinematic charming-gangster manner. "He wants to see something combustible happen."

Cassavetes was laughing violently to himself. Then he cut his laugh off and gave us another intense look. "Peter, Ben, and I would never have been cast together in a film by anybody!" he exclaimed. "For one thing, we all have dark hair." He laughed violently to himself again. "So Peter had an idea that I should do a picture with him."

"Where was that, and when?" we asked.

"At the Celtic-Laker basketball game in Los Angeles, at the Sports Arena," said Falk. "I had never spoken to John before, but I saw him at the

Sports Arena. My wife had gone to school with him in Port Washington. So I yelled to him, 'Elaine May has a movie, *Mikey and Nicky*, about two hoods! Do you want to be in it?' It was the first time I ever spoke to John. He yelled back, 'Yes!' Six months later, I'm sitting in the Paramount commissary, and John comes over to me and starts talking about 'our' picture. 'What picture?' So he says, 'I want to make a picture with you, me, and Benny. About three husbands. Their friend dies, and they go to London.' Then I never saw John again, for another year. Then I was in Belgrade, Yugoslavia, making a picture, *Castle Keep*, and I got a wire from my agent saying I was offered a part in a picture about the Mafia, 'At any price,' which John was in. I thought I would call him. He was in Rome. He said, 'You've got the best part!' Without pausing, he said, 'Did you get my offer?' 'What offer?' I asked. 'For the picture that you, me, and Benny are gonna make,' he said. Then he started telling me the whole picture, long distance. I said, 'I'll come to Rome.' So I came to Rome. He tells me the whole story. Not bad, not good. Some terrific stuff. Some terrible stuff. More than the material, I felt *him*. I felt his presence. The excitement. The belief in himself. I felt his honesty. Then I asked him to tell the story again. He left out some of the best parts. But he added some good things. All in all, I was impressed by his fertility. He's incredibly fertile."

"What happened after that?" we asked Cassavetes.

"Pete is our spokesman," Cassavetes said. "Benny's got the loudest voice, but Benny's not here." He went off again into his very private laughter.

"John has a rebellious perversity, but it's an intelligent rebellious perversity," Falk said to us.

Lustig said, "I think, John, you might want to tell what happened when you gave the script of *Husbands* to one of the heads of one of the big companies to read."

Cassavetes looked angry. "That has nothing to do with it," he said. "Only one thing makes it exciting. That Peter and Ben and I can express something that's intimate, personal, and clean. Are we going to fulfill our promise to *ourselves*? We want everyone to see this picture. We want this picture to make money. We all want to make a lot of money. That's what we want."

"Yes," we said, trying to keep out of *Faces*. "How did you arrange the financing, so that you have the freedom to—"

"Freedom!" Cassavetes shouted. "Freedom! We begin by being un-free and conforming! We are slaves to ourselves! We're frightened little things! All of us!"

We couldn't hold on any longer. We *were* in *Faces*.

Cassavetes rocked with laughter.

Falk put his head close to ours. "What do you think of John?" he asked softly. "Isn't he real?"

"Very," we said.

"He's *healthy!*" Falk said. "John is incredibly healthy. He's really healthy. The healthiest man I know."

## McLuhan's Child

November 21, 1970

Goin' Down the Road is a movie produced and directed by a thirty-two-year-old Canadian named Donald Shebib. Most of the critics not only admired the movie; they exulted in it, as an example of a kind of trend-turner away from the current vogue for sex and violence. Some critics even became very emotional about the movie. Their reasons: it was made for $82,000, or $24,918,000 less than *Tora! Tora! Tora!*; the film is not sophisticated; it shows real feeling for real people, and both are completely different from the people and feeling of *Easy Rider*; it tells an honest story about the adventures and frustrations of a couple of poor, inexperienced, uneducated young men from Nova Scotia who go to Toronto hoping to find a better life. Enthusiasm for the movie has been contagious among movie critics. The *Times* was prompted last week to publish a favorable review of it—a couple of weeks after the *Times*' regular movie critic had given it an unfavorable review. The favorable review was three times as long as the unfavorable one and called the movie "the most impressive new work of realist cinema in years." *Newsweek* called it "one of those movies which, with every success, assault a film establishment that too often has relied on money instead of talent."

Last week, Donald Shebib came down from Toronto, where he lives, and we had a talk with him over a drink at the Algonquin, where he was staying. He is a pleasant young man, stocky and muscular, with a number of timely props—long hair, beard, boots. He had a quiet non-fire-breathing manner.

"What kind of name is Shebib?" we asked him.

"Lebanese," he said. "My grandfather was a chemical engineer, and he came over around 1900. There wasn't any opening for an engineer, so he went to work in a steel mill in Sydney, Nova Scotia. He spoke nine languages. He was very well educated. He died when my father was fifteen. My grandmother was basically a peasant, from Damascus. I guess their marriage was arranged. They had fifteen children. My grandmother is now eighty-seven, and she still lives in Sydney. I met her twice—once when I was ten, and again when I was sixteen. She used to make an annual pilgrimage to the site of Ste. Anne de Beaupré, a five hundred miles northeast of Toronto, and once she came and visited us. Another time, we made the thousand-mile trip to Sydney. My mother came from a fishing village in Newfoundland—Jersey side, in Placentia Bay. Her father was a fisherman; he died when she was ten. My parents met in Toronto. Neither one went to high school. My father has had a lot of jobs. During the Second World War, he was a foreman in a defense plant making submarine detectors. Then he was a barber—he's been a barber, on and off, most of his life. Then he had a couple of restaurants. Last summer, he ran a variety store in a cottage area, selling things like rubber rafts and swim suits. I have one sister, a year and a half younger than I am, who teaches English in a high school in Toronto. But I was pretty dumb in school. I got good marks, but I had no interests other than baseball. The way kids are today, if I'd met the kind of sixteen-year-old kid around today when I was that age, he'd have seemed like forty to me."

"What did you do after high school," we asked.

"Got a summer job as a bank teller, for forty dollars a week," he said. "It was 1955. Then I wanted more money, so I got a job in an insurance office for fifty dollars a week. In Canada, the pressure to go to college was not as great then as it was in the United States. The philosophy of education was different in Canada. A university education was for a select few. Academic requirements to get into the University of Toronto were very high. The tuition was four hundred dollars a year. But I saved up the money myself. I worked in the insurance office a year, and then I started out studying chemical engineering at the University. I stayed with it from September to Christmas. Then I quit. I didn't like it at all. It was forty-eight hours a week—six days, from nine to five. In one exam, in a Logic course, I got a grade of six out of a possible one hundred. It was the kind of course, naturally, that requires an extremely logical mind. It wasn't for me. I preferred a general yukking-it-up during class. I used to clown around a lot. So I quit college and went to work for another insurance company. I figured 'What the hell?' at the time. But I was becoming more aware of political things. And at eighteen I went through a big change in my life. I got interested in music after I bought my sister a record of *Oklahoma*—with Alfred Drake—for Christmas. I had been watching television for about four years; we bought our set in 1951. We got all the American channels, plus all the Canadian ones. I began to learn things from television. For instance, the first record I bought for myself was a ten-inch Decca record of *The Desert Song*. I had seen *The Desert Song* on television—not one of the movie versions but a television special with Nelson Eddy, and I became more and more interested in music and operettas, and started spending a lot of money on records. I re-enrolled in the university in 1957, in liberal arts, and I graduated in 1960. In my last year at college, I decided to try my hand at films, and I found out I could get into the film school at U.C.L.A. It was really television that changed my whole life."

"How?" we asked.

"It got me interested in old movies. I developed a romantic fascination with the nineteen-twenties and nineteen-thirties. I would look in the *TV Guide*, and if I saw a movie listed that was made before 1940, I would watch it. Then I found out that there were two film societies in Toronto that showed old movies, and I saw a lot of them there. The old movies got me interested in movies. One day, in my last year in college, I read in the newspaper that a producer named Julian Roffman was making a movie in Toronto. I wrote to him asking how I could get into making movies, and he wrote back advising me to go to film school at U.C.L.A."

"Did television do anything else to change your life?" we asked.

"You bet!" said Shebib. "See, I was reared a Catholic. But when I was nineteen, I gave up on the church. Television had a program on Darwin in a series called *The Nature of Things*. The series ran for twelve or fifteen weeks, and, believe me, it was an eye-opener for me. I wouldn't have missed a single program of it. About that time, American television was starting to come down from its glory, and Canadian television was putting on all kinds of education programs. The Canadian Broadcasting Corporation was putting on Shakespeare. Not that I liked Shakespeare. I never have. It's always been too difficult for me to follow. I'm a real McLuhan's child. I haven't read a novel since I was twelve. I haven't done *any* reading for enjoyment in a generation. I do read the *New York Times*, but only the sports section. I get the news off television. You can go through life not reading at all. McLuhan gave a course in philosophy at the University of Toronto. He wasn't famous then—he just gave this course. I sat in on it instead of taking an English course. In the English courses, you had to read a book every week. To read a whole Dickens novel in a week was incredible to me. So I found out that you don't have to do English—they try to keep that quiet—and I attended McLuhan's course in philosophy. But it was more of a course in Roman Catholic philosophy, and I preferred sitting around arguing religion. I went two or three times, and then I quit. It was years afterwards that I found out I am a McLuhan's child."

"How did you find out?" we asked.

"I saw him on television," Shebib said. "I never read his book. I'm such a perfect goddam McLuhan's child I couldn't even read *his* bloody book."

"Could you tell what he believes from seeing him on television?" we asked.

"You get an idea of what he's saying," Shebib said.

"How did you find life at the U.C.L.A. film school?" we asked.

"Rather scary," said Shebib. "I didn't know anything about film at all. I had a lot of insecurity about the medium. Everyone else seemed to be so much more aware of cinema than I was. Looking back, I think they were all pretty pretentious. In those days, they were sort of a beatnik crowd. Now they're hip. Very, very hip. I was actually in California for four years. Two years in the film school. My thesis was a ten-minute film called *Revival*, which I made in Toronto in the summer of 1963. It was about a group of people who stand on street corners in Toronto and preach. I spent a good deal of my time surfing. Then I met a C.B.C. producer, Ross McLean, who asked me to make a film about surfers. It ran for twenty-five minutes and cost three thousand dollars. After that, I made six other films—all documentaries—for McLean. The one I like best is *Good Times, Bad Times*. It's about old war veterans, about men loving each other in war. It's a very abstract film, a kind of collage made up of old war footage, war stills, and shots of members of the Canadian Legion. It's a poetic, lyrical film. I think it's a much better film than *Goin' Down the Road*."

"What's wrong with *Goin' Down the Road*?" we asked.

"I'm not happy with it," Shebib said. "I just don't feel good about it."

We asked him to tell us a little about the making of the movie.

"I started working on the script in 1967, with a couple of writers, but it just wasn't right," he said. "Bill Fruet, a friend of mine who is a film editor, then said, 'Let me write it.' He finished it in the spring of 1969. I got a grant of nineteen thousand dollars from the Canadian Film Development Corporation for it. I shot it in sixteen-millimeter, in color, and then a producer invested twenty-eight thousand dollars, so I could pay my bills. I put in five thousand dollars of my own money, and after the film was finished the C.B.C. invested thirty thousand dollars more. I'd carried the idea for the film around with me for a long time. To me, it was like *The Grapes of Wrath*. The movie. Not the book."

"And your next film?" we asked.

"It's about the friendship of four high school boys," Shebib said. We'll shoot it in a big high school in Toronto. I got a hundred and fifty thousand dollars from the Canadian government for it, and a hundred and fifty thousand dollars from the distributor. But the difference between three hundred thousand dollars and eighty-two thousand dollars in making a film is more like a ratio of ten to one."

"Do you prefer making fiction films to making documentaries?" we asked.

"Yes," said Shebib. In a documentary, you're limited. In fiction, you have more control over your material. My way, however, is to let what's around me influence me, too. What I really want more than anything else is to make period films. As a kid, I read the *Classic Comics* books. All the great novels were in *Classic Comics*. Comic books are a form of movie, you know. One I read was *The Three Musketeers*. I've never read the book. I've never read any of the books. I'd love to do *The Three Musketeers* as a movie. You could make a film of it for a million dollars. Hollywood would spend ten million dollars, and it wouldn't be right. It would be spectacular. Making a big film doesn't mean it can't be a personal film. I'd get down to the nitty-gritty of life in the seventeenth century. They made *They Shoot Horses, Don't They?* for maybe five million dollars, and it wasn't right. It was supposed to be about the nineteen-thirties, but there was no feel of the nineteen-thirties about it. It looked like the nineteen-sixties. I feel I could make a film of *The Three Musketeers* and it would be right."

"How do you know if you've never read the book?" we asked.

"The comic book is deadly faithful to the book," Shebib said.

"How do you know?" we asked.

"I can guess," he said. "You can guess what the feeling of the book was."

# Revels

August 5, 1972

HUSTON: JOHN HUSTON was in town last week for the opening of his twenty-ninth movie, *Fat City*. Huston is, of course, an original. He moves, as we've noted more than once in the past twenty-odd years, like a bigger-than-life character in one of his own movies, and it's always a pleasure to watch him go. He's the quintessential American artist-as-movie-director, and he has placed his unique stamp on every one of his twenty-nine movies. Like Ingmar Bergman, like Satyajit Ray, like Federico Fellini, and just a few others, he does it effortlessly, without big prior announcements that he's doing it, and he does it without forcing the issue, without pretension, without those damn irritating look-at-me mannerisms, and always with enjoyment and with humor. Also, not to leave anything out, we like the way, years before hippies, he was far hippier than the hippies in doing what came naturally to him, such as wearing comfortable safari suits, smoking slender Montecristo Cuban cigars, and loving whatever was beautiful—animate or otherwise. So we were delighted to accept his invitation to accompany him, his twenty-two-year-old son, Tony, and a few other well-defined characters, to round out the scene, to the opening of—and later a party for—*Fat City*. Both were held at the Museum of Modern Art.

There was the usual limousine transportation provided by the producer—in this case, Ray Stark. We rode with the two Hustons, both of whom were wearing crisp seersucker jackets, the father with a white shirt and a rakish black bow tie, the son with a brick-red shirt and a multicolored Art Nouveau tie. The son, six feet four, has a couple of inches on his father. Both men have beards, Tony Huston's being new, spare, and black, and John Huston's gray, scraggly, and somewhat shorter than the one he wore as Noah in his movie *The Bible*. Also in the car were three handsome, elegantly attired, horse-loving non-movie friends from California—Celeste Shane, Darlene Pearson, and Bill Gardner. They talked about how *Harper's Bazaar* had said there was a beautiful woman to be found on every street corner in New York but they couldn't see any. It was apparent that they liked California better. John Huston listened, laughed with them, smoked a Montecristo, and saved his conversation for later. We complimented Tony Huston on his appearance. (We might add that Tony, whose full name is Walter Anthony Huston, and his sister, Anjelica, both have faces that remind us of their mother, the late Enrica Soma Huston, who was a strikingly beautiful woman.)

"I just got this jacket at Abercrombie & Fitch," Tony said, in a kind of light and subtly mixed English-Irish-perfectly-enunciated way of speaking that sounded all his own. "I came over here from London to keep Dad company, and I brought London summer clothes—thick tweeds, suitable for the Highlands."

"Tony's been going to all the museums," Huston said, regarding his son with unconcealed admiration, very much the way the late Walter Huston and John used to look at each other. "While I stay behind and do what Ray Stark and Columbia, the distributor, want me to do for *Fat City*." The two Hustons laughed in their individual ways.

"Today, I talked to Frederick Dockstader, at the Heye Foundation, about some American Indian art I've started collecting in my little flat in London," Tony said. "I've always been interested in antiques, but I'm only learning now. I thought prices in London might be better than they are here, but I learned today that the reverse is true."

Huston *père* again laughed appreciatively.

In the few remaining blocks to the Museum, we asked Tony to bring us up to date on his activities in general and his falconry in particular.

"I've trained about thirty birds of prey since I was about ten," he said. "Falconry is the blood sport that intrudes least upon nature. I've read just about everything ever written about the art. It hasn't died in me at all. And I'm still writing poetry, which I started doing when I was seven or eight. My interest has never died out. But I'm writing more prose now. When I graduated from Westminster School, I went to London University to study English Literature. I ended after a year feeling that one way *not* to end up as a writer was to study English Literature."

Two more Huston laughs.

"I wasn't a dropout," Tony continued. "I can always go back. But I felt I might have got into a hole. An opportunity came up for me to travel around America with Buckminster Fuller, going with him from campus to campus. I was transcribing his tapes. I ended up with three hundred hours of tapes. I stayed with him for six months. I feel that Bucky Fuller is one of the very few great men I've ever met. He's got so many things. This great energy. And what you might call his optimism. It was quite wonderful to be with him."

"How did you find the response to him at the colleges?" we asked.

"Very good among the young people," Tony said. "The faculty people were different. I was disappointed by quite a number of them. They would be a little bit mean in the way they tried to find fault with him."

Out of the car at the Museum. Tony stepped aside quickly and the friends from California faded into the Museum as a small crush of young admirers—bearded, blue-jeaned, long-haired, and sweaty—advanced on John Huston and told him they had been watching the free day-long showings of many of his old movies at the Columbia I and II, and thought the movies were great. Into the Museum's lobby, where the movie business took over. Columbia beaters. Assistant beaters. Ray Stark. Leo Jaffe, president of Columbia Pictures Industries, and his wife. Stanley Schneider, president of Columbia Pictures Industries, and *his* wife. Distributors. Theater owners. Agents. Television reporters with TV lights, portable cameras, and portable mikes. Still photographers with flashbulb cameras. Rich supporters of the Museum of Modern Art. Publisher Sam Newhouse and his wife. His son Donald Newhouse and *his* wife. Everybody milling around John Huston and shaking his hand and making remarks.

"*Fat City* isn't my subject, but I'm here anyway."

"Let's hope to God it gets them coming to the theater."

"The film was a smash at the Cannes Film Festival."

Then the head of the Museum's film department, Willard Van Dyke, came over. "I'm Willard Van Dyke," said Willard Van Dyke to Huston. "I'm going to introduce you tonight. This is my wife, Barbara."

Huston smiled, laughed, posed for the cameras, shook everybody's hand, and looked at his watch.

"It's about eight o'clock," Huston called over to Ray Stark, who was separated from him by a four-foot-high ribbon. Stark, a very friendly stocky man wearing a royal-blue jacket and horn-rimmed tinted glasses paused in front of the ribbon.

"Ray, jump over that thing!" Huston called to him. "Jump!"

Ray Stark hesitated.

"Jump!" Huston called, giving one of his throaty laughs.

Ray Stark jumped. Huston received him with a hug.

"Say, I have a cast of that sculpture," Stark said, of a piece of sculpture in the Museum garden.

"Let's go look at it!" Huston said, making a whole production of his brief line, and guiding Stark into position in front of the Gaston Lachaise figure of a flying woman. The photographers had a field day getting pictures of the sculpture behind the two men.

"This is *John's* night," Stark said happily, moving back toward the lobby. "The director is the important one."

"They're the artist. Right, Ray?" A heavily suntanned man said to Stark.

"Right," Stark said.

"I hope to Christ it goes, this picture," said the suntanned man. "I hope this is the year for pictures about fighters."

Ray Stark looked a little worried.

Late arrivals. The stars of *Fat City*. Stacy Keach, with the singer Judy Collins. John Huston hugged Stacy Keach, and vice versa. Then came Keach's co-star, Susan Tyrrell, escorted by her agent, Bill Barnes. Huston hugged Susan Tyrrell. Everybody hugged everybody else. Tony Huston appeared again and shook hands with Judy Collins.

"Stacy is wonderful, just wonderful," Tony said to Judy Collins. "Not only as an actor, I mean, but as a person." Everybody in the vicinity expressed agreement.

"I'm from Columbia Pictures," a calm, bespectacled woman said to us. "I met John Huston when he was making *We Were Strangers*. There's Beverly Adams. She was a Columbia starlet. She's with her husband, there—Vidal Sassoon, the famous hairdresser. She married him and just stopped working. Boom! Just like that."

TV lights were on Huston. Kevin Sanders, the WABC-TV critic, was asking him, "Mr. Huston, just what does the expression 'fat city' mean?"

"It's a jazz musician's term," Huston said. "It's a dreamer's term, meaning no boundaries to the possibilities. It's the pot of gold at the end of the rainbow."

"Everybody into the theater!" a Columbia man was yelling.

Standing in front of the screen, Willard Van Dyke made his introduction: "I want to welcome one of the most favorite of all film directors, Mr. John Huston."

Big applause from the audience, which looked like Museum of Modern Art members and goers. We saw more celebrities, including Mr. and Mrs. Otto Preminger.

"I have a peculiar nostalgia tonight," Huston was saying in front of the screen. "I was coming to the Museum of Modern Art when it was in the old Heckscher Building...."

The light dimmed, and the movie started. Lovely pictures. Terrific characterizations. Wonderful faces. Good acting. Real Huston stuff.

The end. Applause. Everybody into the garden for the party, described in the invitation as "a champagne supper and reception for Mr. Huston."

There was plenty of curried chicken and rice and shrimp salad and drinks, all catered by Robert Day-Dean's and there was plenty of talk about *Fat City*.

"Very authentic."

"A beautiful picture."

"It's too down. I don't like down movies. I like up movies."

"How come Henny Youngman is at *this* party?"

"I'd book it. How about you, Al? You book it?"

"It's like one of those goddamn foreign pictures. No pace. No momentum."

"I loved the picture, John," Otto Preminger said to Huston.

"We loved it," said Mrs. Preminger. "It's beautifully done."

There were a lot of critics there, official and unofficial, and all gobbling chicken and rice and shrimp salad. Everybody eyed everybody else. Woody Allen stood off to one side with his own private group of friends, but they all eyed everybody, too. Almost everybody came and talked to Huston about one thing or another. A young man named Mike Sragow, of the *Crimson*, told Huston he was writing an honors thesis at Harvard about him and his movies. Leo Lerman, a bearded editor of *Mademoiselle*, came over and told Huston he loved the picture. "And I love your beard," he added.

Anjelica Huston, who works as a model in New York, a knockout in a white chiffon shimmery gown and pearls, hugged her father from behind, and Huston looked happy. Mike Sragow asked Huston if it was true that he might make a picture with Leslie Fiedler. Huston laughed deeply. At least seven heavily suntanned men came over and introduced their wives to Huston. One of the men said, "Good luck on the picture. I hope for your sake it makes money."

"Thank you very much," Huston said, graciously making his usual big production of the line.

Huston ducked out of the party fairly early. Tony Huston walked out of the Museum with him. The sidewalk was now empty of fans. Tony's face was glowing with enthusiasm.

"Good night, Dad," Tony said, and the two men hugged each other. "It was the best, Dad," Tony said.

Huston drew away slightly from his son, looked at him, and then drew him close again and gave his deep laugh over the younger man's shoulder.

Tony then drew away and looked straight into his father's eyes. "It was really the best, Dad," he said. "And you know I don't lie."

## Truffaut, Part V

October 18, 1976

FRANÇOIS TRUFFAUT'S VISIT to the Fourteenth New York Film Festival, which opened with the showing of his nineteenth movie, *Small Change*, was also the occasion of our fifth talk with him since 1960, when, at the age of twenty-eight, he made his initial visit to the city, in connection with his first feature-length movie, the now famous *The 400 Blows*. By this time, Truffaut, at forty-four, feels like a kind of relative, so we started by picking him up at Kennedy Airport on his arrival, via T.W.A., from Paris, and bringing up to date our chart of Truffaut statistics.

General appearance: Practically the same as it was sixteen years ago. Hair a mite more iron gray. Horn-rimmed glasses worn almost constantly. Complexion showing hardly any exposure to fresh air or sunshine. Midriff with perhaps a hint of a paunch.

Use of the English language: Terrific. Proved the effectiveness of the intensive course in English that he took in the U.S.A. just before our last talk, in 1973, when he practiced his grammar by watching the Watergate hearings on television and memorizing key phrases like "To ze best of my recollection at zis point in time." He reads books in English. ("I read *Ze Final Days*," he told us. "*Extraordinaire!* I also read *I Remember Eet Well*, by Vincente Minnelli. But I cannot read ze novels in English. Ze *vocabulaire*! Ver-ree difficult.")

Use of an interpreter: During public appearances and during long interviews, as a time-saver. Accompanying him this time was his longtime interpreter and colleague Mrs. Helen Scott, who did the English subtitles for *Small Change*.

His daughters: Laura, now seventeen, is very serious, wants to be a professor of literature, and has just finished reading Simone de Beauvoir's *Memoirs of a Dutiful Daughter*. Eva, now fifteen, wants to be a fashion designer. Both girls have parts in *Small Change*.

Interest in clothes: His main concern is still wearing shoes that don't hurt his feet. He has them made to order. He was wearing a Francesco Smalto suit of oatmeal-colored linen, made in Italy. (Explanation, given to us with an almost wicked grin: "My Cardin period ees *over*. When Cardin bought a theater and renamed eet Espace Pierre Cardin, I objected. Verree pre-tentious. Ver-ree stupid. I would not wear Cardin to ze best of my recollection from zat point in time." And from zis point in time we will drop the accent.)

Interest in, and judgment about, food: Nil. ("T.W.A. food very good. Very good chicken.")

Watching television in France: "Our television is cultural, our films are frivolous. The opposite of television here. I do not like the color television here. I have on my television set a gadget for turning off the color."

Self-appraisal compared to the way he felt ten years ago: "I feel the pressure of not having much time ahead of me when I am not pleased with my work. I have so many films in my mind to make. It becomes urgent to make progress."

Compared to self in 1960: "I was more timid. I was more worried."

Practical differences in his working life between then and now: "Lately, it has been much easier to obtain the money for the films. All they ask is 'How much does the kid want this time?'"

Freedom to make whatever he wants to make the way he wants to make it: The same as it has been all along—complete. "But I have the advantage of giving them the scripts in French, and they do not read French."

How he thinks about each new film he makes: "It is one more stone in the wall."

How much his films cost to make: *Small Change* cost about seven hundred thousand dollars, which is seven times as much as *The 400 Blows* cost. About one-twelfth of the cost of *Jaws*. About one-twentieth of the cost of *The Godfather, Part II*.

How many movies he has seen since 1973, when he told us he had seen, since he was eleven, four thousand nine hundred and fifty: Five hundred more.

How many movies he has directed since then: Two more—*Small Change* and *The Story of Adéle H.*

How he happened to get into Steven Spielberg's movie so far entitled *Close Encounters of the Third Kind* as an actor, playing the part of a French scientist, a specialist in U.F.O.s, for which he will have to go to Benares, India, in January, and for which he has already had to go to Mobile, Alabama, and Gillette, Wyoming, where some of the movie has been shot: Spielberg telephoned him in Paris and told him he liked the way Truffaut wore an old-fashioned wristwatch and always wore a necktie. "I told Spielberg, 'I am not an actor. I can only play myself.?' He said, 'Good.'

The picture started filming on May fourteenth, and, oh, my goodness, it still is not finished. I wanted it clear they could fire me if I am not good. I never asked any questions. I made it a point not to bother Spielberg. Jeanne Moreau once told me, 'On every picture, you must love everybody except the one who becomes the scapegoat.' I followed Jeanne Moreau's advice. I made Julia Phillips, the producer, my scapegoat. Every time I find something not to my liking, I say I am sure it is the fault of Julia Phillips."

Where he goes for a vacation: Only to the Beverly Hills Hotel. He sits by the Beverly Hills Hotel pool and reads. He finds the place calm and appealingly quiet. He never goes into the pool. He does not swim. He does not play tennis. He does not go to the beach. He does not go to parties. He does go to visit Jean Renoir, who lives in Beverly Hills, and who recently finished writing an autobiographical novel, entitled *Friends, I Have Just Become 100 Years Old*, and they talk endlessly about movies and people involved with movies. And he does visit the Larry Edmunds Cinema & Theater Bookshop, on Hollywood Boulevard. ("It is the best shop for film. *Fantastique!*")

Interest in going back to Mobile, Alabama, or to Gillette, Wyoming: Nil. "I might as well go to Cherbourg as to Mobile. The countryside near Gillette is beautiful, but compared to the French countryside you think you are on the moon."

Interests outside of movies: Nil.

Interests in movies: Still all-consuming.

Patience and seriousness with which he meets questions from interviewers: Incredible. Question from Joseph Gelmis of *Newsday*: "How do you renew the man so that the artist can function?" Answer: "One works with what happens to one in the first twelve years of life, and this base is inexhaustible."

What he did this time in New York: He watched *Small Change* at the Film Festival, attended an opening night party, and had a press conference and half a dozen interviews.

After we had met him and driven with him to his hotel, he did not come out for forty-eight hours. When he did come out, we took a taxi with him and Mrs. Scott to Cinemabilia, a bookshop and gallery at 10 West Thirteenth Street, where Truffaut wanted to look for new books about movies.

"You should see the pileup of film books at his home and in his office!" Mrs. Scott said in the taxi. "But he knows where everything is."

"It is a good collection, yes?" Truffaut said mildly.

"He's a compulsive file-keeper," Mrs. Scott said. "He has everything arranged on shelves and in drawers, *alphabetically*. When he comes over to my flat in Paris, he goes around fixing up *my* books alphabetically."

Truffaut shot into Cinemabilia like a retriever. He didn't waste any time on small talk. He concentrated completely on the business at hand. Quickly, he picked up the new issue of Andy Warhol's magazine *Interview*, because it contained an article on Jeanne Moreau. He also took *Film Fan Monthly*, issue of June, 1968, because it had a list of Alfred Hitchcock's films for TV; *A Standard Glossary for Film Criticism*, by James Monaco; the new issues of *American Film* and *Women & Film*; *The Name Above the Title*, by Frank Capra; *Harlow*, by Irving Shulman; *Don't Say "Yes" Until I Finish Talking*, by Darryl Zanuck; and greeting cards that had still photographs from old movies on the front. "Nice," Truffaut said, taking five *Design for Living* with Fredric March, Gary Cooper, and Miriam Hopkins. An Ernst Lubitsch Production cards, and three *River of No Return* starring Robert Mitchum and Marilyn Monroe cards. He flipped through a bin of vintage-movie stills, mostly of *The Little Rascals*, but passed them up. He glanced without interest at a book entitled *Focus on 'Shoot the Piano Player'* and passed it up, along with a dozen other books about him or his movies. He autographed a paperback edition of the script of his movie *The Wild Child* for the bookshop owner, and then, looking disappointed, he retraced his steps and glanced over the stock again. "Nothing new," he said.

"Film students were in here a few days ago and bought practically everything," the proprietor of the bookshop said.

Truffaut had accumulated what looked to us like an enormous load of stuff, but he still looked somewhat disappointed. On the ride back to his hotel, however, he immediately started paging through the books and magazines, and seemed to feel better. We dropped him at the entrance. Before going through the revolving door, he turned around, held his load of books aloft in a kind of farewell wave, and lifted his head to them in triumph.

## Kurosawa Frames

December 21, 1981

# MONDAY, JOHN F. KENNEDY AIRPORT.

The Japanese movie director Akira Kurosawa lands around 11 a.m., after a thirteen-hour flight from Tokyo, for a visit as the guest of the Japan Society, whose Film Center is about to put on a two-month retrospective of Kurosawa's movies—twenty-six, all told. Kurosawa emerges into the Japan Air Lines reception area: seventy-one years old, six feet tall, slightly stooped, gray-haired; wearing dark-tinted, horn-rimmed glasses, a dark-green-and-tan plaid wool sports jacket, a tan silk shirt, a necktie patterned in brown and beige, wrinkled tan slacks, and well-worn brown shoes; carrying a small brown leather-and-canvas bag; and looking expectant. Accompanying him is Teruyo Nogami, who has been his chief production assistant for the past thirty years—from the time he made *Rashomon*, in 1950. She is a short, chubby woman with wild, frizzy black hair, and her expression is dead-pan. She is wearing floppy gray flannel pants and a brown leather jacket with tassels. Greeting Kurosawa on behalf of the Japan Society is Peter Grilli, the director of the Film Center—a stocky, sharp-eyed, friendly, Japanese-speaking American in his late thirties. His father, Marcel Grilli, who is a music critic for the *Japan Times*, an English-language newspaper in Tokyo, took Peter there to live at the age of five. Peter attended the American School in Tokyo, Harvard University, and Tokyo University. He started the Film Center about three years ago. He is obviously very intelligent and very fluent in Japanese. With Grilli are David Owens, another thirtyish Japanese-speaking American—from Indiana, and open-faced, sandy-haired, with a hearty air—who works as Grilli's assistant, and Audie Bock, a rangy, authoritative young woman with a mop of ringlets on her head. She is from Berkeley, California, and she has translated Kurosawa's autobiography, which covers the years up to 1950 and has been serialized in the Japanese magazine *Shukan Yomiuri* in twenty-five installments. Kurosawa, somewhat formal and stiff in manner, speaks only a few words of English, and Miss Bock is slated to be his official interpreter during his visit. Grilli and Owens are wearing tweed jackets and slacks, and Miss Bock is wearing a white fleecy coat over a beige tailored dress. The three Americans bow to Kurosawa, and he bows back. Everybody shakes hands.

Grilli then gives Miss Nogami a heartfelt hug.

"*Yoku irasshaimashita, ne*," Grilli says. Translation: "Welcome. It's great to have you here."

Bows and smiles all around. As they start outside, all three Americans say "*Dozo*" ("Please"), indicating that the Japanese should go first.

MONDAY. 1 P.M. UNITED NATIONS PLAZA HOTEL. ROOM 3701.

A two-room suite reserved for Kurosawa is not ready. Three chambermaids are working silently at vacuuming, ashtray-emptying, and bedmaking. Kurosawa, followed by Grilli, Miss Nogami, Miss Bock, and bellboys carrying luggage that includes a cardboard box tied with a rope, nods politely to the chambermaids and shows no sign of displeasure at finding the room not ready. He glances briefly at the view: the Chrysler Building. He looks over the furnishings, which are ultra-modern, in beige, and among which is a small bar covered in a kind of fake wolf fur; he gives a faint smile. The two women go off to their own rooms, and Kurosawa takes off his jacket and necktie and unbuttons his shirt collar, then sits down with Grilli to look over the schedule of activities for the retrospective.

Tuesday:
    6 p.m. Dinner at Japan House, with Japan Society directors and special guests.
    8 p.m. Opening of Kurosawa Retrospective with screening of *Throne of Blood* (*Kumonosu-jo*). Francis Coppola will introduce Mr. Kurosawa. Mr. Kurosawa will introduce the film.
    Reception in Mr. Kurosawa's honor following the film.

Wednesday:
    9:45 a.m. Japan House—Kurosawa photo portrait session with Arnold Newman for cover of Knopf autobiography.
    12 noon Press luncheon at Japan House—Stanley Kauffman presiding.
    3 p.m. Dick Cavett TV interview.

Thursday:
    6:45 p.m. William Friedkin dinner, for Mr. Kurosawa, at his midtown apartment.

Friday:
    10 a.m. Special screening of *Ikiru* for members of the Film Directors

Guild, with open discussion with Mr. Kurosawa.
7:30 p.m. Public Opening of Kurosawa Retrospective—screening of *Yojimbo*.

Kurosawa asks Grilli how many people will be at Friedkin's dinner party. About twenty-five, Grilli says, and he starts naming them: Mr. and Mrs. Arthur Penn, Mr. and Mrs. Martin Scorsese, Peter Hamill, Linda Ronstadt, Bud Yorkin. Grilli pauses to explain that Bud Yorkin is a very successful producer and director of movies and television shows, including *All in the Family*, which he co-produced with Norman Lear, and also of films, including *The Night They Raided Minsky's*, which was produced by him and directed by Friedkin. Kurosawa nods affirmatively and says nothing, lights a Seven Stars cigarette. Grilli resumes: Mr. Elia Kazan, Frances FitzGerald, Mr. and Mrs. Michael Arlen, Mr. and Mrs. Norman Mailer, Mr. and Mrs. Sidney Lumet—

"Ah, Sidney Lumet," Kurosawa says, interrupting. "I'd like to see Sidney Lumet's film *Prince of the City*."

"We could go tonight," Grilli says. "If you're not too tired."

"Yes, yes, yes. I want to see *Prince of the City*," Kurosawa says.

## MONDAY. 6 P.M. CINEMA III, THE SMALL THEATER AT THE PLAZA HOTEL.

An usher stands near the box office looking bored as Grilli hurries over, followed by Kurosawa, Miss Nogami, and Miss Bock, and buys four tickets, at six dollars each; with quick "*Dozo*"s, has the others go ahead; and hands the tickets to the usher, who gives no sign of recognizing Kurosawa. Kurosawa, Miss Nogami, and Miss Bock are still wearing the clothes they were wearing at the airport. It is dark in the theater. The three of them and Grilli take seats in the rear, Kurosawa with Miss Nogami on one side, Miss Bock on the other. The picture starts immediately. No sound. On the screen:

An Orion Pictures/Warner Brothers Release

Cut to scene of the hero, Danny Ciello (played by Treat Williams), in bed with his wife (Lindsay Crouse). Some music comes up, together with sound effects like a heartbeat, which are picked up by timpani. Danny wakes, frightened, says there's someone going to break down the door. His wife says no one is there. As the picture fades out, cards are being flipped on the screen. "Dom Bando—Detective—NYPD" is shown, followed by several others and, last, by the card with Danny Ciello's name on it. *Prince of the City* is superimposed on that card. Kurosawa, still wearing the dark-tinted glasses, leans forward, watching the screen with complete concentration. On the screen, the scene dissolves to one showing a luncheonette, where Danny Ciello looks up as a seedy-looking, nervous man who turns out to be an addict and an informer enters. The informer tells him that "the king" can be found in a telephone booth across the street. Ciello stuffs something in the man's breast pocket. Next, Ciello is shown at the phone booth, where "the king" informs him where "the action" will take place. Each detective named on the flipped cards is then shown telephoning another with the information.

The film takes nearly three hours, in the course of which Kurosawa's full attention never wavers. He doesn't ask for any translations. A couple of times, Miss Nogami and he whisper to each other, without looking away from the screen. The film moves fast. Quick cuts. Lots of action: hitting, running, knocking about, shooting, chasing, getting soaked in the rain, eating—moving the story along. Danny Ciello agrees to work with the United States Justice Department to root out corruption in the Police Department and to destroy a drug ring. He exposes the corruption among the members of his own narcotics squad. Last scene of the film: Ciello, addressing Police Academy students, says, "I'm Detective Ciello," and sees a student get up and walk out, saying, "I have nothing to learn from you"; and the last frame is frozen on Ciello's face. End of the film. Lights go on. Kurosawa, Miss Nogami, Miss Bock, and Grilli stand, stretch, smile with obvious pleasure. Led by Kurosawa, who seems to know his way around, they make a beeline for the Plaza's Oyster Bar.


MONDAY. 9:30 P.M. THE OYSTER BAR.

Kurosawa is seated at a small square table with Grilli, Miss Nogami, and Miss Bock. They are talking about *Prince of the City*. Kurosawa says that he admires the quality of the color, the camerawork, the fast cuts, and, especially, the way Lumet shot the scenes of Danny Ciello driving in the rain, running in the rain, fighting in the rain, and chasing around in the rain in order to get some drugs to give to his addict informer. It is impossible to shoot in natural rain, Kurosawa says. Lots of laughing from the three others as he tells them how much water he had to use up in the last reel of *Seven Samurai*, in the big twenty-minute battle scene that takes place during a rainstorm, with both men and horses, when three cameras were working simultaneously. Grilli says that the way Sidney Lumet shot the scene of Danny Ciello walking past the long iron-grillwork fence, showing the passing iron-grillwork poles, reminded him of the way Kurosawa shot the trees rushing by in *Rashomon*. He tells Kurosawa that Lumet and other good film directors would be the first to say they had learned much from seeing Kurosawa's films. Kurosawa grins and nods in agreement. They order Bloody Marys and drink a kind of toast to *Prince of the City*. The waiter comes over again, and they order oysters, starting with six Blue Points each. They go on to three repeat orders, followed by cherrystone clams. Grilli says that he has seldom eaten raw oysters in Japan. Kurosawa assures him that raw oysters in Japan taste delicious. Kurosawa says that he is rather tired but that he is very happy he got to see *Prince of the City*, and that he plans to sleep late in the morning.

TUESDAY. 3 P.M. ROOM 3701.

Kurosawa, without his jacket but wearing a tie, is having Japanese tea with Miss Nogami, Miss Bock, and Grilli. Miss Nogami is brewing the tea behind the fake-fur-covered bar; Kurosawa is sitting on the sofa, his back to the window framing the Chrysler Building. On a low glass-topped coffee table are packages of Seven Stars and Camel cigarettes. Grilli and Miss Bock sit in straight-backed armchairs at right angles to Kurosawa. Miss Nogami pours the tea into Japanese porcelain cups, which Grilli has brought over from Japan House. She hands a cup to Kurosawa, and he takes a sip. With the tea, he smokes a Seven Stars cigarette, holding it between thumb and forefinger. Miss Nogami sits cross-legged on the floor facing Kurosawa, and she lights a Seven Stars cigarette. Kurosawa says the tea is good, and praises Miss Nogami for using warm tap water to make it. That's the best way, Kurosawa says—not with boiling water. He looks at the cup holding the tea. In Japan today, he says, everything is plastic. "In my home, I have all old cups and bowls and plates and spoons—everything I can—because I want my children and my grandchildren to live with the old things, to know them by living with them," he says. "The most beautiful bowls in Japan are the ancient ones that came from Korea. They were peasants' soup bowls that were used as tea bowls in Japan. There are few left. We don't even know the names of the potters. The later bowls are more famous, but they are not as good." He picks up the teacup and runs his fingers over the base. "The bases of the Korean bowls are completely original," he says. "You can't reproduce them. We know the names of the later potters. They put their names on their bowls." He takes a sip of tea and draws on his cigarette, holding it practically down at the hot end. "As soon as you put your name on a work, something happens to it," he says. "It is lessened." Kurosawa says he thinks it's very important to learn from the past—in the Japanese phrase, "*onko-chishin.*" That is why he is attracted to making films with historical themes. He says that he knows he was greatly influenced by American directors in his filmmaking, and that he has the greatest admiration for the work of D. W. Griffith, John Ford, and John Huston, among others. *Stagecoach* is still one of his favorite movies. What motivates him now, however, is the desire to have modern Japanese learn that the great old powerful samurai left a rich cultural heritage, which means much more than the physical strength and swordsmanship depicted in many Japanese movies. He feels it's important to show the high level of education, the sense of beauty, the spiritual training, and the mental sharpness of the samurai class. That is the spirit of the Japanese heritage.

In Japan today, Kurosawa goes on, children grow up worshiping everything from the West. The most painful thing in Japan today is the artificial democracy. After Japan lost the Second World War, Japan became democratized from the outside. Democracy didn't develop out of Japanese needs; democracy was just laid over Japanese society.

Peter Grilli asks whether the costumes in Kurosawa's latest film, *Kagemusha* (*The Shadow Warrior*), were accurate duplicates of the ones worn in the sixteenth century—medieval times in Japan. Kurosawa says he tried to give a sense of what the costumes were, but it would be impossible to get the same colors, because they were made with natural dyes in those days, not with chemicals. Grilli says he knows about the subtlety of Japanese color differences, and says he was surprised to learn, years ago, that there was a separate Japanese dictionary for colors, which lists about a hundred different words for the color red. Everybody smiles.

"Television is a very harmful influence in Japan today," Kurosawa says. "University students only watch television and read comic books. They don't read the classics. If I'm working with a writer and I refer to a classic and find he hasn't read it, I can't go on working with him." He looks distressed. "Japan today," he says. "It is all but impossible now in Japan for me to make a film—even one film a year."

TUESDAY. 7:30 P.M. THE RECEPTION ROOM OF JAPAN HOUSE.

Japan House is a very modern four-story black concrete building at 333 East Forty-seventh Street, across from the United Nations at the East River. It was designed by the Japanese architect Junzo Yoshimura. Traditional-style *sudare*, or sunshades, but of steel instead of bamboo, hang over the windows on the top two floors. Inside, the lobby floor is of polished black slate. There is a reflecting pool with bamboo trees growing out of planters in the water and with lighted candles floating in it. In an adjoining glassed-in reception room, the Japan Society board of directors is winding up a dinner. There are five large round tables. Kurosawa, in a dark-blue suit and a white shirt with a red-white-and-blue figured necktie, is sitting at a table with Robert S. Ingersoll, the chairman of the board of the Japan Society and a former United States Ambassador to Japan (under President Nixon), who is also wearing a blue suit. At the same table are six others, including Grilli and Miss Bock. The film director Francis Coppola, bearded, wearing a gray rumpled suit and with a dark-green wool scarf tied around his neck, is at the next table, along with Miss Nogami; Lily Auchincloss, a longtime board member; Mrs. Grilli; and Mr. Kenji Tamiya, president of the Sony Corporation of America. Mrs. Grilli, a dark-haired, attractive young woman wearing a black dress and an Egyptian gold necklace, listens quietly as Coppola and Tamiya enthusiastically discuss Sony video equipment and its possible future use for making movies. Ingersoll gives a toast. He thanks Kurosawa for coming from Japan to open the complete retrospective of his films, which is a major event of the Japan Society's Seventy-fifth Anniversary program. He refers to Kurosawa as "Japan's greatest film director."

Kurosawa, who is still wearing his dark-tinted glasses, rises and responds to the toast. He speaks in Japanese, pausing every few sentences for Audie Bock to give the translation: "I am deeply grateful to the Japan Society for collecting all of my films and for arranging for them to be shown in the retrospective film series that is opening this evening. For a filmmaker, there can be no greater joy than to have his films seen widely and by as many people as possible. I am grateful to you for bringing about such an opportunity for me. My first films were made nearly forty years ago, in wartime Japan. Who at the time would have dreamed that such an event as this film series might one day take place in America? I am a filmmaker, and my greatest love is films. My whole life has been devoted to making films. All of them were made with my own Japanese people as their intended audience. Never once while I was making them did it occur to me that they might also come to be loved and appreciated by Americans and people all over the world. To me, it is almost like a dream, and I am profoundly moved that my films should be so well received. And yet—when you think about it—people everywhere share basic human sentiments that transcend all cultural differences and different ways of thought and social patterns. As human beings, we are the same, and our fundamental sympathy for one another as people is the same everywhere. I am often asked in Japan if I make films in some special way that will appeal to foreigners, or, at least, be understood by them. I do no such thing. As a Japanese, I can think only like a Japanese, and I can make only films that are honest and meaningful to Japanese. Perhaps, in some way, it is for just that reason that foreign viewers also admire these films and are moved by them. I find it wonderful that when people of all nations state their thoughts and feelings honestly and directly they can find mutual understanding and a sympathetic response. Today, at a time when the nations of the world too often confront each other with distrust and suspicion and we grope along rather hopelessly in the dark,

I think it all the more important that filmmakers like me exert our efforts to bring the peoples of the world closer together in forthright exchanges of values and honest attempts to understand each other better. Simple though these thoughts of mine may be, I am grateful for the opportunity to express them and to present to you my films. Thank you very much."

Kurosawa sits down. Applause. The dinner guests get up and wander out into the lobby, where perhaps two hundred additional guests are milling about before going into the screening room. There is a mixture of film critics and film buffs, people from the movie business and from museums, and people whose interest in Kurosawa reaches beyond his films: Richard Gere; Mr. Tadao Fujimatsu, of Japan Air Lines; Robert Duvall; Geoffrey Holder; Mr. and Mrs. Thomas Hoving; Stanley Kauffmann; Edwin Newman, of NBC News; Kazuto Ohira, of Toho Films; William W. Scranton, a former governor of Pennsylvania and a Japan Society board member.

LATER. THE AUDITORIUM OF JAPAN HOUSE.

The guests have taken their seats for the showing of the film. On the stage, Mr. Ingersoll again speaks: "As chairman of the board of the Japan Society, I am delighted you could be with us for the start of this retrospective of the twenty-six films of Akira Kurosawa. No other filmmaker has made as great an impact on our young directors. One such director, Francis Coppola, has revolutionized American cinema." Mr. Ingersoll then introduces Coppola.

Coppola says that no one surpasses Kurosawa in the sense of humanity and the sincerity that mark his films. Then he points out that there is some conflict between art and commerce in Japan, as there is in the United States. "It is very difficult for a master like Kurosawa to do his work," he says. "I would like to see this trend reversed."

Coppola introduces Kurosawa, who takes the stage and says, "My profession is that of film director. I hide behind the camera. I don't know what to do when I am put in the spotlight like this. Since I am put here before you, I have to say something. Making a film takes a great deal of effort, and if I don't put this effort into the film it doesn't come out right. So the most painful thing is to think you will come to see the film and then forget it. It is also painful to think that you see the film, remember it for a little while, and then forget it. So I try to keep you from forgetting. I try to present a human being that you are unable to forget. It is very simple, but this is what I have to say."

The lights go out. *Throne of Blood*—a version of the *Macbeth* story—starts.

*Throne of Blood* was made in 1957, with the Macbeth character played by Toshiro Mifune, the most renowned actor in Japan, who worked with Kurosawa for many years. In 1948, Mifune was in Kurosawa's *Drunken Angel*, and it made him a star. He played the bandit in *Rashomon*, the straying samurai in *Seven Samurai*, and the title character in *Yojimbo*. In *Throne of Blood*, Mifune plays a feudal lord, master of a forest castle. The style of the film is based on various techniques of the Noh theater, in which style and story are one. There are many frightening scenes of conspiracy, murder, and treachery, with a horrible witch. There are few closeups. At the end of the film, the feudal lord's own men turn on him and kill him brutally with a hail of arrows.

The film lasts for a hundred and ten minutes. The audience receives it quietly, with an occasional gasp. Robert Ingersoll eases the collar of his shirt and gives a few audible sighs.

TUESDAY. 9:15 P.M. THE RECEPTION ROOM OF JAPAN HOUSE.

The round tables have been removed. At two rectangular tables on one side of the room, two bartenders are at the ready, the wherewithal for champagne drinks all set up. Members of the audience wander into the reception area. They look a bit shaken, but many of them are smiling. It is obvious that at this point, at any rate, all of them are remembering the feudal lord and his ambitious and evil wife. Snatches of conversation:

"The Japanese are suspicious of international success. Some of the critics in Japan hate Kurosawa. The money people there don't consider his films an art. They won't give him money to make a film."

"Francis Coppola and George Lucas got Twentieth Century-Fox to buy the international distribution rights to *Kagemusha*, and that's the only way he got to finish the picture. It cost six and a half million dollars—the most expensive Japanese film ever made."

"Now he's got this incredible script based on the *King Lear* story, but with sons, and he can't get the money to make it. Coppola and Lucas are going to bat for him again."

"He's never allowed himself to go crawling for money to make his movies. As a samurai, money is beneath him."

"Everybody thinks *Rashomon* was his first picture, but he made ten terrific films before *Rashomon*."

"Coppola and Lucas, and Billy Friedkin, too, will help him get the money to make another movie. But Kurosawa has his samurai pride. You know the Japanese saying: 'The samurai, even though he hasn't eaten, picks his teeth.'"

"From here, he goes to Italy, where the President of Italy is going to give him the Second Order of Merit of the Italian Republic. Fellini is going to present him with the Vittorio De Sica Award, and he's also getting the Donatello Award for the best foreign picture of the year in Italy—*Kagemusha*."

"George Lucas invited him out to California to see all the elaborate equipment at his new studio."

"Knopf is publishing his autobiography, and Charles Elliott is editing it. Chuck is here, with his wife."

"The photographer Arnold Newman is supposed to take his picture tomorrow for the autobiography. Newman asked him to pose wearing a cap and other 'working' clothes, to give the impression that he was working. Kurosawa refused to wear a cap or anything special. He said to Newman, "If you want to get a picture of me working, come to Japan.'"

The reception area is now jammed with people. Kurosawa stands near the doorway, Audie Bock by his side, interpreting, as the guests introduce themselves, shake his hand, present him with Film Center programs (there is a photograph of Kurosawa on the cover) to be autographed. Kurosawa works hard at the reception-line chores, shaking hands, smiling, bowing, autographing, and only now and then nervously edging away from popping flashbulbs, which seem to hurt his eyes. He keeps his tinted glasses on. Mrs. John D. Rockefeller 3rd, president of the board of trustees of the Museum of Modern Art and a longtime friend of the Japan Society, arrives late and heads directly over to Kurosawa, apologizing graciously as she shakes his hand. She is slender and tall—in high heels, a bit taller than Kurosawa—and she is wearing a long purple print gown with a ruffled collar. She had to attend a screening of the new movie *Rich and Famous*, she explains, but she rushed over immediately, because she wanted to thank him for coming to the U.S.A., and she is so happy he could come. There is a concentration of popping flashbulbs as most of the photographers take a shot of Kurosawa with Mrs. Rockefeller. There are at least a dozen photographers, half of them Japanese; they take pictures of Kurosawa posing with this one and that one, and also take candids. Kurosawa produces a Seven Stars, and a photographer lights the cigarette for him and then takes his picture smoking, as he again holds the cigarette between thumb and forefinger. Around him, several Japanese are saying "*Dozo*," each indicating that one of the others should take the path to Kurosawa's handshake first. A number of the guests hug Miss Nogami. A Japanese man, short, with a gray goatee, and wearing a black wool jacket, black slacks, and a gray turtleneck, comes over to Kurosawa, accompanied by a woman, taller than he, with a long face and with black hair pulled straight back. They are Mr. and Mrs. Takehiko Kamei. Mrs. Kamei wears a beautiful purple kimono—the only kimono in sight. Kurosawa hasn't seen them in several years. He and they beam at each other, bow, and shake hands. No hugs à la Hollywood. Kamei addresses Kurosawa as "Sensei," which means "teacher" and is used as a term of affectionate respect. Kamei is a painter, an illustrator, and an animator who made commercials for television in Japan before moving, with his wife, Yoko, to Toronto. He met Kurosawa originally while making a documentary about filmmakers. Kamei and his wife have come down from Toronto in order to attend the opening of Kurosawa's retrospective. Before the other handshakers move in on Kurosawa again, he invites the Kameis to come over to his room at the hotel after the reception. Coppola, still wearing the dark-green scarf, wanders around among the guests, giving jolly hugs and greetings to many, and looking over frequently to see how Kurosawa is doing.

As the reception thins out, Coppola and Kurosawa go off to one side of the room, the older man regarding the younger with undisguised admiration and affection. With lively gestures, Coppola describes his use of the new electronic equipment in his studio—Zoetrope—in Hollywood, in preparing and in shooting his next movie, *One from the Heart*. Video, Coppola explains, is about to evolve into what he calls the electronic cinema, and *One from the Heart* was an experiment in its use. Kurosawa, nodding with interest, gives a few vigorous puffs on a cigarette. In particular, Coppola goes on, he organized the production of this experimental movie from the start with a kind of electronic storyboarding. The script was placed in an information processor, which then became the central link to all the many activities and departments of the studio. He goes on to explain that his art department made sketches. The actors read the script as if it were a radio play. The budget was calculated. Everything was done to the constantly changing text circulating through the various departments, Coppola says, as though a clothesline were running through the entire studio, with each department hanging messages on and taking messages off simultaneously, until the clothesline itself became the movie. Kurosawa looks fascinated. Eventually, Coppola says, the flexibility and intimacy of the system will give us a new instrument, capable of doing things that were not possible before.

Kurosawa nods, and says that he made hundreds of sketches and paintings for *Kagemusha* before that movie was started. He then listens, deferring to what Coppola is saying.

Coppola says that the possibilities for future use of electronic technology in moviemaking are mind-boggling, reducing many of the enormous costs of filmmaking by cutting down the time needed by technicians and talent—collapsing the traditional pre-production, production, and post-production periods into a single-design production process. Since photographic film is a physical material that has to be handled, cut, and Scotch-Taped together, it is obviously slower and more rigid than video, which is pure energy.

Kurosawa says pensively that *he* is still using, for editing in Japan, the same small, primitive Moviola he has been using for years and years.

Almost *all* moviemakers in the world are still using an old-fashioned Moviola or something quite like it, Coppola puts in quickly. Now the same company is making a Videola, a new machine for handling film-to-videotape, and it's part of Zoetrope's editing system.

Kurosawa looks impressed.

Before parting, the two men discuss Kurosawa's plan to go to California after the opening of the retrospective, and meet with George Lucas and then with representatives of Twentieth Century-Fox about financing Kurosawa's

*Lear* movie. Coppola is in high spirits and is reassuring. Kurosawa is subdued and thoughtful.

TUESDAY. NEARLY MIDNIGHT. ROOM 3701.
Takehiko and Yoko Kamei are having drinks with Kurosawa. They are sitting on chairs and a sofa. Miss Nogami again sits cross-legged on the floor, and passes around a dish of peanuts. Everybody takes some. A bottle of Scotch and a bottle of bourbon, along with packs of Seven Stars and Camels, are on the coffee table. The atmosphere is quiet and comfortable. They are talking about various shots in *Throne of Blood*. Kurosawa tells how tiring it was to get one of the long shots of the feudal lord's castle, which he took with a telephoto lens. In order to give instructions to his actors, Kurosawa says, he had to hike all the way down a long road to the castle and then hike all the way back. No walkie-talkies in Japan? Kurosawa says he doesn't like to use walkie-talkies to give instructions to his actors. Kamei says he was much impressed by the sequences in which the murdered man's ghost appears as a vision to the lord. Kurosawa laughs, takes a sip of his drink, and says that the print is so washed out that it makes the ghost look even paler and much scarier than he might look in a better print of the film. He smokes, laughs, and shows no sign of tiring of the talk about his film. For the final scene, he says, in which the feudal lord is showered with arrows—with the last arrow going in one side of his neck and coming out the other—he called in an archery expert to demonstrate how to use real arrows for the shooting. Kurosawa says he insisted on authenticity. Toshiro Mifune, playing the lord, was so frightened as he was shot, even though he had on ample padding, that he had *real* terror in his eyes. Everybody laughs, and the guests agree that they saw the real terror in Mifune's eyes. At 3 a.m., still talking, they finally make a move to leave.

WEDNESDAY. MIDMORNING. A CONFERENCE ROOM ON THE SECOND FLOOR OF JAPAN HOUSE.
Under a skylight stands a dramatic abstract sculpture of black granite by Masayuki Nagare. Kurosawa, wearing the plaid wool jacket and tan

slacks he has worn before, with shirt and tie and tinted glasses, has been placed next to the sculpture. Arnold Newman, portly, gregarious, cheerful, talking with a strong New York accent, is photographing him. Newman has two jeans-clad young men—both of them eager, polite, and deferential—assisting him, and they make their way around Kurosawa, studying him, photographing him with several cameras, including a small one on a tripod. Kurosawa is very restless and ill at ease. He complains that he doesn't like to sit as a subject, to be on this side of the camera. He makes no attempt to hide his dissatisfaction.

THURSDAY EVENING, BILLY FRIEDKIN'S MIDTOWN APARTMENT.

Friedkin, the forty-one-year-old director of *The French Connection*, *The Exorcist* and *Cruising*, had the apartment built to his specifications. It is comfortable, spacious, and handsome, with English-oak floors throughout, and huge safety-glass windows. A large room given over to a billiard table has two nine-foot-high English-oak paneled doors separating it from a sixty-foot living room, which is furnished with eighteenth-century and nineteenth-century English antique tables and chairs, and goosedown sofas with Porthault coverings and embroidered Japanese silk pillows. Over a marble fireplace in the living room hangs a nineteenth-century French mirror with a gilt frame. There's a lot of original art on the walls: a small Turner watercolor of Sidon fishermen drawing in their nets; nineteenth-century Japanese prints from the series *100 Views of the Moon*, by Yoshitoshi; a large Degas watercolor of horses and jockeys at Longchamp; a George Grosz; a Picasso. In a corner of the foyer leading to the living room is the cardboard box that Kurosawa had with him on his arrival at the airport. For this evening, Friedkin has placed small Japanese-boxwood plants here and there in the foyer and in the living room.

Kurosawa, Grilli, Miss Nogami, and Miss Bock have arrived before most of the other guests and are sitting with Friedkin in his study. The furnishings here include a nineteenth-century French table and black leather Charles Eames chairs. On the walls are a Matisse crayon drawing of a woman's face; a George Grosz drawing of a sailor kicking a woman;

several Daumier prints; two large, signed photographs of Red Auerbach, the general manager and president of the Boston Celtics (Friedkin's favorite basketball team); a Boston Celtics pennant; and large, framed stills from *The Exorcist*. Several small Japanese-boxwood plants have been placed around this room, too.

Friedkin is a trim, volatile, friendly, good-natured, and likable man, his eyes alert behind glasses with thin gold frames, and his manner warm and hospitable. He is making a big effort to see to it that everybody feels comfortable. He is dramatically dressed in black pants, black boots, a black shirt, a beautiful tie of red Japanese silk embroidered in pink and red. Kurosawa has on his dark-blue suit and his tinted glasses. Others in the study are Bud Yorkin, who is serious, polite, and watchful, and who also wears a dark-blue suit; and Frances FitzGerald, a tall, blond, attractive, and gracious young woman, who is wearing a black pants suit.

Drinks are served. Friedkin raises his glass to Kurosawa and says, "*Kono go o-kampai!*" He translates, "Let's drink to the future," and adds, "What we all want is for you to make more pictures." Friedkin speaks precisely and clearly, like a confident student in an elocution class.

Kurosawa seems to understand him even before Audie Bock translates for him: he is nodding and saying "Thank you" in English while she is still translating.

"Everyone owes him a debt. Everyone," Friedkin says.

"In *Kagemusha*, in that fantastic battle scene where you had two hundred horses all being shot and falling down at the same time, how did you get them all to fall down simultaneously?" Frances FitzGerald asks Kurosawa.

He responds with great enthusiasm, explaining that he had lined up two hundred people, one for each horse, to give the horses an injection of a soporific at a certain signal. The horses were all put to sleep, and then were filmed as they were getting up, stumbling, falling down. All around the horses, he adds, were actors who were supposed to act dead. Very difficult to do, with horses kicking and failing all around them. He pauses, then says that all the costumes and armor that were used in *Kagemusha* will be very useful in his *Lear* picture, if he can get it made. He learned so much, with *Kagemusha*, about the culture of that medieval period, he says, and he wants to use all that he learned when he makes *Lear*. He looks around at the

pictures on the wall and indicates one of a scene from *The Exorcist*.
"Did that picture scare you?" Bud Yorkin asks.
"I wasn't scared," Kurosawa replies. "But I took my daughter, and she was so scared she couldn't eat for two days."
"Do many of your pictures end up on Japanese television?" Yorkin asks.
Kurosawa nods glumly.
The doorbell rings. Friedkin gets up to admit new arrivals: Mr. and Mrs. Arthur Penn; Mr. and Mrs. Norman Mailer; Mr. and Mrs. Michael Arlen.
"The last time I did this was fifteen years ago—gave a whole dinner," Friedkin says from the doorway. "It was for Harold Pinter."

LATER. THE LIVING ROOM, WHERE THREE ROUND TABLES HAVE BEEN SET FOR A SEATED DINNER.
Sidney Lumet, wearing brown cords, a heavy white turtleneck, a tweed jacket, and black-rimmed glasses, enters and makes straight for Kurosawa. They shake hands, and Kurosawa, grinning widely, holds on to the younger director's hand and keeps pumping it. He tells Lumet immediately that he has just seen *Prince of the City* and thinks the film is wonderful.
"From you, that is very, very special to me, and I don't say that often," Lumet says.
"And I, too, am not given to flattery," Audie Bock translates after Kurosawa, still holding Lumet's hand, makes his reply.
"Beauty many people can do, but beauty with meaning very few people can do," Lumet says, falling in oddly with Audie Bock's translation rhythm, and speaking as though he himself were giving a translation.
What impressed him so much, Kurosawa says, was the physical beauty of the cinematography in the movie and how it related to the story. Also, he was impressed by the way Lumet used light.
Lumet looks as though he were going to weep with joy. "For you to recognize these things!" he says. "These things we worked so hard for. In the first third of the film, the people are separated from the backgrounds; the light is not on the people but on the backgrounds—the neon signs, for example. In the second third of the movie, the light is on both the people and the backgrounds. In the last third, the light is on the people in the

foreground; walls are stripped bare, and the focus is fully on the people."

"And in the last shot," Kurosawa says, becoming as excited as Lumet, "you have the sea of blue shirts at the Police Academy, and then you show just that one face, the face of Danny Ciello. Superb!"

"For you to recognize all that..." Lumet says. "I've never seen one fake frame in your films." Turning toward the other guests, he adds, "To achieve the beauty he achieves without falseness is incredible."

"I don't feel I've yet achieved everything you describe," Kurosawa says.

"One always feels that way," says Lumet. "There were two directors after the silents who changed movies. One was Carl Dreyer, and the other was Kurosawa."

"Now I'd like to go back to making silent films again," Kurosawa says. "There's still a great deal to learn. How to make the words, the talking passages, shorter."

Billy Friedkin comes over. "In Japan, he's a prophet without honor," he says to a guest on the edge of the group around Kurosawa.

Friedkin listens politely as Kurosawa continues to talk to Lumet about *Prince of the City*. Kurosawa says that the rain scenes in the movie looked like real rain, but he knows that it is impossible to shoot in real rain.

Lumet replies happily, "We created blocks and blocks of rain. We had four hundred-foot cherry pickers, with hoses and metal pipes extending for thirty-two more feet. Four pipes were crossed with spinning nozzles, and we let the natural wind carry it. We used tens of thousands of gallons of water."

While Audie Bock struggles to get the information about the cherry pickers and the water translated into Japanese, Billy Friedkin tells Lumet, with what appears to be genuine admiration, "You did it this time, baby. Beautiful!"

The dinner is being catered by Eli Zabar's E.A.T., and canapés—black caviar, Scotch salmon—are passed around by pretty young waitresses wearing dark skirts and white silk blouses. Young waiters wearing dark pants, white shirts, and neckties serve glasses of champagne.

"Gadg!" Friedkin says, greeting the director Elia Kazan. "You look great."

While Kazan and his host are hugging each other, Kazan asks Friedkin whether he has ever met Kurosawa before.

Friedkin says no, but that when Grilli asked him if he wanted to give the dinner he said he'd be delighted to do it, because of his tremendous admiration for Kurosawa.

"For directors, his work is almost like a textbook," Grilli says.

"Kurosawa is one of the figures in world cinema I respect," Friedkin says. "Last January, when I went to Japan on a promotional tour with my *Cruising*, I wanted to meet him, but I was then being spirited around so fast from place to place that I never had a chance. In Los Angeles, I used to go to the Toho La Brea to see his films, but that theater doesn't exist anymore. It's hard to see a Japanese film in this country now."

"The Kurosawa film I want to see is the one he made in Russia—*Dersu Uzala*," Kazan says.

"We're showing it in the retrospective," Grilli says. "We're showing *all* of them. What I find exciting is the way he follows everything the American directors are doing."

"And he's so nice about us," Friedkin says. When *The French Connection* opened in Japan, he wrote me a letter about it from there. It just came in like that, over the transom. He said *The French Connection* was one of the most visually exciting films he'd ever seen. That meant so much to me, when I'm just overwhelmed by his work."


LATER. SEATED DINNER.

On each of the three tables are a couple of small Japanese-boxwood plants in terra-cotta pots. Kurosawa remarks on how nice they look. Along with everybody else, he relishes what turns out to be one of E.A.T's great dinners: ziti with Nantucket bay scallops and wild chanterelles; aged filet of beef with a tart raspberry jelly or bearnaise sauce; Manor House rolls baked without yeast in a brick oven; French-field-lettuce salad; giant chocolate-covered strawberries; giant stem strawberries with crème fraiche; fresh raspberries; California white wine (Spring Mountain Chardonnay); California red wine (Jordan Cabernet); chocolate truffles; chocolate cake. Sitting with Frances FitzGerald, Sidney Lumet, Elia Kazan, and Audie Bock, Kurosawa is now relaxed, even jovial. Right after the ziti, he takes off his tinted glasses for the first time in company since his arrival three days before. He talks easily about his own background.

He was born in Tokyo, the youngest of eight children. His father, who was a descendant of one of the best-known samurai families, the Abe Sadato, dating from the eleventh century, was a physical-education teacher at Toyama Army Academy; he had come to Tokyo from Akita, in the north. Kurosawa went to schools in Tokyo. He got into the movie business by accident. His father loved going to the movies and took his children to see them. One of Kurosawa's older brothers was a narrator of silent films. During the Depression, Kurosawa started out as a painter, trained in Western painting at the Doshusha School, in Tokyo, but he couldn't make a go of it. He answered an advertisement for young people to take an examination for the job of apprentice to a film director, got a job as apprentice to a director he couldn't admire, wanted to quit, but was persuaded by friends to stay. Then he worked under Kajiro Yamamoto, a fine director of comedies and action films, who was the best teacher he ever had. Yamamoto told him to work on writing scripts and to learn editing if he wanted to become a director. Before he directed his first film, he took part in every phase of filmmaking: lighting, set design, props, camerawork—everything. At the age of thirty-three, he directed his first film, *Sanshiro Sugata*. It was 1943, and because of the war the censorship bureau was being very strict about what could and couldn't be made, so he had decided to make a very old-fashioned film. He wasn't taken by the Army for service, because one of his brothers had been killed, and the Army held to the principle that the loss of one son in a family was enough. *Sanshiro Sugata* was a success. It is about a young student of the martial arts, apprenticed first to an arrogant jujitsu teacher and then to a teacher who stresses spiritual ideals and moral discipline. For his second movie, Kurosawa was asked in 1944, by a representative of the Information Ministry, to make a film to inspire the young people at home to work for the war effort. The film is about three factory girls, and he actually put the three actresses playing the roles to work in an optical-instruments factory, to make them lose their self-consciousness as actresses. They became hardworking factory girls, did lose their "actress" qualities, and, after the film was finished, got married and settled down. The leading actress, Yoko Yaguchi, got married and settled down with *him*. They have a son, Hisao, and a daughter, Kazuko, both in their mid-thirties. Kazuko is a housewife, married to an automobile designer who is the son of an actor who appeared in many of Kurosawa's movies. They have two little boys. Hisao, who is also married and has a two-year-old son, has done many things—he once had an interest in a basketball team, for instance, and he has acted for television—and he is now forming his own film company, with the intention of making films that are less difficult to make than Kurosawa's.

Kurosawa has a plate of giant chocolate-covered strawberries, giant stem strawberries, and fresh raspberries in front of him. A waitress offers him some chocolate truffles and some chocolate cake, and he helps himself and contemplates his desserts with obvious pleasure. Elia Kazan, a few seats away at the table, catches his eye. "The film I want to see again is the Russian one—*Dersu Uzala*," Kazan says, looking at Kurosawa with boyish admiration. "I saw it five years ago, when it came out. Did you work with the author? How does a script like that come to be?"

Kurosawa nods several times and laughs, putting back on his plate a chocolate-covered strawberry he was about to eat. "The Soviets came to me and said, 'We want you to direct a film in Russia. Whatever you want to do.' I suggested the Russian novel by Vladimir Arseniev. I had read it thirty years before. The Russians were amazed that I knew this book, and accepted it immediately. The Russian writer Yuri Nagibin kept coming in. We did the screenplay together, working in Russia. That is"—Kurosawa gives a mischievous kind of grin—"his ideas were not usually acceptable, so we stayed mainly with ideas that were mine." He pops the chocolate-covered strawberry into his mouth.

Someone at the table wants to know what *Dersu Uzala* is about.

"A Russian Army captain and his team of surveyors come upon Dersu, an old Mongolian hunter, in the forests of Siberia," Kurosawa says. "Dersu agrees to become their guide. While he is showing them how to find their way through the rugged terrain, he tells them of his philosophy of life—to respect all living things, because man must live in harmony with nature. Five years later, the Army captain and his team return to Siberia and again find Dersu. This time, he shoots a tiger that has been following the group, and falls into a deep depression over having violated his principles. Because Dersu is losing his eyesight, the captain takes him to live with him in Khabarovsk, but Dersu can't stand civilization, returns to the forest, and dies. The film was a big success in Russia."

"I want to see that again," Kazan says.

Kurosawa eats another chocolate-covered strawberry and courteously tells Kazan he greatly admired his film *Splendor in the Grass*.

Kazan looks a couple of decades younger and gives a boyish smile. "Trying to make films in this country now is much too difficult," Kazan says. "Trying to raise those millions of dollars to do what you want to do. So in recent years I've written two novels and now I'm finishing a third."

Kurosawa looks sympathetic. Turning to Lumet, he says, "It would be impossible to make *Prince of the City* in Japan today."

"How much political pressure is applied on your movies?" Lumet asks.

"It depends, one, on what the film is, and, two, not on the government but on who runs the government," Kurosawa replies.

Lumet says, "In Hollywood, if it can make money there are no limitations on the money. Is that true of Japanese financing?"

"Pretty much the same pressures but more complicated," says Kurosawa, and he samples a chocolate truffle as Audie Bock translates. "In 1960, I made *The Bad Sleep Well*, a film critical of corruption and bigness in business which destroyed the lives of men working for corporate structures. When I submitted the original script, the producers disagreed with everything. I had to make cowardly compromises. I couldn't show what I wanted to show—that the real and final source of the corruption was at the top. I had to settle for a faceless voice on the other end of a telephone line. Even so, it was surprising even then—about twenty years ago—that I could go that far. I don't think I could make that film today. It might appear that I could make anything I wanted today if I had the funds. Actually, it is not so. My 1952 film *Ikiru* was critical of bureaucrats, but it was respected, and it was given an award by the Education Ministry. Today, that film could not be made. Now I want to make films about the past. The past is important to me, of course, and I can say what I want to say. But Japanese critics attack me for not making films about present-day society, and the attacks take the form of saying 'He spends too much money on those big historical films.' They don't understand why I feel forced to make films about historical subjects. They don't understand that the problems I like to deal with are *human* problems, which are ageless."

"Do they consider you a reactionary in Japan?" Lumet asks.

"Yes," Kurosawa says, looking sad.

"When you hold on to where you came from and what you are, it's impossible for young people to understand," Lumet says. "Young people like labels."

"Yes," Kurosawa says, still looking sad but starting in on the fresh raspberries. "I just keep on doing what *I* can do," he adds.

Martin Scorsese and his wife, Isabella—a beautiful young woman, who looks very much like her mother, Ingrid Bergman—come over to Kurosawa and greet him. Kurosawa says that he saw Scorsese's movie *Raging Bull* and liked it very much.

Isabella Scorsese tells Kurosawa that she is hardly ever taken to the movies. "When I was a child, both my parents were working at acting or directing for the movies, and when they came home they always wanted to do something other than take me to the movies," she says. "Now I'm married to Marty, and he never wants to take me to the movies, either!" Everybody laughs.

Before leaving the table, Kurosawa stands and drinks a toast to his host. "I wish to apologize for my lack of education in not knowing English," he says, in Japanese. "I am very much overwhelmed that all of you gathered here for my sake." In English, he adds, "Thank you."

Billy Friedkin comes over to the table as Eli Zabar, the creator of the delicious dinner—a slender, slightly built man wearing an oversized white apron—peeks from behind one of the tall paneled doors. Friedkin turns from Kurosawa and calls out, "Eli! Mr. Kurosawa wants to tell you that it was one of the best dinners he has ever eaten in his life."

Miss Nogami drags Kurosawa's cardboard box into the room, opens it, and takes out copies of glossy-paper picture books, with Japanese text, dealing with Kurosawa and his movies. She hands them to Kurosawa, and he signs one for each of the guests. Billy Friedkin then presents Kurosawa with gifts: the large National Museum of American History book on folkcraft and art (from the first American flag to the first Model T Ford), a book on American art with a front section in which everybody at the party has signed his name, and albums of thirty-six of Mozart's symphonies, performed by the Academy of Ancient Music under Christopher Hogwood. Kurosawa says he loves Mozart. Billy Friedkin looks very pleased.

FRIDAY. 10 A.M. THE AUDITORIUM OF JAPAN HOUSE.

About a hundred members of the Directors' Guild of America have come here on a beautiful, clear, sunny morning and are attending a screening of *Ikiru* (*To Live*), Kurosawa's movie, made in 1952, about a petty official in a city ward office who is told he has only six months to live and decides to use his remaining time to do something good; namely, fight red tape and bureaucracy and so push through to completion the construction of a playground for children. The role of the official is played by Takashi Shimura, and it is a memorable and famous performance. The last half of the movie shows an all-night wake held by the official's colleagues, where some of the politicians present try to take credit for what the official did but are shown up by his friends. It is a heartrending movie. When the lights in the auditorium go on, the audience is very quiet, very shaken. Billy Friedkin is sitting in one of the last rows with Frances FitzGerald. Like the others in the audience, they sit waiting, not even talking to each other.

Kurosawa appears at a microphone set up on the stage, with Audie Bock at his side. He speaks in Japanese, and she translates: "My name is Kurosawa. Thank you very much for coming to see my film today. When *Ikiru* was first released in Japan, it did very well, but the distribution company felt that it would not be understood by foreigners. Especially the second part, the wake, they felt, would be incomprehensible. But I kept after them. Finally, they agreed to submit it to the Berlin Film Festival. At the Berlin Film Festival, it was very well received, and I won the Silver Bear, the prize for the best film. This experience served to confirm my belief that film is international and humanity is universal. I am often asked if there is anything special I do to make my films understood by foreigners. I reply that I am making my films as a Japanese as honestly as I can. So these films are understood by other people and sometimes are loved by them. It seems that everyone becomes closer to everyone else through cinema."

A FEW MINUTES LATER. THE RECEPTION ROOM OF JAPAN HOUSE.

Several long rectangular tables have been set up facing the speakers' table, at one side of the room. The tables are set with black lacquer boxes holding a typical Japanese lunch—several varieties of raw fish, meat, rice, vegetables, salad. Kirin beer. Tea. Chopsticks. No forks. Billy Friedkin is at the speakers' table. His clothes look sharp, snappy, and becoming. He wears a brown corduroy jacket with tan suede patches on the elbows; gray slacks; a red-and-tan checked shirt; a solid-red necktie; and dark-tinted aviator glasses. Kurosawa, also at the speakers' table, wears a well-pressed beige jacket and tan slacks. Audie Bock is on one side of him, Peter Grilli on the other. Everybody opens a lacquer box, eats rapidly with the chopsticks, and drinks the Japanese beer and tea. Time is not wasted. Then the talking starts.

Billy Friedkin is the master of ceremonies, and he introduces Kurosawa. As usual, Friedkin is warmly good-natured and speaks with emphatically clear diction. He takes off his dark-tinted glasses. Kurosawa keeps his on. "One thing Akira Kurosawa and I have in common is that we both got into the movie business by answering an ad," Friedkin says. "He was given an oral exam, and he was also asked to write an essay on the subject 'State the basic defects of the Japanese film industry and how they should be remedied.' His answer was. 'If the defects are basic, they can't be remedied.'" Friedkin pauses. Lots of laughter. "He got the job," Friedkin says. "For which we are all grateful." More laughter, and applause. Friedkin makes a few remarks about Kurosawa's apprenticeship to the film director Yamamoto and about his list of twenty-six movies. "He is always engrossed in separating what is real from what is false," Friedkin says. "Now here is Mr. Kurosawa."

"Thank you very much for your welcome," Kurosawa says. "In front of so many people, I'm not very good at speaking, but I'd like to say what is important to me in directing. What I fear is we'd put all our energy into our film, then people would come, see the film, walk out the door, and forget it. Throughout my career, I have tried to present human beings on the screen that you will not be able to forget. With that philosophy, I'd like to continue trying to make new films. If any of you have questions, I'll be glad to answer them."

Young woman wearing a tweed suit and horn-rimmed glasses: "Is Mr. Kurosawa working on a project now?"

Kurosawa: "I do have a project. And it came to me through my study of Japanese history. There is a medieval warrior, a marvelous man who had three marvelous sons. What would it be if three sons were not marvelous, if two of them were like King Lear's daughters! That is my idea for a film I'd now like to make."

Young man wearing bluejeans, who says he directs commercials for NBC: "Why did you choose *Ikiru* for today's screening?"

Kurosawa: "It is one of my better-made films, I think."

Older man: "Are you more at ease with contemporary or historical themes?"

Kurosawa: "I don't feel particularly more at ease with one or the other. Today, it is very difficult to make contemporary films. If I were to submit the kind of contemporary-film idea exemplified by *Ikiru* to the film companies in Japan, they would be likely to refuse it."

Youngish man: "You made hundreds of elaborate sketches and paintings for *Kagemusha* before you made the film. Is that a new way you have of preparing a film?"

Kurosawa: "The sketches for *Kagemusha* are unusual. I had submitted my *Lear* idea for a film, but it was rejected, partly because the budget was too high. I began to feel that it would never get on the screen, so I began doing the sketches—paintings—for *Kagemusha*. I always do sketches for the film continuity, but I had never done anything as elaborate as this. I had plenty of time. I thought the *Lear* film would never be made. I ended up with four hundred paintings, which will also be very helpful for preparing the *Lear* movie now. I've prepared a deep study of the armor and the costumes of those medieval times."

Woman: "Why, after the success of *Rashomon*, did you have problems getting your films made?"

Kurosawa: "Immediately after *Rashomon*, I made *The Idiot*, based on Dostoevsky's novel. This movie was viciously attacked by every critic in Japan, so I couldn't get any projects off the ground. As I was resigning myself to eating cold rice for the rest of my life, the Venice Film Festival gave *Rashomon* the Grand Prize. Suddenly, everything changed, and I made *Ikiru*."

Young man: "Have you ever considered doing a series for television, like Ingmar Bergman's *Scenes from a Marriage*?"

Kurosawa: "No. The way television films are made and the way theatrical films are made are fundamentally different, and I only know how to make theatrical films."

Strong applause from the audience. Kurosawa bows his head and lights a Seven Stars cigarette.

Older man: "Are your films autobiographical?"

Kurosawa: "My films contain what I have felt and thought about in my life, but no events of my personal life have been taken directly into my films."

Older woman: "You always seem to bring out unique acting talents from your actors. How do you do it?"

Kurosawa: "What's most important for all of us involved in any film I'm making is to get to understand each other, so that we can work together. When we sit together and chat over food, that's the most important part of the job for me. From everyone who works with me on a film, I demand total concentration on the film twenty-four hours a day for as long as we have to work together. For many years, I worked with the same actors on many films. They became almost a repertory company of great actors. But now many of them have died. Most of today's actors are forced by various pressures to work in television, a medium that destroys their talents as film actors. I do not like to have spoiled-by-television actors. It is very difficult to re-train them for my films. Instead of re-training, I prefer to find new, inexperienced actors. For *Kagemusha*, we held open auditions and advertised in the newspapers for actors. More than ten thousand inexperienced actors applied. About three top-quality, talented actors came out of that episode, and there were many others whom I'd like to have again in minor parts. Their *Kagemusha* training qualifies them for me."

Friedkin: "Is there an equivalent of the Directors' Guild in Japan? Does it work for creative rights and better salaries, as ours does here?"

Kurosawa: "There is an organization, but it doesn't do much. The great film directors in Japan seem to have died, and the directors who are left are without energy. The younger ones seem interested only in fitting into the pattern of turning out routine, money-making products."

Man with a big black mustache: "Would you share your thoughts about color versus black-and-white in films?"

Kurosawa: "I think that black-and-white is beautiful. I also think that color is beautiful. But we have longer experience with black-and-white, greater artistic capacity. Color is still in the future."

Young woman: "Have you been influenced by directors outside Japan, or do you admire them?"

Kurosawa: "I have loved movies from the time I was a very young child. I greatly admire the work of directors all over the world. My admiration is not limited to my seniors. I also admire many directors who are younger than I am."

Man wearing bluejeans and a sweater: "Would you make films outside Japan? In the United States, for example?"

Kurosawa: "It depends on the subject matter. The subject comes before the country."

Man with a beard: "Your films have this overriding theme of love for man and people who become reformers. Do you identify with these people?"

Kurosawa: "I don't think that I am myself such a wonderful person. I admire the people in my films. That's why I put them in my films."


AN HOUR LATER. AN ART GALLERY ON THE SECOND FLOOR OF JAPAN HOUSE.

Figures and other art objects, dating back to the sixth century A.D., are exhibited in glass cases. The art has been sent over from the famous Horyu-ji Temple, in Nara. Built in 607 A.D., it is believed to be the oldest wooden building in the world.

It is dark in the museum. Accompanied by Grilli, Miss Nogami, Owens, and Miss Bock, Kurosawa, wearing his tinted glasses, clasping his hands behind his back, stands before a gilded and lacquered camphorwood figure of Kwannon, a god or goddess of mercy, dated late seventh century. "Figures like these are often hollow," Kurosawa tells the others. "They used to put the religious documents inside the figure for safekeeping and to make the statue holier." Looking solemn, he remains standing in front of the figure for a long time. "This one is really fine, really fine," he says with a sudden smile.

Kurosawa then explains patiently that the technique of lacquering these statues involved putting on gold foil and then hundreds and hundreds of layers of lacquer. He points out to Grilli and Owens that they must be very careful to maintain the correct temperature and humidity in the room, because the lacquer is so sensitive to both that it could crack in a moment under adverse conditions. Grilli assures him that they monitor the humidity with the utmost concern, using gauges and other equipment brought over from Japan.

Kurosawa smiles and puts a hand on Grilli's back in a restrained gesture of approval.


THAT NIGHT. THE AUDITORIUM OF JAPAN HOUSE.

The first public screening of the retrospective. The movie being shown is *Yojimbo* (*The Bodyguard*), which was released in 1961. Toshiro Mifune plays the role of the bodyguard. In the movie, the bodyguard, an unemployed and masterless samurai, in the nineteenth century, comes to a town where the two richest men—one a sake merchant who runs the prostitution business, the other a silk merchant who runs gambling—are fighting each other for control of everything. The samurai sells his services first to one, then to the other, deceiving both gangs, playing them off against each other, and getting them to wipe each other out. Kurosawa, who is an admirer of *Stagecoach* and other American Westerns, made in *Yojimbo* the model for what have become known as "the spaghetti Westerns." *A Fistful of Dollars*, with Clint Eastwood, an American-type Western filmed in Italy a couple of years later, was a remake of Kurosawa's movie. *Yojimbo* goes over smashingly with the audience at the retrospective. The applause is loud and prolonged.


THAT NIGHT. NEAR MIDNIGHT. ROOM 3701.

Kurosawa is entertaining his Japanese friends again. Mr. and Mrs. Takehiko Kamei have been joined by a striking-looking woman named Eiko Ishioka—Japan's foremost graphic designer, who is in New York studying English. Miss Ishioka has shiny black hair that hangs down to her shoulders. She wears black mod pants and a loose-fitting matching blouse. As before, Kamei addresses Kurosawa as "Sensei," and they remark to each other that their shared understanding and appreciation of art draw them together in friendship in New York. The Kameis say that tonight they are going to stay only briefly—none of this business of staying until 3 a.m.

The guests have brought Kurosawa a present—some fresh avocados, a fruit not grown in Japan. Mrs. Kamei suggests trying some avocado with soy sauce. Miss Nogami finds the soy sauce and prepares the avocado with it. The flavor is something like that of raw tuna, Kurosawa says, and he reports that he likes it. "*Umai*," he says, which means "Delicious."

Kurosawa says that he should feel tired but he doesn't. The guests say that they don't feel tired, either—*Yojimbo* was so stimulating. Kurosawa tells them how he happened to think of the opening scene of the movie: the shot of a dog trotting across a dusty road with a human hand held in its mouth. It's a grotesque scene Kurosawa says, but he wanted to set the mood of the film, to demonstrate what the samurai might have in store for him. One of the actors had a pet dog on the set, and one day Kurosawa saw the pet dog walking with a glove held in its mouth, and that gave him the idea for the scene.

For the next five hours, they talk mostly about *Yojimbo*. How Nakadai, one of Japan's leading actors, who plays a pistol-carrying gang member in the movie, suddenly decided, one day, to wear a British muffler tied around his neck, above his kimono, and how that touch gave the character a special kind of dash. How Kurosawa wanted the film's music to have a contemporary sound, and, because the mambo was popular in 1960, he had mambo music played by Japanese instruments—very effective. They wind up the visit with a discussion of how to bring freshness to old ideas in movies by doing the photography in an unusual way. The guests leave shortly before dawn.

A FEW DAYS LATER. JOHN F. KENNEDY AIRPORT.
AMERICAN AIRLINES TERMINAL.

Kurosawa, accompanied by Miss Nogami, arrives from Los Angeles, and they are met by Grilli. Kurosawa has made a quick visit to George Lucas, at his new studio, near San Francisco, and to officials at Twentieth Century-Fox, in Los Angeles. He has shown them his script for his new movie—the one based on the *Lear* story. Audie Bock has stayed on the West Coast, at home in Berkeley, California. Kurosawa is pretty much on his own in English. He looks very cheerful. Miss Nogami looks very cheerful, too. Grilli bows to both of them, then gives Miss Nogami a hug. He shakes hands with Kurosawa and waits for the older man to speak. Kurosawa grins. Grilli asks, "*Umaku ittemashita ka?*" which means "Did it all go well?" "*Umaku itteru*," Kurosawa says, grinning again and taking off his tinted glasses. "Very O.K.," Kurosawa adds, in English. Then he puts an arm around Grilli's shoulder, in his own kind of Hollywood hug.

## Some Figures on a Fantasy

November 8, 1982

FRANCIS COPPOLA, THE talented, original, volatile forty-three-year-old moviemaker, who is a movie writer (*Patton*, *The Conversation*, and other pictures), a movie producer (*American Graffiti*, *The Black Stallion*, and others), a movie director (*The Godfather*, *Apocalypse Now*, and others), a movie impresario and distributor (Abel Gance's 1927 epic *Napoleon* and others), and a fan of other people's movies (Michael Powell's *The Thief of Baghdad*, Alexander Korda's *Things to Come*, Andrzej Wajda's *Ashes and Diamonds*, Akira Kurosawa's *Yojimbo*, Stanley Kubrick's *Dr. Strangelove*, and about five hundred others), started working on his movie *One from the Heart* in 1980. The year before, Mr. Coppola had bought Hollywood General Studios, built in 1919—one of the oldest movie studios in town. Harold Lloyd started making *his* movies there in 1922. The studio occupies almost nine acres of land in the heart of Hollywood, one mile from the Goldwyn studios and two miles from Paramount. Mr. Coppola paid seven million two hundred thousand dollars (some cash, many mortgages) for the studio and renamed it Zoetrope Studios—after his production company, American Zoetrope, which he had founded in 1969, in San Francisco, as a center for young filmmakers. "The Zoetrope was an early device to create the illusion of a motion picture," Mr. Coppola explained recently to a visitor at his studio. "In the eighteen-sixties, it was a popular toy—a revolving cylindrical box with slits in it, making pictures appear to move—but I'm sure it was used much earlier. In Greek, *zoe* means 'life,' and *trope* means 'turn,' or 'movement,' so the word really means 'life movement.'" Two of American Zoetrope's early movies were *THX 1138* (1970), co-written by George Lucas, with Walter Murch, and directed by George Lucas, and *American Graffiti* (1973), written and directed by Lucas, who then went out on his own to make *Star Wars* and its sequels. At Zoetrope in Hollywood, Mr. Coppola had nine sound stages; several one-story and two-story buildings; four bungalows, including one that was used by Harold Lloyd and is still named for him; and plenty of wardrobe space and rehearsal space. He borrowed an additional three million dollars and spent it repairing and renovating the place, with new roofing, new air-conditioning, new lighting, new carpeting, and a large assortment of the latest kinds of electronic equipment (some of it designed by him), for making movies in a new way, which he called "the electronic cinema." He gave the studio streets and parking area new names, among them Federico

Fellini Lane, Akira Kurosawa Avenue, Buster Keaton Boulevard, Raoul Walsh Alley, and Sergei Eisenstein Park. He hired a hundred and eighty-four people, including a number of electronics technicians and experts, to work with him at Zoetrope Studios. One of the most dramatic components of Mr. Coppola's technology was a custom-designed twenty-eight-foot-long image-and-sound-control van, complete with kitchen and bath. "The concept behind this unit is that movies are like music and should be composed along the same lines," Mr. Coppola said when he introduced his van to people at Zoetrope Studios. The van was filled with a good deal of unusual electronic equipment. "Much the same as a twenty-four-track music-recording studio booth," Mr. Coppola said. "But here we include image as well as sound, and we can use it in the way that best suits each production. I'm rarely in the van during an actual take, but in the van afterward I can review each shot, make immediate cuts, and know right away whether I want to shoot additional material or make a change in a scene." The system enabled Mr. Coppola to edit *One from the Heart* while it was being shot.

Before, during, and after the making of *One from the Heart*, Mr. Coppola did considerable talking to everyone involved in the movie and to others, interested in moviemaking in general, about the meaning as well as the practical uses of his new technology. A notably unpretentious man, who, like most artists, follows his feelings together with his ideas in creating his work, he found himself from time to time sounding oddly philosophical. He is burly, untrim, overweight—two hundred and thirty-five pounds at five feet eleven inches—and he has none of the health-conscious, life-preserving habits, disciplines, or self-indulgences of many of his Beverly Hills, Pacific Palisades, or Malibu peers, who diet, exercise, get plenty of sleep, and have an obligatory daily massage between work and dinner. Mr. Coppola eats too much and is always short on sleep. He has a three-inch-long curly black beard and long, wavy black hair, and he wears horn-rimmed glasses for nearsightedness. His clothes invariably look rumpled and slightly out of season. He has remained untouched by most of Hollywood's social patterns, including the need to go to A parties, to sit in special seats in certain restaurants, and to get there in the most expensive cars. On the infrequent occasions when he has free time, he likes to stay home and practice on one or the other of two musical instruments he plays: the tuba and the string bass. He also likes to cook; his veal Marsala and his spaghetti with his own marinara sauce have a great reputation among his friends. In cooking Japanese food, he prides himself on his ability to fillet a tuna and then make tuna sashimi. He does not measure his words. He is not cautious in expressing his ideas, or his uncertainties about them. He likes to throw out his ideas—to try them out on people who he thinks might share his deep interest in motion pictures. Using a tape recorder, he often makes oral notes to himself in the middle of the night, after his co-workers are asleep. Occasionally, on request, he has offered transcripts of his rough notes to magazines concerned with movie technology; to the press; and to colleagues. "I worry about content," he said in one of his messages to himself. "I worry about story.... The talent for writing a good tune is especially admirable when we think how composers have been arranging and rearranging those few notes into something that sticks as a melody. A story must be like that—a specific talent to come up with the sequence of events, the unfolding of information that captures us and has us eagerly awaiting the outcome, as though we were children. And even if we already know the story, we enjoy going through it again." In another of these messages, he said, "There is and can be content in technology. New tunes that we've never heard before, because they've never been possible before."

Ray Stark, the producer of *Annie* and many other expensive Hollywood movies, who describes himself as "one of the *oldest* working movie producers in the business," feels that technology is of less importance than some other elements of moviemaking. "Francis Coppola is one of the unique talents in the business," he said to a recent visitor in his office at Columbia Studios, in Burbank. "But the only things that matter in the movie business are: one, a good story; two, interesting casting; three, a good director. A computer and all the technology in the world can't create a story, can't feel as an actor, can't think as a director. It's the human element that makes a motion picture. The basic problem in the movie business is still the expense of lighting and of camerawork, all the time it takes to set up a shot. Technology has not changed that—at least, so far."

"Ray is correct about the expense," Mr. Coppola says. "My point is, with a new technology we're going to make that cost much lower."

One night recently, Mr. Coppola stated to himself, "I am more interested in technology than I am in content. Technology is one aspect of today that is truly fresh, brimming with new tunes and story turns. Ones that we have never heard or thought about before. But my interest in technology is a temporary phase, a vehicle taking us from the old world... into still another new era of art and thinking."

Not long ago, in the Harold Lloyd bungalow at Zoetrope Studios, sitting alongside a newly purchased bass that he had not yet had the time to practice on, Mr. Coppola said, "The adventure of *One from the Heart* was simply my trying to own the rights to my movies." By then, *One from the Heart* had come and gone on public screens. Mr. Coppola was in Hollywood for a few hours, to see a screening of his new movie, *The Outsiders*, and was about to leave for Tulsa, Oklahoma, where the image-and-sound-control van—along with much of the other technological equipment and some of the personnel of his company—was waiting for him. He had made *The Outsiders* there and was about to put the finishing touches—including music composed by him, with rhythm tracks worked out by Stewart Copeland, the drummer in The Police—on another movie, *Rumble Fish*. He had made both pictures after the release, early this year, of *One from the Heart* . "I think it's wise to separate the earning of money from the making of a movie, but I wanted to own the *rights* to my own movies—to be the one to decide what to do with what I make," Mr. Coppola said, giving his bass a wistful look. "At the same time, I was trying to use new methods. Everyone seems to be encouraging you to be ordinary, to tell the same old story the same old way, package it this way, package it that way. Just get the money. All that doesn't interest me. I like to experiment—to push the techniques of moviemaking forward and simultaneously find the most economical methods of making a film. I tried to make *The Outsiders* as I imagine fifteen-year-olds and sixteen-year-olds would like it to be. In making *One from the Heart* , I was trying for something different. I wanted the scenery, the music, and the lighting, for example, to be *part* of the film, not just a background for the action."

*One from the Heart* took about twenty-two months to make, including time that Mr. Coppola spent working on the screenplay with Armyan Bernstein, the original writer of the story, and working with the actors and dancers in rehearsals of one kind or another as well as the time he spent shooting the picture. Development of the music and art concepts began in September, 1980. The actual filming began on February 2, 1981, stopped on March 31, 1981, resumed after three weeks, and finished on June 29, 1981. The movie was released about seven months later, on February 11, 1982. Its cost came to twenty-seven million dollars. At the start, M-G-M was slated to distribute the movie domestically, but M-G-M had provided none of the money for making it, and in February, 1981, because Zoetrope had differences with M-G-M over the question of "completion" responsibilities, Zoetrope made a distribution deal with Paramount. The completion agreement, one of the elements in some distribution deals, is like an insurance policy covering all concerned to guarantee completion. With a completion agreement in hand, a moviemaker can obtain financing—the financing in this case being a loan from the Chase Manhattan Bank. "Still no money up front," Mr. Coppola recalled recently of the Paramount deal. "But a very favorable distribution agreement. A four-million-dollar advertising budget, a low distribution fee—better than the average, which is generally thirty percent—and six hundred prints out to theaters across the country on February 10, 1982." On January 15, 1982, Mr. Coppola announced that he had terminated the agreement with Paramount, mainly because Paramount, he claimed, refused to live up to its completion agreement, and also because of what he felt was poor handling of a screening for exhibitors. On January 29th, Columbia Pictures became the distributor of *One from the Heart*. On February 11th, the movie opened in San Francisco, Los Angeles, Denver, Chicago, Washington, Boston, New York, and Toronto. By April 1st, the only theater it was playing in was the Guild, on West Fiftieth Street, in New York. At that point, Columbia was willing to release several hundred prints of the movie in a hundred markets around the country. Mr. Coppola said no—he wanted to withdraw the picture entirely. Columbia agreed to the withdrawal. For the next seven months, *One from the Heart* couldn't be found in any theater in the United States.

Before *One from the Heart* was withdrawn from distribution in this country, it had generated a disappointing one million two hundred thousand dollars in gross box-office revenue. Zoetrope's share of the gross revenue was almost negligible. In theatrical motion-picture distribution, the amount of money that a distributor receives from the theater owners is called "net rentals." Net rentals—in movie-business jargon, "the remittance from film exhibitors to film distributors"—are a percentage of box-office receipts (it is usually negotiable but generally begins at ninety percent for the distributor and ten percent for the theater owner, the percentage changing as a movie plays out) calculated after subtraction of the "house nut." The house nut is the amount of money that theater owners claim it costs them just to open the doors of their theaters. When people in the movie business use the term "house nut" or "house expenses," they usually give it a somewhat melodramatic reading, occasionally accompanied by a bit of a leer. Distributors reluctantly tolerate this deduction. After the theater owner's house nut and his percentage and the distributor's lion's share of the gross have been taken into consideration, the split between distributor and theater owner is likely to be about fifty-fifty. The producer's percentage comes out of the distributor's fifty percent. Film distributor's take a "distributor's fee," the norm for which is generally acknowledged to be thirty percent of the net rentals; and mention of this is often accompanied—especially when the mention is made by the few highly talented filmmakers who have written, directed, and produced movies and then handed them over to distributors—by a considerable show of agitation. In addition to the distributor's fee, distribution deals usually allow the distributor to recover, on a dollar-for-dollar basis, all money spent on prints and advertising, and may also allow the distributor to handle negotiations for other rights, such as cable-television, network-television, television-syndication, video-cassette and video-disc, publishing, soundtrack, music, and merchandising.

Distributors are usually proud of the sub-deals they make in connection with their rights to release a movie. For example, weeks before Universal Pictures released Steven Spielberg's film *E.T. The Extra Terrestrial* the company took a full-page ad in the weekly *Variety* to announce:

> Universal has planned one of Hollywood's most extensive merchandising efforts to support the run of this unique film. We proudly peasant our partners:
> C/C Sales, Posters
> Collegeville Flag & Mfg. Co., Halloween costume
>   and mask
> Davis-Delaney-Arrow, School posters
> Everything bicycles, Kuwahara Motorcross Bicycles

Hershey Chocolate Co., Products, premiums and
    promotions for candy
Kamar International, Puppets and stuffed toys
Lin Toys, 4" to 11" action figures
Photo-Lith International, Iron-on-transfers and
    T-shirts
Terrimondo, Inc., Towels
Simon & Schuster, Three activity books
Texas Instruments, Electronic learning hardware,
    firmware or software
Topps Chewing Gum, Bubblegum picture cards and
    stickers

After the opening of *E.T.*, the returns from the merchandising off-shoots, like the movie itself, assumed Herculean proportions, which already fall into a special—and, in the movie business, profoundly admired and envied—class, shared to date only by *Star Wars*. Among other things, there is an *E.T.* talking doll—capable of saying "Ouch," "Home," and two other words—which the manufacturer estimates will bring in fifteen million dollars in 1982 all by its extra-terrestrial self. These "merchandising efforts"—together with books based on the movie, and records and tapes of the soundtrack—represent just the beginning of offshoots that may, according to some movie-business experts, gross three times as much as the movie's net rentals.

*Star Wars*, released in 1977, has been the most profitable movie in motion-picture history so far. According to the weekly *Variety*, *E.T.*, *The Empire Strikes Back*, *Jaws*, and *Raiders of the Lost Ark* are close behind, in that order. *Star Wars* cost nine million dollars to make and at the end of 1981 had earned net rentals of more than a hundred and eighty-five million dollars in the United States and Canada. Money from the rest of the world and from games, records, books, and toys, and future money from television and video cassettes, has not been estimated by anybody in the movie business. (CBS paid twenty-five million dollars for the privilege of showing *Star Wars* only three times.) As the result of a particularly advantageous arrangement, George Lucas receives forty percent of the net profits of *Star Wars*. *Gone with the Wind* cost three million nine hundred thousand dollars and has earned seventy-six million seven hundred thousand dollars in net rentals, together with twenty-five million dollars for showings on network television. The 1933 version of *King Kong* is estimated to have cost a million dollars and to have earned five million dollars in net rentals in one year. The 1976 version cost twenty-four million dollars to make and now has a net-rentals figure of thirty-six million nine hundred thousand dollars. *Towering Inferno* cost fifteen million dollars and has a net-rentals figure of fifty million dollars.

Movie distributors like to publicize their products in terms of their "grosses," and when the grosses are high they like to publicize how much higher they are and how much faster they are realized than the grosses of other high-grossing movies. One press release from Paramount, for example, stated, "Paramount Pictures' record setting summer release, *Star Trek II: The Wrath of Khan*, has grossed $53,201,334 in its first twenty-eight days of domestic release." It went on, "Currently playing in 1,250 situations in the U.S. and Canada, the film topped the $50 million mark at a faster pace than either *Raiders of the Lost Ark* or *Grease*, the two most successful releases in the company's history." According to the weekly *Variety*, the record-setting box-office film, exhibited under the most favorable terms in its premiere run, has been *E.T.*, which, to quote a story in that paper, "has become the number two picture in *Variety*'s ranking of the all-time film rental champs of the U.S. and Canada." It earned close to a hundred and forty million dollars after sixty-five days of release. The movie opened on June 11, 1982, and in the first fourteen days of its release took in just over forty-four million dollars. In its first weekend, it grossed about thirteen million dollars. According to *Variety*, the producer-directors Steven Spielberg and George Lucas have, between them, made the top five earners: Lucas' *Star Wars*, at rentals of about a hundred and ninety-five million dollars, *E.T.*, at about a hundred and seventy-five million dollars; Lucas' *The Empire Strikes Back*, directed by Irvin Kershner, at about a hundred and thirty-five million dollars; Spielberg's *Jaws*, at about a hundred and thirty-four million dollars; and *Raiders of the Lost Ark*, produced by Lucas and directed by Spielberg, at about a hundred and ten million dollars. There is often some disparity in the figures—depending on who is issuing them—for movies that cost more than, say, fifteen million dollars to make. One example is *Annie*. Columbia Pictures, the distributor and backer, says that *Annie* cost forty million dollars, and that Columbia, as distributor, will receive ninety percent of the box-office receipts but is paying fifteen million dollars for prints, advertising, and promotion, and will break even at sixty million dollars. Ray Stark, the producer of *Annie*, adds that the movie will take in at least seventy million dollars in worldwide film rentals, and that it has a two-and-a-half-million-dollar advance on the soundtrack album, a ten-million-dollar network-television sale, a ten-million-dollar cable sale, and a ten-million-dollar estimated profit from toys and other merchandise. He says that *Annie* will break even at between sixty and sixty-five million. He has already planned for a *re*-release of *Annie* next August, which he figures will bring in from seven to ten million dollars over several years. He likes to point out that half of the audience for *Annie* consists of children under twelve, who pay half price. "Otherwise, we would have taken in an additional *fifteen* million," he said recently. "*Annie* will do forty million in domestic net rentals by Christmas." According to *Variety*, which keeps its own records, the movie cost forty-two million dollars to make, will cost twenty million dollars more to advertise and promote, and will have to earn at least a hundred million dollars in net rentals before it breaks even.

"The exhibitors' share and the distributor's fee come off the top, and then, depending on how much is spent on prints and advertising, what's left is used for recoupment," Mr. Coppola has explained. "If there's anything left after you break even, it's usually a small pool, and it's divided up among the people who own shares of the movie. *One from the Heart* will have to earn two and a half to three times its cost, or—according to a broad rule of thumb—about sixty-eight million dollars, before we break even."

*One from the Heart* runs for a hundred minutes. As Mr. Coppola describes it, it is "a fable about love and show business." As Columbia Pictures describes it, it is "a romantic comedy, a musical fantasy, and an erotic love story." It takes place in Las Vegas. Because Mr. Coppola wanted to get away from realism, and achieve certain effects of fantasy, he decided to make the entire movie at Zoetrope Studios—a procedure counter to the pattern that most movies have followed for the past thirty years or so, of being shot on location, and more like the moviemaking pattern of of the nineteen-thirties and forties. *One from the Heart* stars Frederic Forrest, Teri Garr, Raul Julia, and Nastassia Kinski, and features Lainie Kazan and Harry Dean Stanton.

The cinematography is by Vittorio Storaro. Among the other credits: songs and music by Tom Waits, sung by Crystal Gayle and Tom Waits; costume designer, Ruth Morley; production designer, Dean Tavoularis; executive producer, Bernard Gersten; co-producer, Armyan Bernstein; producers, Gray Frederickson and Fred Roos; screenplay by Armyan Bernstein and Francis Coppola; directed by Francis Coppola. Technical credits are given to one hundred and eighty-four people, including set decorators, sound editors, re-recording mixers, camera operators, grips, leadmen, a visual-effects editor, a miniatures supervisor, casting directors, a script supervisor, choreographers, costumers, still photographers, electronic-cinema technicians, publicity people, a production coordinator, special-effects coordinators, transportation coordinators, title designers, color technicians, and numerous assistants. Credits are also given to the Sony Corporation; to Colossal Pictures (title designs); to Dreamquest, Inc. (motion-control photography and matte paintings); to The Optical House, Modern Film Effects, and Zoetrope Images (opticals); to Technicolor, Metrocolor, and Dolby Stereo; and to Columbia Records (original-soundtrack album).

Francis Coppola was born in Detroit, Michigan on April 7, 1939, and he grew up and went to school in Queens, New York. His father, Carmine Coppola, is a composer and conductor, who once played flute under Arturo Toscanini in the NBC Symphony Orchestra, and who since early 1981 has been the conductor of the sixty-piece symphony orchestra providing live music at the screenings of *Napoleon*. Francis Coppola's maternal grandfather, Francesco Pennino, was one of Enrico Caruso's accompanists; he came over from Naples and settled in Brooklyn. Detroit was Francis's birthplace because Carmine Coppola had taken the family there from New York when he got a job as a flutist, arranger, and assistant conductor of the orchestra for the *Ford Sunday Evening Hour* on radio. Francis Coppola was originally known as Francis Ford Coppola, having been named after the *Hour* and his father's boss. A few years ago, Mr. Coppola decided that he liked his name better without the Ford. Distributors, however, are still attached to it, and use it in his name most of the time.

When Francis was nine, he was stricken with polio, and the disease left him paralyzed for a year in his left leg, arm, and side and in his entire back. He was unable to walk during that year, and he spent most of the time in bed, cut off from other children except for an older brother and a younger sister. "My greatest pleasure during that year was to watch Horn & Hardart's *Children's Hour* on television every Sunday morning," he recalled recently. "I loved little children very much then, as I do now, and I dreamed of being involved with them someday in theatrical activities. I had a Jerry Mahoney puppet that I could make talk and sing, and I had a tape recorder, a record player, and other equipment I could use to make up shows with. I am sure that from those shows came the idea of my studio—a place where we could work together like children, with music, puppets, scenery, lights, dramatic action, whatever we wanted to do." At the age of fifteen, because of some proficiency playing the tuba, Francis was awarded a band scholarship at the New York Military Academy, at Cornwall-on-Hudson. He was there for a year and a half. Then, while his parents were on the road with the musical *Kismet*, for which his father conducted the orchestra, Francis ran away, made his way to the family's home, in Great Neck, and enrolled in Great Neck High School. He graduated in 1956.

In collaboration with Francis, Carmine Coppola composed the music for *Apocalypse Now*, in 1978, and for *The Outsiders*. Talia Shire, Francis's sister, who is an actress, played in *Rocky* (the part of Sylvester Stallone's girlfriend) and in *The Godfather* (Al Pacino's sister). Francis's brother, August, runs an educational and apprenticeship program for Zoetrope Studios. Gian-Carlo Coppola, Francis Coppola's eldest child, who is nineteen, has been working with his father as an assistant for a couple of years and is an associate producer of *The Outsiders*. Roman Coppola, Mr. Coppola's second child, who is seventeen, worked as an assistant sound mixer in the making of *The Return of the Black Stallion*, a Zoetrope production, which was filmed in Morocco last winter. Sofia Coppola, Mr. Coppola's youngest child, who is eleven, sings, dances, and acts (non-professionally) with a group called the Dingbats, which she founded a year and a half ago with Jilian and Jenny Gersten, twelve and thirteen respectively—the daughters of Bernard Gersten. The girls have also published a summer newspaper, the *Dingbat News*, which has been more or less the official Zoetrope newspaper. Eleanor Coppola, Francis's wife, who is a designer in various media, works outside the movie industry. She helps out unofficially in many capacities in Mr. Coppola's productions, however, and she supervises the logistics of taking the Coppola family along on locations where Coppola movies are being made. "Francis wants his family with him," Mrs. Coppola says. "We travel together like a circus family, with Francis on the tightrope and the rest of us holding the ropes."

In 1956, Francis Coppola enrolled in Hofstra University, where he majored in theater arts. Two of his classmates were Ronald Colby, a cherubic, good-natured man, who is now a Zoetrope producer, and Robert Spiotta, now the president of Zoetrope Studios. Mr. Spiotta, who is forty-five, is an athletic-looking six-footer and, unlike Mr. Coppola, is very well groomed, with a neatly trimmed beard, and, unlike many Hollywood executives, is addicted to Eastern, almost preppy clothes. He played end on the Hofstra football team and acted the part of Stanley Kowalski in a school production of *A Streetcar Named Desire*, which was directed by Mr. Coppola. Also at Hofstra, Colby directed an original musical by Mr. Coppola called *The Delicate Touch*, about a school for pickpockets. Lainie Kazan, who plays Maggie in *One from the Heart*, was another classmate who participated in Mr. Coppola's Hofstra productions. In 1960, after graduating from Hofstra, Mr. Coppola enrolled in the film school of the University of California at Los Angeles. While he was still attending the film school, he worked as an associate producer, sound man, and writer for Roger Corman, a producer-director of low-budget, money-making horror films with such titles as *The Masque of the Red Death*, *Attack of the Crab Monsters*, and *The Terror*, and also a kind of classic, *The Day the World Ended*. Mr. Coppola worked on movies called *The Premature Burial*, *Tower of London*, and *Battle Beyond the Sun*, and then, in 1963, he wrote and directed his own horror film, *Dementia 13*, for Mr. Corman. In 1967, he won considerable acclaim for his first important directorial effort, *You're a Big Boy Now*, which was shot entirely on location in New York City. After that, he directed *Finian's Rainbow* and *The Rain People*, and was co-author (with Edmond North) of the screenplay for *Patton* (directed by Franklin Schaffner and starring George C. Scott). In 1971, being under considerable financial pressure as the owner of American Zoetrope, which he had established two years earlier, he somewhat reluctantly worked for Paramount Pictures as the co-author (with Mario Puzo) of the screenplay for *The Godfather* and director of the movie based on it. As co-author and director, Mr. Coppola was paid a fee of seven hundred thousand dollars and was given a six-per-cent profit participation in the movie, which was released in 1972, and which has set box-office records that are among the highest in movie history. As of last month, the movie had grossed almost two hundred million dollars in the United States and throughout the world. In 1974, also for Paramount, Mr. Coppola directed *The Godfather, Part II*, which, like Part I, earned a great deal of money. Mr. Coppola's share of the profits of *The Godfather*—both parts—has been about seven million dollars so far.

Between making *The Godfather* and *The Godfather, Part II*, Mr. Coppola, among other things, wrote, directed and, with Fred Roos, produced *The Conversation*, starring Gene Hackman. The movie, which was about a professional eavesdropper, cost a million eight hundred thousand dollars to make. It was financed by Paramount in an agreement with Mr. Coppola, together with two other directors, William Friedkin and Peter Bogdanovich, who had joined forces with the Directors' Company, an experimental effort that turned out to be short-lived. *The Conversation* has still not earned back its cost, but it has earned much acclaim and several awards, including the Palme d'Or, for best picture, at the 1974 Cannes Film Festival.

In 1972, Mr. Coppola undertook to produce *American Graffiti*, a small film to be directed by George Lucas, who had been unable to get any major company to finance it. Mr. Coppola wanted to invest his own money in the movie and own it himself. "Everybody advised me *not* to invest my own money," Mr. Coppola has recalled. "So I turned the film over to Universal and lost the chance to earn enough money to set up my own studio. That movie could have brought me over twenty million dollars. After that, I decided that I would try to finance all Zoetrope films myself."

In 1976, Mr. Coppola started making *Apocalypse Now*, about the Vietnam War (screenplay by John Milius and Francis Coppola). He produced and directed the movie, which starred Marlon Brando, Robert Duvall, and Martin Sheen. For *Apocalypse Now*, as for *One from the Heart*, Mr. Coppola's cinematographer was Vittorio Storaro, and his production designer was Dean Tavoularis. *Apocalypse Now* took sixteen months and cost thirty-two million dollars to make. The movie has grossed just over a hundred million dollars to date. *Apocalypse Now* won the Palme d'Or award (shared by *The Tin Drum*), for best picture, at the 1979 Cannes Film Festival. Thus, Mr.

Coppola became the only director to win the award twice. "It takes years and years for the value of a movie to be revealed," Mr. Coppola explained recently. "My guess is that *Apocalypse Now* is worth between ten and fifteen million dollars to me. We got four million nine hundred thousand dollars in 1980 for the cable-television rights. It was shown only once in Japan on television, and for that we got a million one hundred thousand dollars. It is still to be sold to the television networks here for major release, and to the affiliates, and then for television syndication. There are many important values not yet exploited. We owe United Artists, the film distributor, only three million dollars of the twenty-seven million we originally owed them. That movie will bring in a lot of money over a long period."

In the late seventies, Mr. Coppola and Steven Spielberg gave each other one "point"—one-per-cent ownership of net profits-for the help each had given the other in their respective movies: *Apocalypse Now* and *Close Encounters of the Third Kind*. Because the profits of *Apocalypse Now* are still in the future, while those of Mr. Spielberg's movie are in the past, present, *and* future, Mr. Spiotta often kids Mr. Coppola about the deal, describing it as "the *best* deal you ever made." Mr. Coppola's one point has so far brought him $365,072.

*One from the Heart* was rated "R" by the Motion Picture Association of America. It is the story of an unmarried couple, Frannie and Hank, who have been living together in a small house in Las Vegas for five years and are dissatisfied with each other. Frannie works for a travel agency, and daydreams about going to Bora Bora and finding a man to go there with her. Hank runs an automobile-repair shop and junk yard, and daydreams about having a romantic alliance with a glamorous girl. They have brief alliances with other partners, Frannie with a singing waiter who does indeed want to go to Bora Bora with her, and Hank with a seductive young tightrope walker from a circus family. Hank then wants to get together with Frannie again. After some resistance and turmoil, she returns to him, and that's that.

Because Mr. Coppola wanted the movie to be what he called "theatrical" instead of "naturalistic," he decided against making it on location in Las Vegas. Instead, he created his own, stylized version of Las Vegas at Zoetrope Studios. "The real Las Vegas is like Burbank," Mr. Coppola said at the time.

"We're going to tell this simple story in a fantasy way, so we'll make our own fantasy of Las Vegas, which for me is a metaphor for America itself, and like the *Mahagonny* of the world."

It took more than two hundred carpenters and other craftsmen to build the studio Las Vegas, which consisted of six paved streets, seven houses, a motel, a travel agency, a department store, the Strip, an automobile-repair shop and junk yard, and a replica of McCarran Airport. "I want to do something that people haven't seen before," Mr. Coppola said. "I'm so happy we're all acting out this fantasy. A company like this can make twelve movies a year like this one, each better than the last." He set his electronic-cinema methods in motion to that end, and, in addition, found new ways of bringing the optical effects, the dancing, and the songs together with the acting so as to realize his particular vision on the screen. The electronic-cinema method, which Mr. Coppola says he has developed and improved further in the making of *The Outsiders*, included what Mr. Coppola calls the "previsualization" of the movie. The pre-visualization was accomplished by means of tapes of the actors reading their parts, videotaped rehearsals, Polaroid stills, artists' sketches, and a filmed walk-through of the story in the real Las Vegas—all of which enabled Mr. Coppola to rewrite and edit the script while the movie was still being shaped and before the actual filming started.

All the music for *One from the Heart*, including twelve songs and their lyrics, was composed by Tom Waits, a jazz-style singer well known for his records *Blue Valentine* and *Foreign Affairs*, and for his songs about transients hanging around in seedy bars and motels. Waits and Crystal Gayle, a country-and-Western star, did all the singing in *One from the Heart*, which was recorded during the making of the movie. The record was just brought out by Columbia Records a few weeks ago. Mr. Coppola's idea was to have the record make a kind of detached comment on what was happening to the characters in the movie, and to have it give a truer sense of the soundtrack. "The record didn't work out that way by the time the movie was released, so I stopped it until it sounded right to me," Mr. Coppola said the other day. "It's really nice now, even though Columbia insisted on making the cover look like a Tom Waits-Crystal Gayle record instead of one from the movie." Gene Kelly, the actor, dancer, and choreographer, whom Mr. Coppola had engaged as "executive for musical production and development" for Zoetrope Studios, worked as a kind of over-all consultant on the dances for *One from the Heart*; Mr. Kelly starred in *An American in Paris* (1951), which was directed by Vincente Minnelli, and *Singin' in the Rain* (1952), which he co-directed with Stanley Donen. "We're going to use color the way *An American in Paris* did," Mr. Kelly said at the start. "We're going to *paint* the picture." Vitorio Storaro, the cinematographer for *One from the Heart*, who was born, in Rome, the year after Mr. Coppola, was also the cinematographer for Warren Beatty's *Reds* and for several movies directed by Bernardo Bertolucci, including *The Conformist* and *Last Tango in Paris*. "Storaro's use of color and form is always imaginative, always sensual," Mr. Coppola said. "Just what we want for this picture."

Among the major trips that Mr. Coppola took in connection with the making of *One from the Heart* were five from Los Angeles to New York, four from Los Angeles to Las Vegas, and two from Los Angeles to Rome; he was accompanied on a few of them by his cast and crew. The making of the movie took seventy-nine rehearsal days and seventy-two shooting days. There were several "wrap" parties for everybody involved in making the picture. Usually, in moviemaking, the wrap party is held after the shooting has been completed. For *One from the Heart*, Mr. Coppola said, they might as well have a party at the end of each week's shooting, because there was perpetual doubt whether there would be enough money to continue shooting the following week.

Right before starting production of the movie, Mr. Coppola, who lives in the Napa Valley, just north of San Francisco, gave a big party at his home, which occupies some seventeen hundred acres, including two hundred acres of vineyards. The party was a barbecue, with about three hundred and fifty guests, among them everybody working for Zoetrope and everybody working on *One from the Heart*. At the party, everybody talked eagerly about the making of the movie. Late in the afternoon, while toasting marshmallows, Mr. Coppola said exuberantly, "Something incredibly great is about to happen." The executive producer, Bernard Gersten, said, "You just begin to smell the movie around the corner." Before joining Mr. Coppola, Mr. Gersten had been, among other things, an associate producer of the Shakespeare Festival in New York. Because his wife—the Eliot Feld company's dance manager, Cora Cahan—and their two children stayed behind at their home in New York, Mr. Gersten made thirty-two commutation trips between Los Angeles and New York during work on the movie.

When the movie was finished, Mr. Coppola said, with satisfaction, "The entire film has so many long takes—one goes on for ten minutes. The average hundred-minute film has hundreds of cuts, and the takes are much shorter."

For these long takes, two hundred thousand feet of film was shot, of which ten thousand feet was used in the movie. For the entire movie, twelve hundred and thirty-one video cassettes were used, three hundred and eleven storyboards were made, and thirteen hundred photographic stills were taken—many in the pre-visualization stage. Eight wind-making machines and eight rain-making machines were used, and nobody counted the gallons of water spilled for the scenes in the rain. "After making *Apocalypse Now* in the Philippines, I felt this was a better way of making movies than slogging through the jungles," Mr. Coppola says now. "We did everything in relatively small spaces right in the studio."

Technically, Mr. Coppola owns *One from the Heart*. (*The Godfather*—both parts—is owned by Paramount. Mr. Coppola is a profit participant in *The Godfather*, receiving six per cent of the net profits of Part I and a larger percentage of the gross profits of Part II, but he has no say in what Paramount does with the movie. To own a movie is to own the negative, the copyright, and the right to show it or arrange for a distributor to show it.) From the start, he was intent upon arranging financing and distribution deals that would enable him to retain ownership rights. Although he kept informed about proposals for deals, the job of day-to-day negotiations for them fell to Robert Spiotta, Zoetrope's president. Mr. Spiotta, a patient, calm, good-natured man, is adept at following the rhythms and speech patterns of corporate executives, including the practice of turning almost any noun or adjective into a verb (in the movie business one "strategizes" what one is doing for a movie, "finalizes" it, and then "platforms" it), while trying simultaneously to tune in sympathetically to Mr. Coppola's artistic intentions and resolutions. Mr. Spiotta graduated from Hofstra the year after Mr. Coppola, and worked for Mobil Oil for the next sixteen years, winding up as an international marketing manager in Europe. In 1978, he quit that job to join Zoetrope. Mr. Spiotta recently explained to a strictly non-business type how a movie must earn two and a half times its negative cost to make a profit, and he proceeded to review as simply as possible the very complicated and somewhat elusive history of the financing and distribution arrangements he made for *One from the Heart*.

"The twenty-seven-million-dollar cost will ultimately be provided from several sources," Mr. Spiotta said, having explained that he was using the future tense because of yet-to-be-collected guarantees from foreign distributors. "To start with, the Chase Manhattan Bank lent eight million; it later expanded that loan by four million, and lent an additional seven million against foreign contracts. Then, we borrowed three million from Jack Singer, a Canadian investor, who is primarily in the real-estate business, and we put up the studio as collateral. But though we also got some smaller loans, from other sources, including Paramount, Security Pacific National Bank, and Norman Lear, we wound up two million dollars short of the twenty-seven. We still owe two million in outstanding bills to various creditors. The preliminary budget for *One from the Heart* was for fifteen million dollars, but in September, 1980, when Francis decided to make the whole movie on the lot, we had to budget the movie at twenty-three million one hundred thousand dollars. In early March of 1981, after M-G-M dropped out, we made our distribution agreement with Paramount. The agreement stated that the film would complete photography by mid-April, according to the original shooting schedule, and provided for an unspecified completion amount, if that was needed, after the budget had been exhausted. But Francis found that additional shooting was required. Instead of going to Paramount for money at that point, we went ahead to finish the film. We didn't know in April what the over-budget would be, and we thought that Paramount would be more likely to give us some completion money once the figure became definite. Francis shot an additional thirty-two days, and after that the film went into what is called post-production. The titles were more expensive than we had figured on, and so were the special effects. By October, we were over budget by four million dollars, so we deducted the cost of the extra shooting days from the four million, and asked Paramount for less than two million dollars—less than half of the over-budget. That's when communication with Paramount broke down. Paramount felt there was no obligation for it to put up any money, because we had exceeded the

"I'd rather not," Mr. Coppola said. "I'd rather be free just to hang around the house."

Soon after that, Mr. Coppola settled down on the floor at the back of the center aisle. On the screen, Teri Garr and Raul Julia were dancing a tango. "It's very romantic," Mr. Coppola said to a companion next to him on the floor, pushing his glasses up on the bridge of his nose.

When the movie ended, Hank and Frannie were together again on the screen. The audience applauded. Not a shattering ovation—just appreciative applause. Then, for five minutes or so, almost everybody in the audience stood up and stayed put, staring at the white, still screen, apparently reluctant to leave. Slowly, people began filing out. Mr. Coppola picked up his parka and quickly headed for a large rehearsal studio backstage, where the press conference was to be held.

About seventy-five people were at the press conference, including many photographers and television-news cameramen as well as people who write about movies. Most of their questions carried with them heavily inside information.

No. 1 was "How do you feel, now that everyone dislikes the picture?"

No. 2: "Doing this the way you have done it, what is your purpose, and have you, in your opinion, accomplished your purpose?"

No. 3: "But will this film be commercially successful?"

No. 4: "How important is the success of this movie to your future ventures—to your future movie productions and movie ventures?"

No. 5: "Is this film your homage to Fellini?"

No. 6: "Is there an agreement with Paramount on this film as to its distribution?"

No. 7: "Mr. Coppola, do you feel you love this movie as much as Hank liked Frannie?"

No. 8: "Mr. Coppola, why do you take these kinds of chances?"

No. 9: "Mr. Coppola, you helped create George Lucas. Why hasn't he helped you?"

Visibly trying to remain calm, Mr. Coppola replied.

To No. 1: "A lot of people in there looked as though they *did* like the movie. They seemed to laugh throughout the picture; they stayed pretty motionless and intent throughout the picture; there weren't many walkouts.

At the end, there was a play of emotion and enthusiastic applause that lingered throughout the titles and even after the titles. That's what I saw. If someone saw it a different way, then maybe that's so."

To No. 2: "A lot of people who spoke to me told me it was a very unusual and beautiful picture. When I make a film, I take a jump into something I am interested in. In this case, in the film, I was interested in show business, in gambling, I was interested in love, and I was interested in fantasy, and I was interested in music. Those are the things I worked with in my film. I am very proud of it, and I imagine that years from now, just as in my other films, people will see something of these elements and see it as an original work. It's not a copy of anything. It entertains people, and it is innocent."

To No. 3: "How the hell do I know?"

To No. 4: "I know very specifically what I want to do and where I am going. It's just two different roads I can travel to get there. The result of the success of this film determines maybe an easier road."

To No. 5: "No."

To No. 6: "About a week ago, I saw the film in Rome and then in Paris. I showed it to a few friends, filmmakers, directors, people, kids. I felt real good about their reaction, and, more important, I felt real good about my own reaction to it, which is all that really matters, I guess. At that time, because of a series of business discussions going on with Paramount, I became frustrated, and I decided that I didn't care whether Paramount released the picture or not. At that point, I terminated Paramount's release of the film. But Barry Diller, the chairman of Paramount, asked us not to announce the termination until we had a chance to discuss it further. I had to finish the film. I had to bring it to a stop, because we were involved with the bank and these various things that had to come to a close. I was very concerned about the sloppy way the film was shown to the exhibitors when it wasn't finished, and I was concerned about the way the film was being prejudged. And I just wanted a chance to show it clean to an audience. The thing with Paramount is a tricky situation, because I terminated them. I had hoped that that would bring us around to make an agreement. Whether that happens or not depends on the reaction of people to the film, so I don't really know what's going to happen."

To No. 7: "I love this movie, because I like to watch it, and I like the music, and I think it is beautiful."

To No. 8: "I'm a guy who's been around for twenty years. I've made a lot of films, and you know them. I've also produced a lot of films. You know them, too. I've written a lot of films and I've discovered a lot of new talent. I was the one responsible for making Part IIs, if you want to consider *that* something. Every time I want to make a movie, every time I want to make a film, every time I want to sponsor a filmmaker, I have to go, hat in hand, to a series of studio executives who don't have my background and my experience. So I find that frustrating. So, since I don't have any money really, to speak of, I use what little I have to try to get to the point where we can have our own studio, where we can make films like the films we've made over the last twelve years—all of the quality that this film has. I will stand by this film, because I know what went into the making of it. That's what I want. But I can't do that if I have to be controlled by people who say what film you can make and who's going to supervise what. So if I have my own studio, to keep the control and supervision to myself, it is taking a risk. Taking risks like this one creates some excitement. You may not have been excited, but others were. I don't know, but it was something."

To No. 9: "I don't need to be bailed out. My friendship with George Lucas is such that I know that's not his style of doing things. He would help me in other ways. George is a good friend, not in a money-lending way but more in the way of giving me a lift to the airport if I needed it." Without missing much of a beat, he went on, "I'm a guy who feels, Let's get out and take some chances. What I really don't understand is why you guys don't seem to like that. Why don't we all cheer the moviemakers *on*?"

A bit later, Mr. Coppola went back into the theater, where the second screening of *One from the Heart* had started, and he moseyed around, observing both his movie and the audience reaction to it. Then, along with six hundred and forty-seven guests, he went to the party celebrating the event in the Tower Suite of the Time-Life Building. Over their drinks, shellfish, cabbage soup, pasta, cold cuts, and desserts, the guests told Mr. Coppola that they had enjoyed his movie very much. Norman Mailer told him it was "an extraordinary film." Joseph Papp told him it was "a pioneering film, as big in its way as *Star Wars*." Robert Duvall told him it was "a lot of fun and technically dazzling." Thomas Hoving told him, "I liked it. I liked it very much." Andy Warhol told him, "It's really lovely." Carly Simon, Richard Gere, Susan Sarandon, Christopher Walken, Robert De Niro, and Martin Scorsese all told Mr. Coppola they enjoyed and admired the movie.

Mr. Coppola did a lot more kissing and gave a lot more hugs. The orchestra played "One," from *A Chorus Line*, about fifty times, and the Dingbats did their dance routine to it a couple of dozen times; many of the guests rewarded their efforts with generous applause. Everybody seemed to have a good time at the party, and most of the guests, when they left, kept their "I was at *One from the Heart* Radio City Music Hall" buttons on.

Before the evening was over, some television stations included reports on the *One from the Heart* preview in their news programs. One station reported on the preview by interviewing four people who walked out on the movie before it was over, and who, like most early walkouts, made negative pronouncements on what they had walked out on. The United Press issued a report that was published in newspapers around the country. One of the papers headlined that story "ANGRY COPPOLA DROPS PARAMOUNT AS DISTRIBUTOR FOR MUSICAL."

The next morning, Mr. Coppola held a meeting with about a dozen of his associates at his New York apartment, which is at the Sherry Netherland— four rooms with a kitchen. It has Art Deco furniture in the rooms and French theatrical posters on the walls, and that morning a vase filled with large red tulips occupied a non-working fireplace in the living room. Mr. Coppola, who had just awakened, sat barefoot on a sofa wearing a green silk dressing gown and his horn-rimmed glasses; sipped a cup of espresso; and listened to reports indicating that *One from the Heart* might not be greeted by the kind of enthusiasm that had been expressed the night before by many of those in the audience, including Robert De Niro, Joseph Papp, Robert Duvall, Martin Scorsese, and Thomas Hoving.

"It looks as though the press is lining up against the movie," said the publicity woman for the New York area. "But Jonathan Cott, of *Rolling Stone*, loved it. Rex Reed hated it. *Variety* will do a long interview with you any time you say, and you will have a platform for what you want to say."

"I don't want a *platform*," Mr. Coppola said. "From what I saw last night, the audience was interested in this picture. They could see that this picture is different. I think this picture will be like *Apocalypse*. *One from the Heart* will change the way people look at movies. Just as *Apocalypse* eventually did. In my opinion, the people who liked the movie the least were the critics—the people who want to tell you how you should work, what you should do. It seems to me that journalists who write about the entertainment business have a tough row to hoe. They need to stay on top, to set the tone and rules for what *they* say is or is not a good film. When a good film comes along, one that they think will work out with the public, they act a little bit like Danton, who when the rabble rushed by his house to make a revolution ran out behind them to lead them. When a film is successful, many journalists seem to feel as though they had made the filmmaker. Then, in the future, if that same filmmaker does not seem to be respectful of these journalists they seem to want to unmake what they think they have made."

"The Paramount thing keeps getting in the way," a publicity man said. "Every time you come out with a picture, people want to talk about all your financial troubles instead of just looking at the picture. Maybe it was a mistake to hold the preview."

"I *had* to show the picture," Mr. Coppola said. "I was trying to say to the public, 'Endorse this picture as collateral, so that the banks will allow me to go on.'"

"I'll work on the distribution, and in two weeks you'll have a distributor," said the president of Zoetrope Studios.

"What we've got to decide now is when to hold a preview in Los Angeles and where," said a vice-president.

"Los Angeles is a real cow town," said an older Zoetrope executive working in the realms of publicity and advertising. "Monday through Thursday, Los Angeles is asleep, so we ought to hold it on a Friday, Saturday, or Sunday."

"The best thing with this movie might be to make it impossible for people to see it, and let people imagine what it is," Mr. Coppola said. "Maybe I'll just withdraw the picture. Five years from now, I'll show it."

"If we give too much notice for the preview, the movie companies will buy up all the tickets," said Zoetrope's director of special projects. "We don't want an audience full of people in the business."

"These things only work when you spring them," Mr. Coppola said, without great interest.

"How about having the preview on Wednesday?" said the company president. "The next day, we can have a deal in place."

"They don't come out on Wednesday. They come out on Friday," said the older executive working in the realms of publicity and advertising.

"It doesn't matter when you have the preview," said the company president. "They're going to come out no matter what."

"I'm tired of making films so that people can come out and try to shoot them down," Mr. Coppola said. "I don't know whether I want people to see this picture. Why can't I just put the studio up for sale? Liquidate everything. Can't a guy opt out? Can't I just liquidate? All I have to do is give the bank back twenty million bucks. Right?" There were some uneasy laughs all around, but Mr. Coppola looked serious. "I think the artist still has a right to show his work or not to show it," he said.

"You have risked everything to make this picture," the New York publicity woman said. "You wanted to make what you wanted to make."

"I like the idea of pulling the movie," Mr. Coppola said. "And then maybe showing it thirty years from now."

The executive producer said, "Please, Francis, don't decide what the entire press is going to say about the picture. Let's think about the previews. Can we do two cities? I would not do central U.S.A.—I'd do Toronto after Los Angeles. We'll see what happens. *Then* we'll decide."

Mr. Coppola said, "Right at the point when the movie industry, by its own admission, is falling apart, you try to do something different, something to bring it away from the television mentality—the quick cuts, the hyped-up action, the cut to her, the cut to him, the warmed-over stories, everything done in the editing room instead of by the maker of the movie. And people ridicule you for making the effort. That's what gets me upset."

There was a brief silence.

"*Treasure of the Sierra Madre*, directed by John Huston, was a big flop at the previews," the older executive said. "I was there. I remember. It was 1948. If Warner Brothers hadn't owned their theaters themselves at that time, the picture never would have been shown. Then it went on to win three Academy Awards."

"*Traviata*, the first time out, bombed," the executive producer said.

"They tried to murder Stravinsky's *Sacre du Printemps*."

"At the press conference, the first question they asked me was 'How do you feel now that everyone dislikes the picture?'" Mr. Coppola said. "Why do I have to put up with that? I feel dirtied by it."

"You let that guy get to you," said the Zoetrope president.

"From the start of this movie, I felt I was a cat on the griddle," Mr. Coppola said. "It's not the way I felt when I was a kid and we put on plays. The show would open. People liked it. Then we would all go to the dance. I like the idea of telling the bank, 'Take the studio. Take everything. I'll just keep one little can of film.'"

Mr. Coppola's associates gave weak smiles.

"It's probably the most interesting movie I've ever made," Mr. Coppola said. "I feel the movie will be studied thirty years from now. Maybe I just ought to transfer it to a cassette and release it as just that."

Again, there were weak smiles from the associates.

"Why can't I just pay all the money back?" Mr. Coppola asked.

"Because it's not twenty million only," the Zoetrope president said. "It's seven million more on the foreign contracts. Just because some ass asks you a dumb question…"

"The best way I can use my energy, is in trying to make a beautiful film," Mr. Coppola said. "Instead, if you want to make a film you are thrown into merchandising. If the truth were known about distribution methods, the distributor wants and gets cable, network sale, cassettes. Distributors have delayed bookkeeping. They are marketing executives. And they all have lawyers. Hollywood is infested with lawyers. With big egos. They don't know about making pictures."

"When the picture starts making money, all those guys will slip back into the mud," the co-producer said.

"I can't try to make movies the way they do for television, which is the bargain-basement way," Mr. Coppola said. "I'm not going to do all that. My father always told me it's tough to get people to try something new. They're like kids resisting a new kind of food. Once they try it, he told me, they'll get to like it. But you have to *give* it to them to try. The things you come to love best are the things you didn't love at first. I've got to make the films my own way."

"You make them, and I'll worry about the distributors," the Zoetrope president said.

"I'm in no rush," Mr. Coppola said. "The distributor is merely what bus you're going to get on."

The West Coast preview was to be held on the following Wednesday, January 20th. In the meantime, Mr. Coppola read some additional press comments on the New York preview. Rex Reed's piece, in the *News*, was headlined "HERE'S ONE FROM THE HEART: HOGWASH!" and Stephen Grover's, in the *Wall Street Journal*, "COPPOLA OFFERS UP ONE FROM THE HEART TO WARM RESPONSE." Janet Maslin wrote in the *Times*, "At the film's end, it was greeted with measured, if not wildly enthusiastic, applause. So the evening, with its two sold-out previews, could in no way be viewed as a fiasco. But neither was it the triumphant debut Mr. Coppola had doubtless hoped for two weeks ago, when he hurriedly planned this unorthodox unveiling of his ambitious new musical movie."

In Los Angeles, full-page ads were placed in the January 20th Los Angeles *Times* and U.C.L.A. *Daily Bruin* announcing two screenings for that night, to be held at the Village Theater, in Westwood, an upper-middle-class neighborhood near the university. The theater's capacity was fourteen hundred and seventy-seven, and the tickets were sold out. The response of the audiences was enthusiastic—much *more* enthusiastic, Mr. Coppola and his Zoetrope colleagues thought, than that of the audiences at the Music Hall. "How can you figure these things? Maybe the difference was, at the Music Hall there was no popcorn," Mr. Gersten said, with a grin, to a reporter. "At Westwood, there was popcorn. So the response was very, very good."

Then, on January 22nd, came what the Zoetrope people called "a breakthrough review." Sheila Benson, the film critic for the Los Angeles *Times*, wrote a review that began, "It's so easy to love *One From the Heart*; you just let yourself relax and float away with it. A work of constant astonishment, Francis Coppola's new film is so daring it takes away your breath while staggering you visually." Mrs. Benson also wrote, "The picture comes from the same artistic impulses that inspire airbrush art, three-dimensional pop-up greeting cards, and the delicately beautiful new neon that illuminates L.A. shops. It is post-Warhol, where everything is 'pretty,' all slickness and sleekness, and it cherishes its surfaces even more because of the hollowness they cover.... Coppola's leap into years-ahead technology is sure and dazzling. 'It's artificial,' he seems to say. 'Isn't it gorgeous?' Indeed it is—sumptuous, sensuous, stunning.... Two kinds of audiences will accept *One From the Heart* easily, *naifs* and sophisticates. Those in the middle will worry too much about the silhouette-thinness of the characters. They shouldn't. Musicals have been far emptier than this in terms of real emotion, and very few have dared this greatly."

By now, Robert Spiotta, Zoetrope's president, was working day and night to make distribution arrangements for *One from the Heart*. Mr. Coppola was in hiding, working on the screenplay for *The Outsiders*, which he was scheduled to start directing in three weeks. For the next eight days, Mr. Spiotta met with executives and lawyers of motion-picture companies that put up or obtain money to make movies and then distribute them or else just make the deals to distribute movies whose financing has been arranged by others. Lawyers and marketing experts on both sides had their own meetings with each other. With valiant attempts to be matter-of-fact, Mr. Spiotta described his negotiating efforts to a reporter. "In this industry, the greater your need, the worse your deal," he said. "Money is very powerful, and power is used to the hilt. These people are corporate animals. We have three viable alternatives. One, we can make a two-picture deal with Warner Brothers for *One from the Heart* and Francis's next picture, *The Outsiders*. We're reluctant to make the two-picture deal with Warners, because they are more interested in *The Outsiders* than in *One from the Heart*. Two, we can make a deal for *One from the Heart* with Columbia and a separate deal for *The Outsiders* with Warner Brothers. Three, we can make a separate deal for *The Outsiders* with either Warner Brothers or Columbia and distribute *One from the Heart* ourselves. We want to develop a good relationship with Warner Brothers, because they will distribute *The Escape Artist* and *Hammett*—two pictures produced but not directed by Francis. The situation at Columbia is also favorable, thanks to their recent successes. On a lesser scale, there's Filmways, which is being acquired by Orion, whose key people liked *One from the Heart* very much. Filmways has become a much more serious consideration, because of the Orion involvement. But that would be a back-end deal, which means no money up front. There would, however, be a low distribution fee and tremendous input by us in the marketing campaign. What we'd like to get is a negative-pickup deal, with a low distribution fee—lower than twenty-five per cent—and a substantial advance up front. All deals are different. Some deals have distribution fees tied in to box-office grosses. The better the business at the box office, the lower the fee for the distributor. If a picture does badly, the fee is higher. Deals should be made quickly. It's important to pick the optimum time."

A couple of days later, Mr. Spiotta, sounding wearier, reported, "Columbia is very eager to have *The Outsiders*, but it has less than the required enthusiasm for *One from the Heart*. We want to deal with a company that is enthusiastic. The trouble is, distributors are greedy. They want everything. For example, Universal has shown a late interest in *One from the Heart* and has offered us a deal that would give us six million dollars up front, but it wanted too much in return. It wanted all domestic rights—cable-television, network-television, cassette, and disc—but we want to retain as many rights as we can. We want to keep *something*. Most producers don't have the stature or the audacity to keep many rights. For example, Francis controlled the rights to *Apocalypse Now*, which was distributed by United Artists. That picture has already brought in a hundred million dollars. The cost was thirty-two million dollars. We still owe three million dollars, but the value of unsold rights will far exceed that amount. We may have terminated our distribution deal with Paramount for *One from the Heart*, but nobody in this business stays on the outs with anybody else. Eventually, we all need each other. Warner Brothers are still high on our priority list. I believe we can agree on a distribution fee. The more serious issue with Warner Brothers is the license terms. They would like to have the distribution rights in perpetuity, and we're attempting to restrict them to ten years and the guarantee on the number of prints and the amount of money spent on advertising. We want very much to duplicate the guarantee we had from Paramount, which was for six hundred prints and four million dollars guaranteed in advertising."

The next day, Mr. Spiotta, sounding still wearier, said, "I saw Francis and explained the level of interest of each studio and the problems with each deal. He said, 'Let's distribute it ourselves.' At this point, there's a great deal of risk and uncertainty in doing that, and Francis is not pigheaded when it comes to business. We want three things. One, we want the best long-term distribution deal in respect to economics. Two, we want restriction of distribution rights to domestic theatrical—no cable, no cassettes, no foreign deals. Three, we want to be comfortable with the distribution. Attitude is a very critical area. The number of prints, what theaters, the advertising budget—all reveal attitude."

The next day: "The Warner Brothers deal fell apart. Warners would not back down on the issue of perpetuity, and although we were close on the distribution fee, it was not as low as we wanted. At this point, time is working against us. We're very eager to get the film released according to the original schedule. We decided to engage Irwin Yablans, the independent film producer who made *Halloween*, and who worked as a consultant for us on the distribution of *Apocalypse Now*. Yablans has an exceptional knowledge of the theatrical-distribution business, and he also has great esteem for Francis. He quickly started getting in touch with theater owners directly to explore the possibility of opening *One from the Heart* ourselves, without a distributor. Within one hour, Henry Plitt, of the Plitt chain, in Los Angeles, offered us the Century Plaza Theater, and Bernie Myerson, of the Loews chain, in New York, offered us the Tower East and Loews Paramount. During the next twenty-four hours, we also secured key theaters in Denver, Las Vegas, Boston, Chicago, Washington, northern New Jersey, and Long Island. At this point, we don't necessarily intend to *distribute* the film ourselves, but we do intend to release the film *without* a distributor, to demonstrate our ability to get playing time directly from exhibitors. Francis would love to distribute the film himself. But, from a practical point of view, distributing this film beyond an initial limited release without a distribution organization would be madness—and we could never attempt it on a film that cost twenty-seven million."

"They know that a Coppola movie is out of the ordinary," Mr. Gersten said a few days later, when he arrived in New York to work on advertising for *One from the Heart* with the advertising agency that was already handling the *Napoleon* ads. Mr. Gersten also started working with Howard Deutch, who had been engaged by Paramount to make a trailer and commercials for *One from the Heart* back in the days when Paramount was going to distribute the film. Other Zoetrope executives stepped up plans for the premiere of the movie. Mr. Spiotta, however, continued talks about distribution with Columbia, Universal, and Filmways. Mr. Coppola made some final changes in the negative of the film and, on January 26th, sent it, along with the soundtrack, by courier to Rome for final processing. Twenty-five prints, at a cost of two thousand dollars each, were ordered. Two days later, Mr. Spiotta had some news to report. "At first, Columbia had less than the required enthusiasm," he said to a reporter. "But the people there looked at the film again, and this time they were more encouraged. Columbia is potentially our best bet."

The night of Friday, January 29th, Mr. Spiotta had news of an agreement with Columbia. "We agreed on the deal at 5 p.m.," he said. "I'm sure all the arrangements we've made for bookings will be taken over by Columbia. We want to open on schedule, for starters, with forty-one screens in eight cities. The deal does not involve a great deal of up-front money. None, in fact. We've decided to gamble on the back end to go with a lower distribution fee and retain control of all rights, rather than take the Universal deal, which provided six million dollars up front but meant losing control of all rights."

"We turned down Universal's six million dollars up front because we wanted to retain the rights for ourselves," Mr. Coppola said. "Now it's up to Columbia."

In New York, Mr. Gersten was still working with the advertising agency on the ad that showed the faces of Teri Garr and Frederic Forrest coming together in a kiss, and they had been struggling with the line "Francis Coppola takes a very special look at love" versus the line "Francis Coppola takes a chance on love" for the advertising copy, and also with "A new kind of old-fashioned romance" versus "A new kind of valentine."

The next day, Mr. Gersten and the ad agency were told to stop struggling, because Columbia was taking over.

"The die is cast," said Mr. Gersten. "Columbia's advertising people are coming in with a whole new concept of what we should do. They're planning to show Raul Julia lying on top of Teri Garr, and over it they want to say, 'Francis Ford Coppola, the man who brought you *The Godfather* and *Apocalypse Now*, takes a light look at love in a spectacular way.' And they want to put *One from the Heart* not in script but in Deco type, something like

*Pennies from Heaven*. And under the title they want to say, 'Sometimes you have to break apart to come together.' I don't like what they're doing, and I told them so. I told them that Francis himself has wanted to leave out the Ford in his name, because he himself has said, 'Never trust anyone who uses three names.'" Others at Zoetrope were pleased with Columbia's approach, and said they were impressed by Columbia's ability to create a completely new campaign overnight.

Having been relieved of responsibility for the ads, Mr. Gersten now devoted himself to arranging, and then accompanying Mr. Coppola on, a whirlwind pre-opening promotional tour across the country, starting with an appearance on the Merv Griffin television show in Los Angeles on February 4th: One hour with Merv Griffin in his own Merv Griffin Theater, in Hollywood, answering Merv Griffin questions like "Why did you spend all that money?" Plane to Las Vegas that night. Next morning at nine, in a Caesar's Palace conference room, a press conference with a dozen representatives of television, radio, and newspapers, answering questions about electronic-cinema procedures, about why Paramount did not come across with the *One from the Heart* completion money, and was it after that that Mr. Coppola decided to drop Paramount as the distributor for the movie? Plane that afternoon to Chicago, limousine to the Ambassador East, for what are known as one-on-one interviews in this case, two interviews with Gene Siskel, of the Chicago *Tribune*. Mr. Siskel first did an interview for his Public Television program, with a television crew that was interested in Mr. Coppola's remarks and hung around listening to the second interview, for the newspaper. In reporting on his questions to Mr. Coppola, Mr. Siskel wrote in the *Tribune*, "Why couldn't we just see *One from the Heart* without having to worry about who was going to distribute it?… Why didn't he [Mr. Coppola] act more like his co-equal as the greatest of American filmmakers, Martin Scorsese, who manages to release his extraordinary movies with a measure of dignity and without going nuts in public?" Mr. Coppola's apparently calm answer was "Why does one weigh two hundred and forty pounds and the other weigh something like ninety-six pounds? Obviously, it has to do with a difference in personality.… I finance my own pictures, and Marty doesn't. So I'm usually in a financial situation that he isn't." On the

same day, Mr. Siskel's review was headed "COPPOLA'S LATEST FILM IS MORE FROM THE LENS THAN THE 'HEART.'"
Next day: Press conference at 9 a.m. at the hotel with about forty people, arranged by Columbia Pictures field representatives. Mr. Coppola and Mr. Gersten and also Gian-Carlo Coppola, who was accompanying them on the tour, said they were impressed by Columbia's efficiency. That afternoon, plane to Toronto, with Mr. Coppola carrying three frozen pizzas (gift from Columbia) from Chicago's famous Pizzeria Uno. In Toronto, Columbia field representatives had set up a press conference with fifty people at the Sheraton Centre Hotel and one-on-one interviews with Jay Scott, of the *Globe & Mail*; Bruce Kirkland, of the *Sun*; and Ron Base, of the *Star*. Late that night, still carrying the three Uno pizzas, Mr. Coppola returned home to his apartment at the Sherry Netherland, heated up one of the pizzas, ate some, and went to sleep. He worked all the next day, Sunday, on casting for *The Outsiders*, taking time out only to look at some newly developed high-definition video systems that the Sony Corporation wanted to show him.

On Monday morning, the Columbia people had Mr. Coppola scheduled to appear on *Good Morning America* with David Hartman, and they wanted to show some clips from *One from the Heart* during the interview. Mr. Coppola said he didn't want the clips shown.

"To put a little fragment of the movie on television is stupid," Mr. Coppola said. "Commercials and trailers are different. I'd prefer not to show *any* clips on *any* talk shows. I'd rather just talk about the movie. You sit there, and then you're supposed to look up at where the clips are shown. You feel like a jerk. Besides, this movie is not a conventional movie, and showing fragments is misleading." The clips were not shown. On *Good Morning America*, Mr. Coppola followed Olivia Newton-John singing "Let's get physical..." and Erma Bombeck giving a humorous report entitled "The Cost of Wives." "We are a very small company," Mr. Coppola said to an endlessly smiling Mr. Hartman on the program. "We don't have wealth or power. I'm facing the question now of whether Zoetrope can win the right to exist."

Back to the Sherry Netherland. A breakfast there at eleven-thirty with twelve people who write or talk about movies for a living. Immediately afterward, another breakfast there, with twelve more people who write or talk about movies for a living. Some more casting work on *The Outsiders*. Appearance on another television talk show. Back to work on *The Outsiders*.

Plane to Washington, D.C., the next morning. Appearance as a guest at the Washington Press Club in connection with the opening of *Napoleon* at the Kennedy Center, where the orchestra was to be led by Carmine Coppola. Several one-on-one interviews. Then the black-tie opening of *Napoleon*. Afterward, a midnight party in the foyer of the theater.

Next morning: Plane directly to Los Angeles, where Mr. Coppola, Mr. Gersten, and Gian-Carlo landed in pouring rain. "We were charged up," Mr. Gersten said over the telephone to a friend in New York. "We were finding positive signs wherever we went, in everything."

The premiere of *One from the Heart* was held that night—Wednesday, February 10th—at Plitt's Century Plaza Theater, in a complex of shops across the street from the Century Plaza Hotel. It was still raining. Present were two klieg lights, executives from Columbia Pictures, all the stars and other members of the cast of *One from the Heart*, and some other celebrities. The theater capacity was fourteen hundred seats, and the house was full. Afterward, there was a party in a nearby Chinese restaurant. Celebrities who attended told Zoetrope people that they had liked the movie. "It's lovely. It's charming. He made a hell of a movie," Peter Falk said. And Steven Spielberg said, "I thought it was a great achievement, a complete conceptual design. You know, from the beginning to the end, it's a wonderful dream. It's a dream about reality relationships, but it's very, very entertaining. After all the things I'd heard about it I didn't expect it to be this entertaining. It really sort of took my breath away. All those dissolves and people appearing behind scrims. It was as if Francis went to Broadway and made a movie about it. It's just wonderful."

The movie opened officially the next day, in forty-one theaters in eight cities: San Francisco, Los Angeles, Denver, Chicago, Washington, Boston, New York, and Toronto. The reviews were uneven. Many critics had already reviewed the movie, after seeing one or another of the previews. The day of the opening, the *Times* review, by Vincent Canby, was unfavorable. Mr. Canby wrote, "Nothing had quite prepared me for the staggering number of wrong choices—made by one of our most talented and adventurous film makers—that are contained in the version of *One from the Heart* that I finally saw." Mr. Canby criticized the story, the action, the screenplay, the casting, the acting, the dialogue, the music, and the style, and wound up calling the movie "unfunny, unjoyous, unsexy, and unromantic."

Mr. Coppola did not appear bothered by the bad reviews or by other negative comments on his movie. "It's like the first reaction to *Apocalypse Now*, he said on hearing about the reviews. "Everybody talked against that one at first, too. At first, they didn't like what I had done. A lot of them wanted me to go on making *The Godfather, Part III*, or something. Then everybody came around."

The amount of business a movie does after its first week determines whether it has what is known in the trade as "legs," and the legs are carefully evaluated. After *One from the Heart* had appeared on the forty-one screens in the eight cities, it was regarded as practically legless.

"It's worse than we expected," Mr. Gersten said. "It's disappointing."

The legs situation did not improve during the next few weeks.

Mr. Spiotta said to a reporter, "In San Francisco, Los Angeles, New York, and Toronto, it did well at first, but it was disappointing in Denver, Chicago, Washington, and Boston. Columbia made what is called an exit survey—interviewing at random people as they leave at the end of a screening. Their survey told us that people who went to the movie with some awareness of what to expect liked it, and people who had thought it was something else had a negative reaction. Fifty per cent of those who saw it liked it. The other fifty per cent knew little about the picture beforehand—they didn't even know it was directed by *Francis*. At that point, we decided to get Patrick Caddell, of Cambridge Survey Research—the guy who did polls for President Carter—to do a survey to provide more data on the reasons people liked or disliked the film, thereby enabling us to design a new campaign aimed at the target audience. All of which, of course, should have been done months earlier."

By then, Mr. Coppola was deeply involved in preparations for shooting *The Outsiders*. "*The Outsiders* has been set up as a separate company, and it's in Tulsa," Mr. Coppola said to a reporter. "We brought most of our electronic setup to Tulsa. Our whole methodology is with us. I like to work on a lot of things at the same time. This is going to be the busiest year of my life. I'll be directing at least three more films. I treasure *One from the Heart*. It's an unusual film, and it can be proved only by time. Maybe it's something only *I* cherish. Maybe the film doesn't make itself understood. All I know is that I got twenty-seven million dollars' worth out of making the film, because it represents everything I will want in the next thirty years. There's plenty to learn from that movie. When I decided to preview the movie at the Music Hall, it was a romantic gesture. I wanted to demonstrate to Paramount that it should help me. For me, it was a beautiful evening. It was like being in the theater again. I was running around deciding how to have the house lights. I didn't anticipate the Paramount controversy. All I wanted was to get the money, so that I could finish the film. I don't have any bad feelings toward Paramount. The Columbia people are real professionals. They jumped in with both feet. When the record of *One from the Heart* comes out, a new campaign will be stimulated, because I think the songs, the lyrics, and the singing performances are wonderful and got little attention. Fundamentally, I think what can be blamed for what happened to this film is the way, for a year prior to its release, it was associated with conflict, money problems, the threat of bankruptcy. Right away, it was bad, even before the reviews. The public shied away. The trick now is to encourage good word of mouth. As for me, I have to work in the only way I know how. Some people are quick to tell you how to function, and when you don't do what they want you to do they become angry. I don't know why some of the reaction to what I do is so cynical. I know that I'm for intelligence, creativity, and friendliness, as opposed to greed, power, and hostility. Whether you're the director or the producer or the owner of a movie, as soon as you form an organization to make a picture you're a businessman. The problem is to be in all that and still to be free."

"We made a lot of mistakes," Mr. Spiotta said. "We should have had trailers in the theaters at least two months before release. We did not. The publicity was not right. We had no time for research. We should have had the attention of the public on the film, not on Zoetrope, not on Francis and the financial problems. We didn't bring the music out as an album before the picture was released. In retrospect, the ad campaign was all wrong. After the Music Hall previews, we went on the wrong assumption that we had to get the picture out in a hurry. We should have waited."

One week after the opening—at a cost of about twenty thousand dollars—Zoetrope Studios officially engaged the Cambridge Survey Research organization to make a study of people's views on *One from the Heart*, whether they had attended the movie or not. Cambridge interviewed four hundred and fifty-one moviegoers at theaters in Chestnut Hill, Massachusetts; Paramus, New Jersey; Denver; and Los Angeles. Half the people interviewed had attended *One from the Heart*; the others had seen other movies. The survey found:

(1) "Half of those attending *One from the Heart* considered it a good or excellent film.

(2) "Most people attending the other movies had at least some awareness of *One from the Heart*," because of negative publicity pertaining to the Coppola studio's distribution problems or to negative reviews, or both.

(3) "Coppola commands a strong personal following." Half of those who did not see the film but had heard of it were unaware that Coppola had directed it. Filmgoers who were disappointed in the movie had expected a more realistic treatment of the romantic theme.

(4) Negative reviews and negative publicity dominated the responses of those not attending *One from the Heart*.

(5) People who disliked the film had not expected to see the kind of movie they saw.

(6) "Many of those who attended the film, particularly women, were disappointed with the film's dreamy or surreal aspects." They had expected a more typical love story.

The survey recommended a "marketing strategy" based on its finding that those who liked the movie were sixty-three percent male; sixty-nine per cent single; forty-four per cent between the ages of twenty-six and thirty-five, with thirty-nine per cent twenty-five or under; fifty-nine per cent once-every-two-weeks filmgoers and seventy-three percent college educated. Cambridge Survey Research recommended:

> A marketing strategy which can maximize the box office of this core support group and its word-of-mouth potential must incorporate the following.
> (1) Coppola.

(2) An innovative film which only he can do; which he always does.

(3) A love story or romance captured by an extraordinary atmosphere of fantasy-photography, scenery, lighting, and music.

If in the process of communicating these chief messages the audience infers that the film contains an upbeat message or that a blend of normal, frustrating daily lives and dreams of exotic places and lovers is reached, so much the better. Those themes must be subordinate to the three main messages, however—their impact is not as strong and their cumulative effect will be to mislead people if no other accompaniment exists.

Among further recommendations, the report warned, *"Beware of misleading women,"* and advised using radio to link the film's background music with a message about the film's Coppola-innovative romantic story of realism and fantasy, and having Mr. Coppola make a personal appeal on radio and television, explaining how he had tried to do something different in his new movie. The report concluded, "If people understand better than they have so far just what precisely they might go to see, *One from the Heart* can generate interest, better word-of-mouth, and break through the vicious cycle of bad publicity, mixed reviews, and poor box-office which is now threatening it so severely."

Cambridge also recommended that Mr. Coppola show segments of *One from the Heart* in television commercials.

At Zoetrope, the report was read and studied by Mr. Coppola, Mr. Spiotta, and Fred Roos, one of the producers of *One from the Heart*. At Columbia, James Spitz, the president of domestic distribution, still had confidence in *One from the Heart*. "Box-office grosses for the picture are so far disappointing, but we're tenacious individuals, and we think there's a following for the picture," Mr. Spitz told a reporter. "We'll create a groundswell for the picture. Give it a quote class presentation unquote. That's what we did with *Tess*. Gave it a successful image. One of the great strengths of Columbia is, we believe in the team concept. We all saw the film at the Westwood preview. We all thought it was a unique piece of work. We all thought commercially it had potential. We've probably got the most innovative, most contemporary marketing methods. We brought in new marketing concepts for the picture. We prescribed new ads. We gave the picture a different look ad-wise. We're proceeding to launch this picture like *Tess*. On the basis of that parameter, we're going for the really big presentation in class theaters—New York's Tower East; Mann's Chinese Theater, in Hollywood; and Century Plaza, the Chicago Water Tower, and ten suburban theaters in affluent, middle-class areas. We'll then pull back to eight theaters in eight cities and try to maintain the run as long as possible in New York, Los Angeles, San Francisco, Cincinnati, Seattle, Toronto, and Dallas. We're going at it with renewed vigor. Nothing is written in stone in the film business. We'll profit not only in the film but in the relationship with Francis Ford Coppola."

Others on the Columbia team echoed Mr. Spitz's views on marketing *One from the Heart* with renewed vigor, in the customary noun-into-verb idiom. "We'll platform the picture from eight cities," said Peter Benoit, Columbia's national publicity manager. "We did that with *Absence of Malice*. By the time that picture broke wide, there was an awareness of the picture's content. By the time the picture opened, there was already a groundswell. With *Neighbors*, we knew we had to capitalize on the immediacy of the picture. So we opened it in fourteen hundred theaters. That's called get-the-money. With a special-handling picture, we give it a special-handling release. Like *Tess*. Here we've got something special—our relationship with Francis Ford Coppola."

At Zoetrope, Fred Roos said, "We want to pull back to cities we're comfortable in. A movie's life is years and years. Our concern is that the picture's reputation is solidified for the future."

By April 1st, seven weeks after the opening, when the only theater showing *One from the Heart* was the Guild, in New York, there were forty-three people in the theater at the last showing. The next day, the movie was gone.

"Columbia was willing to release four hundred prints in a hundred markets," Mr. Spiotta recently told a reporter. "But we decided to remove it from release. We didn't want to go through those kinds of motions.

Columbia was very cooperative. A few weeks ago, Francis had a chance to make a few changes in the movie, to polish it here and there. And now he feels it's even better. This fall, we're releasing it in three test markets—in Dallas-Fort Worth, in Minneapolis-St. Paul, and in Vancouver—and with a new advertising campaign. The final chapter is not yet written."

In April, Mr. Coppola announced that Zoetrope Studios—the actual real estate—was up for sale. At about the same time, the big business news about Columbia Pictures was that the Coca-Cola Company stockholders had voted overwhelmingly in favor of acquiring the movie company, thus making Columbia a wholly owned subsidiary of Coca-Cola. "Within the structure of Coca-Cola, Columbia will be tantamount to one can in the overall corporate six-pack," *Variety* wrote in its report of the merger. "That is, Col's annual gross of $700,000,000 will be swallowed up by Coke's annual $5.9-billion gross."

In Tulsa, Mr. Coppola was immersed in working on his two new movies, but he kept posted on developments concerning his past debts. "Chase has been insisting that we sell the studio in order to pay it back," he said, fairly unemotionally, to a friend. "If we sell the studio and other assets in order to repay Chase the thirty-one million they are owed on *One from the Heart*, *Escape Artist*, and *Hammett*, they are willing to cooperate and not foreclose on the collateral. When a bank loan is in trouble, the bank turns it over to 'work-out' people, and they are very, very, *very* tough. We may get them to understand, however, that the best thing I can do to repay them is to go on working. One thing about me, I sure put in the hours."

A few weeks later, Mr. Coppola said, "Whatever happens with *One from the Heart* now may have an effect on how easy or difficult it will be for me to go on making movies, but I know for certain now that making that film the way I wanted to make it has already given me a lot. I've already learned so much from the experience in two major ways: first, about the filmmaking process itself, what I feel a film *is*; and, second, various practical realizations having to do with the things that make it possible to make a film—the raising of the money, relations with the press, and so on. The *most* important single thing I've learned, actually, is to play everything closer to the vest from now on. I enjoy the work I do, and, because I enjoy people, I tend to try my ideas out on them. I always find myself talking, and showing people things and ideas, much the way a playwright wants to get an audience reaction to his play. Bouncing off their reaction, you get a whole new bunch of ideas. So I would find myself telling everyone everything—even things that haven't yet been proved, or things that are only hopes or ideas. In the past, I often found myself in all kinds of trouble that I wouldn't have been in if I had kept my ideas to myself. There are all sorts of storms and turbulences out there in the world, and, because I tend not to be concerned with protecting myself, even though I thought I was only putting a toe in I'd be sucked way out in the storm. People on the outside have their arguments and different positions they're in tumult over, and if they hear a peep out of me I've let myself be sucked into the middle of *their* storms, thus making it very difficult for me to pursue my own business. I therefore jeopardize myself—make my job much tougher than it needs to be. The issues I found myself immersed in during the making of *One from the Heart*—all the trouble about the financing—have always been the thing of least interest to me. Money has never been the most important part of my life, and, of course, that is why I was able to take some risks in order to do my work. Quite ironically, I think that *One from the Heart* was overshadowed in the minds of the public by the money troubles. Few people seemed to look at the movie in just its own light, as a personal film a filmmaker had made in which he was maybe trying to find a new vocabulary for himself. What is important to me about the movie is the way I felt about it and the way I thought film might someday be used.

"Ever since I started making films, I've tried to use the theater director's approach—imagining this enormous production as an event that I want to create—and then I've gone with the camera and sound and tried my very best to record it as I imagined it. There is another point of view—the illustrator-director's approach—which I think is the opposite of my own. That starts with a series of pictures, moving pictures, which you produce, and which, when the pictures are displayed, *becomes* a production."

In May, Mr. Coppola made an arrangement with the Chase Manhattan Bank that required him to increase his personal liability in exchange for an extended repayment schedule; the agreement allowed both Mr. Coppola and Zoetrope the opportunity to liquidate real property, including the Hollywood studio, and various motion-picture rights for the repayment of the Chase loan. Under the circumstances, Mr. Spiotto was satisfied with the agreement. "Banks don't win by suing clients," he explained to a business novice. "Had the agreement not been reached, it would certainly have required a bankruptcy action by Zoetrope and possibly personally by Francis. Now Francis can do the one thing that can turn his financial fortunes around, and that one thing is going on to make other films."

Last month, Mr. Coppola took a quick trip to Europe in connection with the openings of *One from the Heart* in France, Germany, and Sweden.

"At the French pre-opening screenings for critics and others, the response to the movie was so much more alive than it was here," Mr. Coppola told a strongly pro-*One from the Heart* friend on his return to this country. The reviewers were really *interested* in what I was trying to do. Business there has been good—as good as the business for *Blade Runner*, anyway," he said. "But in Sweden the movie is doing very, *very* good business. In Sweden, they really seem to like the movie."

Mr. Coppola was quiet for a moment, looking somewhat puzzled. "I'm bothered by the nagging idea that I failed in what I was trying to do," he went on. "*One from the Heart* had its roots in so many of the aspects of my life that to have had it rejected here with such indignation causes me to wonder about all my preoccupations and ideas. First, there was Theater, and Theater for me was technology: lighting boards and fly systems and trapdoors. There was Remote Control, as demonstrated for me by my Lionel train set when I was a little kid—the way I controlled the milk car and the cattle car, the switch tracks, and, best of all, the direction of the locomotive. Then, there were the Songs. The first time I heard songs in a story I cared about was when my family went to see Sigmund Romberg's *The Desert Song* on the occasion of my brother's birthday. I will never forget it, though I could have been only five or six years old. This, along with the experience ten or twelve years later of watching my father as he conducted the orchestra for the road company of *Kismet*, fixed in me the desire to create fantasy with music and songs. Then, when I was paralyzed, although I loved my brother and sister with a kind of fairy-tale devotion and intensity, I was always hungry to be with other children. When I put on my shows alone in my room, I dreamed about the day when I would put on shows with others and people would come to see them. I was dreaming, I'm sure, about having a place like my studio, where we could learn, and teach what we learned to others."

Mr. Coppola paused, and then he said, "I doubt whether many people understood the depth of my feelings on this subject. I have no doubt that I have the energy and the resourcefulness to keep going with the studio. But sometimes I wonder whether it's worth it in such a cynical and frightened world." He paused again and pushed his glasses up on the bridge of his nose. "I love *One from the Heart* not only for what it is but for where it was going," he said. "I love Zoetrope Studios for the same reason. We were doing all sorts of things for the first time. I'm sure that we have profoundly influenced other moviemakers, and we deserve the opportunity to go on. Every once in a while, I start feeling a bit down, but I'm really enthusiastic about the future. My head is percolating with new ideas about everything. You know, some of those Chase bankers told me *they* liked the movie. I told the bank I'll make the first payment with the money we get from the sale of the studio and the money owed us for the foreign distribution of *One from the Heart*. For the second payment, I'll use the money we get from the cable sale of *One from the Heart*, *Hammett*, and *The Escape Artist*. In the meantime, I'll be finishing everything on *The Outsiders* and *Rumble Fish*. So what if my telephone is turned off again at home? Or my electricity is shut off? Or my credit cards canceled? If you don't bet, you don't have a chance to win. It's so silly in life not to pursue the highest possible thing you can imagine, even if you run the risk of losing it all, because if you don't pursue it you've lost it anyway. You can't be an artist and be safe."

# Generator

February 27, 1984

Soap operas, commercials, specials, documentaries, and other such items made in New York City for television, movies made for movie houses, and live theater, ballet, concerts, and assorted other performing arts—now including musical videos—are worth two billion dollars to the city each year. This impressive fact, based on a Port Authority study of economic development which was issued last May, was given to us the other day by Patricia Reed Scott, the director of the Mayor's Office of Film, Theatre, and Broadcasting. "The performing arts are a major generator of dollars in the city's economy," Miss Scott said, delivering the line with the authority of someone who knows firsthand whereof she speaks, and someone who is clearly determined to be a very active participant in the generation of dollars. Here are some highlights of Miss Scott's history: now in her forties, she was born in Portsmouth, Virginia, and raised in Southern California; was a child actress on a San Francisco radio station (Little Beaver in the radio version of the *Red Ryder* comic strip); graduated from George Washington University, in Washington, D.C. (English-lit major); married the actor George C. Scott and did summer stock with him in Canada; came to New York in the fall of 1956 and lived at 44 Riverside Drive, in an old apartment where, myth had it, John Barrymore had once lived; had two children, who are now in their twenties and are involved in different aspects of the performing arts; started the Studio Duplicating Service (scripts of all kinds) and sold it; acted Off Broadway ("I enjoyed it, and was good at it, as a matter of fact, but I was never driven"); worked in night clubs like the Blue Angel, Bon Soir, Mister Kelly's, and Troubador, as a singer, in tandem with Woody Allen, George Segal, and Mort Sahl; acquired a press agent, a business agent, and a record contract and then freed herself from all of them; went to work under Mayor John Lindsay as a press officer in the Department for the Aging; produced a television series about aging called *Getting On*, which won a couple of Emmys; worked for three years as a deputy press secretary for Mayor Koch; was appointed eight months ago to her present job. She is blond-haired, slightly buxom, good-natured, sharp-eyed, quick to anticipate questions, able to give well-informed answers, and acquainted to some degree or other with thousands of actors, producers, directors, promoters, developers, archivists, and benefactors of the entertainment industries, and also with politicians and strategically placed friends who like what she is trying to do for film, theater, and broadcasting around here and want to help her do it.

"I didn't perceive the breadth of the activity until I read the Port Authority's description of all the components of the performing arts," Miss Scott told us over a cup of tea at the Algonquin. "The permits issued by our office in 1983 numbered six thousand two hundred and sixty-four for filming on locations, mainly exterior, around the city. That's six hundred and twenty-seven more than in 1982. Films made entirely in New York numbered thirty-three, but that many again were partly made here. These productions, which brought eight hundred and fifty-six million dollars to the city, included *Trading Places*, with Eddie Murphy and Dan Aykroyd; *Romancing the Stone*, with Michael Douglas; *Not for Publication*, with Nancy Allen and Laurence Luckenbill; *Unfaithfully Yours*, with Dudley Moore and Natassja Kinski; *The Cotton Club*, with Richard Gere; *Le Bon Plaisir*, with Catherine Deneuve; *The Brother Who Fell to Earth*, with Joe Morton and Dee Dee Bridgewater; *Sweet Ginger Brown*, with Matt Dillon and Richard Crenna; *Ghostbusters*, with Dan Aykroyd and Bill Murray; *Staying Alive*, with John Travolta; *The Goodbye People*, with Martin Balsam and Judd Hirsch: *The Lonely Guy*, with Steve Martin; *Broadway Danny Rose*, with Woody Allen and Mia Farrow; *Moscow on the Hudson*, with Robin Williams; *The Ultimate Solution of Grace Quigley*, with Katharine Hepburn and Nick Nolte; *Once Upon a Time in America*, with Robert De Niro; *Splash*, with John Candy; and *The Muppets Take Manhattan*, with Miss Piggy and Kermit.

"In television, we've got nine soaps, which we call daytime dramas, being produced here, and those bring in two hundred million dollars a year. We've got five one-hours—*All My Children*, *Another World*, *As the World Turns*, *The Guiding Light*, and *One Life to Live*—and four half-hours, which are *The Edge of Night*, *Ryan's Hope*, *Search for Tomorrow*, and our newest one, *Loving*. Each soap gives work to at least a hundred actors, directors, producers, stage managers, gaffers, grips, electricians, camera people, script supervisors, makeup artists, audio technicians, wardrobe people, editors, and others—I have lists of them. What with the soaps and the theater and commercials, we have a great acting pool. There isn't a better acting pool in the world." Miss Scott took a sip of her tea. "I have constant reminders of the opportunity picture for actors," she told us, with a wry smile. "For instance, seventy-five per cent of all major characters in prime-time television are men, mostly white and mostly between the ages of thirty-five and fifty-five. And the women are mostly white and are mostly between twenty and thirty."

Miss Scott continued, "We've made progress on all fronts. Five years ago, we had the following made here: forty feature films, thirty-nine movies or specials for television, three hundred and seventy-five television programs, nine hundred and sixty-one commercials, four hundred and seventy-four educational documentaries, and five hundred and nineteen student films. Last year, we had anywhere from fifty to a hundred percent more activity going on. Over the past eight years, we've made steady progress in the restoration of the old Astoria Studios, among the biggest in the world, with the largest sound-stage—twenty-six thousand square feet. The whole complex is on a twelve-acre site, with fifteen buildings and eight soundstages—with two of the soundstages opening this month. You probably know that over a hundred silent films were made in the Astoria Studios in the nineteen-twenties. The Marx Brothers, Rudolph Valentino, Clara Bow, W. C. Fields, Gary Cooper, and Claudette Colbert all made movies here before they went out to Hollywood. When Hollywood moans and groans about what it calls 'runaway productions,' I always say, 'What do you mean, runaway? It all started *here*.'"

"How do you encourage filmmakers and others to come here?" we asked.

"We've got a great staff in our office to facilitate production," Miss Scott said. "We don't charge for our services. Other cities charge, but we're here to serve. Two of my people have been production managers, and they really know the business. We have four people issuing permits, including a former Parks Department man, Sam Stone, who knows every rock, every tree, every bush in the parks. Four others are experts on television, the theater, film operations, and film development. Benefits to the city often go way beyond the actual production. For example, *The Verdict* used the stairwell of the Tweed courthouse, behind City Hall, as a location. The movie people cleaned and painted the stairwell until it was sparkling, and, of course, that's the way it was left for us. Once a year, I go out to California and see the production heads: Charlie Maguire at Paramount, Fred Gallo at Warner Brothers, Terry Nelson at Universal—all of them. They know what New York looks like. I'm not going to dazzle them with the subway. When they tell me what they need, I tell them what we've got. We have wilderness on

Staten Island that is as good as anything out West. If it's caves they want, we've got caves aplenty in Inwood. As a matter of fact, one young filmmaker just finished *Luggage of the Gods*, set in the time of Neanderthal man, and he used our Inwood caves for the film. The Perry Como Special *Christmas in New York* came here because its people wanted scenes with a fifth-grade class at the United Nations International School and the Neapolitan Christmas tree at the Metropolitan Museum of Art. We offer extraordinary sets."

Miss Scott went on, "The commercial theater is also our concern. This city has the best performing live stages in the world, and we're out to help build an audience for the theater. Early Stages is our program to bring thousands of schoolchildren to see preview performances of shows. Last fall, we bused in eleven hundred kids between the ages of nine and thirteen—one class from each of the thirty-two school districts—to see *The Tap Dance Kid*, and it was such a success that we're getting ten-thousand-dollar contributions from theater-related people to do the same thing for other new shows. Audiences talking their heads off at the theater drive me crazy. That's the influence of television—talking at home no matter what's on the screen. We're going to build a theater going audience that keeps quiet."

We asked Miss Scott to give us an example of one of her successes in bringing a film production to New York.

"A producer came to see me the other day," she said quickly. "He said he represented a big, big star. He wanted to know about production costs, and I told him that fringe benefits are cheaper here than in California. Then he said suppose he wanted to hire a fifteen-year-old actress—what about the rules regulating working hours? I told him that our rules are less stringent than California's. What about union costs, he asked, and I threw all of them at him—I.A.T.S.E. (that's International Association of Theatrical Stagehands and Electricians), N.A.B.E.T. (National Association of Broadcast Employees and Technicians), and the Teamsters, the Screen Actors Guild, the Directors Guild, the Writers Guild. And he was satisfied. He's going to make his movie here, about a psychoanalyst and his fifteen-year-old patient, and the star is Frank Sinatra. I like to send people back to California as happy as possible."

## With Fellini

June 16, 1985

FEDERICO FELLINI, THE one-of-a-kind moviemaker, came to New York the other day to be honored by the Film Society of Lincoln Center in its annual tribute to a film artist, and here with him for a few days was his one-of-a-kind gang: his wife, the actress Giulietta Masina (star of the Fellini movies *La Strada*, *Nights of Cabiria*, and *Juliet of the Spirits*); Marcello Mastroianni (star of the Fellini movies *La Dolce Vita*, *8½* and *Ginger and Fred*, a still uncompleted one, in which he appears with Miss Masina); the actress Anouk Aimée (star of *La Dolce Vita* and *8½*; and also well known for her Claude Lelouch-directed movie *A Man and a Woman*); and various advisers, helpers, and experts on things American and many other things. We hadn't seen Fellini and the gang in several years, and so we were delighted when Fellini asked us to join them as they set out, the morning after their arrival, in a cavalcade of limos heading for Darien, Connecticut, and the country home of Dorothy Cullman, chairman of the F.S. of L.C., who had invited the whole gang, including us, for a typical Sunday-afternoon visit to her remodeled eighteenth-century Colonial house with grounds and pool. The visit was scheduled to include the obligatory swim, the quintessential tour of what-was-there-before and what-is-there-now, and a good meal. Fellini, gray-haired, ageless as ever, and nattily decked out in as preppy an outfit—navy-blue blazer with gold buttons, gray slacks, black loafers, white shirt, red silk tie—as has ever appeared in Darien, directed us to sit in the limo with him, Miss Masina (she was up front with the driver), Miss Aimée, and Mastroianni. Northward we went, followed by the others, who included a full complement of tribute workers, an admirably efficient bunch: Joanna Ney, public relations; Vivian Treves, interpreter; and Wendy Keys, co-producer, with Joanne Koch, of the whole shebang, to be put on in Avery Fisher Hall the following night. There were lots of high-spirited "*Ciao!*"s and laughter and the Italian equivalents of "Get a horse!" from those in our limo to those in the one behind us, and then Fellini settled down. He called to his wife up front, asking whether she was tired, and she replied, keeping her eyes on the road ahead, that she was never tired when she was happy, and she was happy. Fellini gave affectionate pats to the rest of us.

"This is the first time we are all together in New York," he said. "And now we go to Conneckticut," he added, giving a phonetic rendition that was used comfortably by everybody thereafter.

"When we see each other, it is always the same," Miss Aimée said. More pats from Fellini, reciprocal pats from Miss Aimée, pats from Mastroianni to both of them. Mastroianni, who was wearing a cream-colored Panama hat, adjusted it to a more rakish angle. He was wearing an impeccable, creaseless cream-colored linen suit, a black-and-white striped shirt, and a black tie.

"Anouk is a good fellow," Fellini said, in his most playful manner. "She is a famous actress who makes Western pictures," he went on, to us.

"Is that Conneckticut?" Mastroianni asked, pointing out the window at New Jersey as we drove up the Henry Hudson Parkway.

Fellini pointed in the opposite direction, at Grant's Tomb, and we identified it for him.

"Cary?" Miss Aimée asked, looking stricken.

We explained Ulysses S., and everybody looked relieved.

"We go to swim, and we will have a big lunch," Fellini said. "Soon we will see Conneckticut."

We asked Mastroianni whether he had seen any of the rushes of *Ginger and Fred*, which is not about Rogers and Astaire but about two dancers who call themselves Ginger and Fred. Mastroianni said he never goes to see rushes, because they are shown at night, after shooting, at the time he likes to go out to dinner. "Anyway, is *his* problem," he said, with a Mastroianni-charming smile-cum-shrug at Fellini.

"Is *my* problem," Fellini said. "I leave *Ginger and Fred* with four more days of shooting to shoot, and fly to New York, and is *my* problem to go back and finish *Ginger and Fred*. But is worth it to see Conneckticut."

There was a brief discussion about getting into bathing suits in Darien and Mastroianni referred affectionately to the fact that Miss Aimée was still thin. More pats from Mastroianni for Miss Aimée, who laughed and tossed her hair back off her face.

"Do you remember, when we made *La Dolce Vita*, on location in that tough neighborhood, I didn't know Italian then, and I heard the young men hanging around and shouting at you?" Miss Aimée said to Mastroianni. "Then I learned later they were shouting, 'Be careful, Marcello! You will hurt yourself holding her! She has too many bones! Give her food, Marcello!'"

"That place was full of thieves," Fellini said. "We had to pretend we were leaving, and we had to sneak back in the middle of the night, but the thieves all came back, too."

"Look at the trees!" Mastroianni called out, pointing at the countryside. "Look! There's Conneckticut!"

Not yet, we said.

Miss Aimée told us that she was going to work next making a sequel to *A Man and a Woman*, on its twentieth anniversary.

Mastroianni put on a mock-doleful expression. He told us that in the mid-sixties Miss Aimée had called him in Rome from Paris to say she was going to make *A Man and a Woman*, and had asked him to join her, playing the part later taken by Jean-Louis Trintignant. "She say to me a young director, unknown, no money; she plays a widow; I play a widower. I say no. I made a mistake."

"Two Academy Awards," Miss Aimée said, with a laugh. "Best Foreign Movie, Best Original Screenplay."

Connecticut! Everybody looked out at the Colonial-style wooden houses, some painted yellow, most painted white. Mastroianni wanted to know why so many Colonial houses were built of wood, unlike the old houses in Italy, which were built of stone.

Everybody looked bewildered.

"We go to the house of Dorothy Cullman, and we ask Dorothy Cullman why," Fellini said decisively, and everybody looked at ease again.

Destination reached: a light-beige-painted clapboard house with white trim, built around 1720, overlooking a slope of weedless, perfect lawn, as long as a city block, that was surrounded by weeping willow, apple, ash, dogwood, and Japanese white pine trees and led down to a waterfall and a huge, pond like swimming pool with a Japanese-style boathouse in front of it. Here and there on the lawn were wooden sculptures, some of them abstract and some in the shape of people or birds. Up a white-and-tan pebbled walk Fellini and the gang strode—like characters in Fellini movies—toward the house, and we were all greeted on the walk by the hostess, an attractive woman with a very pale face. She wore an ample peach-and-white antique Japanese kimono over a white cotton jumpsuit, and she had on flat-heeled white sandals. On her wrists she wore handsome matching wide antique Indian bracelets of ivory and silver. She extended both hands to the guests.

"An apparition!" Fellini whispered in awe.

"Welcome, Mr. Fellini, I'm Dorothy Cullman," she said. "Lewis, my husband, has just taken our cook to the hospital, because our cook was suddenly taken ill. But I promise you there will be lunch."

Fellini kissed one of Mrs. Cullman's outstretched hands, Mastroianni kissed the other, everybody relaxed, and we were off on Sunday-in-the-country. In a glassed-in addition to the old house, with a complete view of the lawn, trees, sculptures, pool, and Japanese boathouse, we munched on crabmeat on apricot halves and pâté on toast, and chose drinks. Miss Aimée said that water would be fine, but Mrs. Cullman said, "No, no, no, you don't have to drink water—we have orange juice," so Miss Aimée took orange juice. Mrs. Cullman said that it seemed to be hot and the gentlemen might want to take off their coats, but Fellini and Mastroianni said they wanted to keep their coats on. Mrs. Cullman said that she had bought her peach-colored kimono and another one, just like it, to use as covers for her living-room cushions. Glass panels on three sides of the room were sliding doors; Mrs. Cullman slid them open, and everybody exclaimed over the view. Mr. Cullman appeared, wearing bluejeans and sneakers and an Italian striped cotton shirt, and reported that the cook was now healthy, so he had brought the cook back to their kitchen.

Mrs. Cullman sat down next to Fellini and said, "I have only two Italian words—*molto bene*."

Fellini smiled politely and lifted a crab-filled apricot half in a gesture of salute to her. "*Molto bene*," he said.

Mr. Cullman reappeared, now wearing a cream-colored Issey Miyake sweater shirt, cream-colored slacks, and white loafers, and led everybody on a tour of the old part of the house. "This is our pizza oven," he said, with an air of amusement, indicating a large fireplace. "This was the kitchen, and that other room was the parlor, where the minister came, and there are two bedrooms upstairs."

"Pizza oven," Fellini said, looking thoughtfully at Mastroianni, who gave his charming smile and shrug. Everybody regarded the fireplace with admiration.

Gang members from the other limos arrived and joined the tour, which wound quickly back to the room with the view.

"The rooms were small," Mr. Cullman said. "With low ceilings to keep them warm on cold nights."

"Yes, very cold in Conneckticut," Fellini said sympathetically.

Mr. Cullman looked pleased. "The farmhouse, when it was first built, had only four rooms," he said. "Now we've got eleven."

"Very cold on a farm," Miss Aimée said.

Miss Masina said that the pâté on toast was very tasty, and she smiled gratefully at the host and hostess. Mr. Cullman invited Fellini to take off his coat, but Fellini graciously again said no. Mr. Cullman pointed up to the ceiling beams. "I got those beams from this guy who buys old farmhouses," he said to Fellini. "There's this guy Weiss, in Roxbury. Collects old barns, old timbers."

Fellini nodded respectfully.

"Why all the houses made of wood, not stone, in Conneckticut?" Mastroianni asked.

"Plenty of wood in this part of the country," Mr. Cullman said

"I thought wood because the pioneers moved all the time—away from the Indians," Mastroianni said, acting the part of an Indian shooting an arrow at Mr. Cullman.

"Yeah," Mr. Cullman said.

Led by the host and hostess, the gang then trooped down the grassy slope to the boathouse, where Mr. Cullman pointed to a narrow wooden canoe hanging under the Japanese eaves. "It's a New Guinea canoe," Mr. Cullman said as the gang stared solemnly at the canoe. "Dorothy bought it there from a native for six dollars. It cost a hundred dollars to ship it home." He laughed heartily, and the gang cooperatively joined in with mild laughter.

On the boathouse deck, Miss Masina pushed some hanging Soleri bells, and they jangled, so she pushed them harder.

"The Whitney used to sell them," Mr. Cullman said. "Who's for a swim?"

Fellini looked at Mastroianni, who looked at Miss Aimée, who looked at Miss Masina, who turned from the bells, and all shook their heads. One gang member's son, age nineteen, said all right, he'd take a swim, and he did, while everybody else, still looking solemn, silently watched him. Mr. Cullman called to the young man, asking him what he thought the temperature of the water was. About sixty-eight degrees, the young man called back. Mr. Cullman said it should be at least seventy-two degrees, and called to the young man to get the pool thermometer and take the temperature of the water. The lone swimmer took the temperature and reported that it was sixty-eight degrees. The silent gang nodded with distress at this news. Mr. Cullman remarked that the pool held a million gallons of water. Everybody looked obligingly bowled over. Then everybody trooped up the green slope toward the house as Mr. Cullman briefed us on the sculptures. "Recognize the bird?" he said. "It's a Senufo piece, from Africa. Dorothy found it somewhere."

Back in the house, the gang again got to work on the crabmeat and the pâté. Mrs. Cullman sat with Fellini and discussed travel.

"You haven't spent much time here, Mr. Fellini," Mrs. Cullman said.

"In 1957, I came for some producers, as the guest of them," he said. "They gave me people to show to me anything I want to see, and they said, 'Do what you want.' What I want was to go back to Italy, so I left. In the plane, as we flew away from New York, I looked down, and I felt very moved, very guilty that I was leaving."

"Do you find when you travel that you're too close to it, and that later you feel differently about it?" Mrs. Cullman asked.

"Language is the medium for the relationship to reality," Fellini said, looking apologetic. "If I don't know the language, I feel lost."

"Would that be true in another European country?" Mrs. Cullman asked.

"Yes," said Fellini.

"Are you sure you won't take off your jacket?" Mr. Cullman asked.

We had a bite of crabmeat. Fellini came over. "Don't eat too much," he said. "These are only the hors d'oeuvres. There will be a lot of food."

He was right. He knew the script. The meal that followed was terrific: curried chicken, seafood pasta, steamed mussels, steamed clams, green salad, white wine, three kinds of cake, ice cream, candied-ginger sauce, fresh fruit, and espresso. Everybody ate for two hours. Then everybody hugged Mrs. Cullman and shook hands with Mr. Cullman and said very enthusiastically, "Thank you very much. Goodbye."

In the limo on the way back, Wendy Keys, the director and co-producer of the tribute, explained to Fellini how the program in Avery Fisher Hall would go—with projections of clips from his movies interspersed with three-minute speeches from Mastroianni, Miss Masina, Miss Aimée, Donald Sutherland, Martin Scorsese, and others.

"It will be pictures, people, pictures, people, etcetera, and, at the end, you," Miss Keys said.

"I want the Rockettes," Fellini said.

The next night was a black-tie occasion. Before the program started, Fellini ran into Mr. Cullman, whose bow tie, with his tuxedo, had spectacular blue polka dots the size of dimes on a bright-red background.

"It is the tie of a Conneckticut Yankee," Fellini said knowledgeably.

The tribute went off nicely. It was pictures, people, pictures, people, et cetera, and then Fellini, who read a short speech: "My dear American friends: You are truly a simpatico people, as I always suspected since I was a child.... In the small movie house of my village—with two hundred seats and five hundred standing room—I discovered through your films that there existed another way of life, that a country existed of wide-open spaces, of fantastic cities which were like a cross between Babylon and Mars. Perhaps, thinking about it now, the stories were simplistic. However, it was nice to think that despite the conflicts and the pitfalls there was always a happy ending. It was especially wonderful to know that a country existed where people were free, rich, and happy, dancing on the roofs of the skyscrapers, and where even a humble tramp could become President. Perhaps even then it wasn't really like this. However, I believe that I owe to those flickering shadows from America my decision to express myself through film. And so I, too, made some films and gave life to some flickering shadows, and through them I told the story of my country. And tonight I am extremely touched to find myself here, together with my beloved actors, and honored by the people who inspired me in those old years."

# Oliver Stone Has Lunch with His Mom

December 6, 1993

Jacqueline Stone, the mother of the filmmaker Oliver Stone, told us at lunch the other day that her son had made her cry. It happened at a screening of his new film, *Heaven and Earth*, which is about the life of a Vietnamese woman, from her childhood in a rice-farming village, through the Vietnam war and her immigration to the United States, to her return to Vietnam. Oliver Stone wrote, produced, and directed *Heaven and Earth* and he has dedicated it to his mother. "Last night, at the screening, the movie starts, and I see it says 'For my mother Jacqueline Stone,'" Mrs. Stone said, speaking with a throaty French accent. "He made me cry. He did not tell me. Nobody tells me anything."

Her son was in town for a few days, ensconced in the Regency Hotel, to make himself and his film's cast—which includes Tommy Lee Jones, Joan Chen, and Hiep Thi Le—available for advance P.R. And in order to have a relatively quiet rendezvous with his mother, who lives in midtown, Oliver Stone arranged to slip her into the Regency, and invited us to meet her in a small private dining room, where he planned to join us.

Jacqueline Stone, a handsome, elegant woman, was wearing a bright-red blazer with gold buttons, black pants, a black cashmere turtleneck, and black suede boots. On the right lapel of the blazer was pinned a tiny gold angel. She fingered the angel. "This angel protects you," she said. Then, placing her hand over her left breast, she said, "Oliver is a very good boy, he has a very good heart. But that life they lead in this business—that life is crazy. Such a long time I live with him, forty-seven years." She was referring to Oliver's age.

Still waiting for Oliver, she had a glass of water and so did we, and she told us that she was born in Paris; that she was in France with her family throughout the Nazi occupation; that she studied French literature at the Sorbonne; that she loved horses and went riding often in the Bois de Boulogne; that she rode a bike to get to the stables; and that in May of 1945, right after the German surrender, Lou Stone, a lieutenant colonel in the U.S. Army, was riding a bike in the Rue de Rivoli and accidentally on purpose bumped his bike into hers. "Lou said he wanted to know me, and I said that was impossible, because I was engaged, and I was leaving the next day for the South of France. But he followed me to the South of France. I was nineteen. We were married in France on December 3, 1945, and sailed on a victory ship to America. We lived at the Plaza for a month. Oliver was born on September 15, 1946. At Doctors Hospital in New York. (Lou Stone died in 1985.)

Mrs. Stone went on to tell us about how her son left Yale and, in the spring of 1967, joined the Army and went to Vietnam. "He could have gone to Officer Candidate School," she told us. "He insisted on being in the infantry. He was away for fifteen months. I was always thin, but I lost twenty pounds. He was wounded. He got the purple heart. He got the Bronze Star. I wrote to him every week. I sent packages with Hershey bars, which he never got. Finally, he came home." She took another sip of water. "I look at him, and I see his eyes, to me they always look Chinese. Maybe it was because I had a very hard labor when I had him, and the forceps used to pull him out might have done it to his eyes. The slanting, Chinese eyes. The high cheekbones, though—they are mine. Oliver looks like me."

Just then, the subject under discussion appeared, looking mildly harried, but grinning. He wore a blue shirt, open at the collar, and black pants.

"Hi baby," his mother said. "You look good."

"Hi, Mom," he said, kissing her on the corners of the mouth, the French way, and giving her a tight hug. "You look great."

"You look so good, baby," she said.

"I've only got a few minutes, Mom," Oliver said. "I'll just have a Caesar salad."

We all had the salad.

"The dedication," his mother said. "You make me cry. Why didn't you warn me?"

Oliver grinned again, and said, "I wanted to surprise you."

"Nobody ever tells me anything," Mrs. Stone said. "And you gave me only six tickets. All your friends, all the people who knew you as a little boy, wanted to come, and they could not come."

"There will be other screenings," Oliver said, picking at his salad.

"You told me Sixty-sixth and Third. It was Sixty-*fourth* and Third," his mother said.

"Mistakes happen," Oliver said. "It's the movie business, Mom."

"I was talking about your father, in May of 1945, when he followed me to the South of France."

"Lou did that?"

"When I went with him to America on the ship, I did not know I was pregnant. It was a month after we were married."

Oliver raised his eyebrows.

"I was a good girl," his mother said. "I did not sleep with your father before I was married."

"Mom, you were a virgin?"

"I did not say I was a virgin. I said I did not sleep with your father before we were married."

"With the other guy you were engaged to when you met Lou?" Oliver asked.

"No. It was with a movie director. He worked with René Clair," she said.

Oliver laughed. "Did Lou know?," he asked.

His mother ignored the question. "Did you know that you were born on September 15, 1946, at nine-fifty-eight in the morning?"

"Tommy Lee Jones was born that same day," Oliver said.

"I had your astrological forecast done," his mother said.

"I had it done by a *Sanskrit* scholar in Los Angeles," Oliver said in a clearly one-upmanship way. "I've got to get back to work." He grabbed a chocolate-chip cookie, polished it off, and then popped a couple of pills in his mouth.

"What is that you just put in your mouth?" his mother asked, on the alert.

"They're only enzymes, Mom. They break the food down."

"I don't like those things," she said.

Oliver gave her a parting hug. She hugged him back and said, "I was the only woman on board that ship with sixteen hundred men, and all the time I was so sick I had to have the intravenous feeding."

Oliver grinned. "No wonder I am the way I am," he said, and he made for the door.

Huston Chronicle

January 8, 1996

FERVOR AND EXCITEMENT on a movie set at the start of shooting are par for the course, but the fervor and excitement of Anjelica Huston a few weeks ago when she began her first job as director—with the movie version of Dorothy Allison's novel *Bastard Out of Carolina*, in the Carolinas—were over the top. She is now in her early forties, about the same age that her director-actor father, John Huston, was when he began shooting *The Red Badge of Courage*. I wrote a series of articles about that movie—its making and its adventures and its Hollywood milieu—for this magazine in 1952 which became the book *Picture*. Thereafter, the moviemaking lives of John, who died in 1987, and his family somehow became delightfully intertwined with mine, and I continued writing about him, including a piece about him in Brooklyn in 1984 making *Prizzi's Honor*, which starred Jack Nicholson and Anjelica.

"It's scary as hell," Anjelica told me on her set, looking confident and energetic and happy as hell. She was directorially clad in an oversized parka and bluejeans and twenty-year-old cowboy boots. Her good-natured husband, the artist Robert Graham—gray-bearded and sleepy, eyes closed, side of face resting on the palm of one hand (they get up at 4 a.m. in this business)—sat on a canvas folding chair that said:

ANJELICA HUSTON
DIRECTOR

Tony Richmond, the director of photography, looked through the camera at two actors on a dilapidated porch in what was supposed to be the bleak, impoverished rural South. One was the leading character, Anney (Jennifer Jason Leigh)—pretty, desolate, abused, tragic. In a rocking chair nearby sat her granny (Grace Zabriskie), chewing tobacco—cynical, resigned, but still with humor, with spirit. The first assistant director yelled "Rolling!" Angelica, studying the video monitor, said, with even authority, "And action!" The actors spoke their lines. Anjelica called "Cut!" Then she added "Beauty!" and gave a joyous Huston laugh. In fact, after almost every "Cut!" she would add" Beauty!" and give that joyous laugh.

"I've got the best of the young actresses in Jennifer," Anjelica said exuberantly, between takes. "I've got a great D.P. I've got Julie Hoyt, my key makeup person, who worked with me on *The Grifters*. I've got that good actress, Susan Traylor, whose mother, Peggy Furey, was my old acting teacher. I've got Nava Sadan, my dresser for years. I've got my good personal assistant, Daniella Milton. I've got a great story. It's about people. I've never been interested in special effects, in explosions, except human explosions. I like making a movie for television. Everything moves faster. I like the budget—five million instead of thirty-five million. If you drop dead, the show will go on. I like not having the luxury to dabble around. Total freedom gets you in trouble. We're making the movie for TNT, but we're making it for theatrical release simultaneously. I like to learn on my feet. You're responded to. You're listened to. It's a pretty elevated position you find yourself in. Ready, Tony?"

Richard motioned to her to look at the actors on the video monitor for the shot. She looked, and then, glancing up, she smiled at him. They exchanged nods of mutual approbation. Richard said that he wasn't accustomed to working with women directors. Then he grinned at Angelica and said, in an earthy North London accent, "I *like* it."

Another "Cut!" Another "Beauty!" Anjelica rejoined me. This certainly beats doing a prequel or a sequel to *Prizzi's Honor*, which they wanted me to do," she said. "I didn't want to do more *Prizzi's Honor*. *Prizzi's Honor* belongs to Dad. I want to do something of my own."

## Wes Anderson in Hamilton Heights

May 21, 2001

Last week, Wes Anderson, the director, was working up in Hamilton Heights, filming the final stretch of *The Royal Tenenbaums*, his third movie (this one budgeted at a "modest" twenty-five million dollars). He celebrated his thirty-second birthday on the set—over a peanut-butter-and-jelly sandwich, his daily staple meal—with his crew and with his actors, Gene Hackman, Anjelica Huston, Ben Stiller, Bill Murray, Danny Glover, and Owen Wilson, who appeared in Anderson's movie *Bottle Rocket* and who also co-wrote the *Tenenbaums* script. Everyone except Anderson ate a regular meal, and then they brought out a traditional cake, a "Happy Birthday" banner, and presents.

"He's the first director who doesn't scare me," Anjelica Huston said. "This is the first time a director asked me what I think of something. I suggested wearing my grandmother Rhea Gore's locket in the movie."

"Most directors only want it their way," said Bill Murray, who appeared in Anderson's last movie, *Rushmore*. "This guy wants it to be right."

The object of their ruminations may be the most waifish-looking film director since François Truffaut. He has, from the top, nondescript brown hair, sharp features, clear-frame glasses, shoulders permanently hunched in behind-the-camera position, and no noticeable hips. On the set, he was elegantly clothed in mauve corduroy pants, a maroon corduroy sports jacket, and red sneakers.

Bill Murray said, "This guy has his own tailor. It's so nice, for a change, to like a guy and not begrudge him anything."

"There aren't even restrictions in his clothes," Anjelica Huston said. "His pants are custom-made with the crotch coming down about four inches above his knees. He's so skinny, and he gets skinnier by the day. We all want to hold him and mother him. We're so proud of him."

The movie, Anderson said, "is about a family of talented people who peaked early and got short-circuited. They fell apart, and then they try to get together again in new ways. It's not about my own family, but I use tons of stuff about us. I'm the middle of three boys. My older brother, Mel, was a doctor in the Air Force. Eric, four years younger than me, is an artist, the concept illustrator of my movies. We're from Houston, Texas. My parents are divorced. My mom is an artist and an archeologist, but now she works as a real-estate agent. My father was an amateur race-car driver, but now he's in public relations."

The main set for *The Royal Tenenbaums* is a nineteenth-century red brick townhouse a few blocks from City College, near Alexander Hamilton's house. Last week, Anderson was directing a technically difficult forty-five-second outdoor shot at the house with a Panavision camera at the top of a huge crane on a dolly. Most of the key cast members participated, as did a wrecked white 1967 Austin-Healey convertible, a fire engine, firemen, a Dalmatian, and a number of cops. With all this going on, only one person raised his voice. It was the Dalmatian's handler: "On your feet! On your feet!" The dog complied. The shot was a success.

"Very brave shot," the producer, Barry Mendel, said.

"Wes can tell a personal story in a moving but still comic way," Bill Murray said. "Usually, these stories are sentimental or vicious. He makes me feel different, almost like I'm not obliged to be entertaining. I don't find myself pushing or selling my scenes. My own persona is greatly diminished."

"He's so stylized," Gene Hackman said. "This picture has a sense of fable."

An old Indian man named Kumar, who moved from Bombay to the United States as a juggler during the Second World War ("I can still juggle twelve or thirteen plates at a time"), is in the movie, too. He met Anderson in Dallas in the early nineties. "I ran the Cosmic Cup, a health-food restaurant and yoga center with jazz," Kumar said. "As a college student, Wes used to hang out at my Cosmic Cup with Owen Wilson. Now he puts me in all his movies. I play Gene's buddy in this movie. Wes lifts me up. He has trust, an interesting mind, and humility. That's the beauty of him."

Anjelica Huston said, "I've started smoking again. When I stopped smoking, I was so depressed, I cried for months. Now I'm happy. This picture gives me license to be myself. I'm fatalistic."

# Nothing Fancy

March 24, 2003

CLINT EASTWOOD RECENTLY began directing a new feature film, *Mystic River*, but, just days before starting, he embarked on making *Piano Blues*, one of seven parts of a documentary about the blues which Martin Scorsese is producing for public television. Eastwood was going to shoot *Mystic River* in Boston, but he got his blues film under way at the Mission Ranch, an inn that he owns in Carmel, on California's Monterey Peninsula, where he also owns a great deal of other property. Out there, he seemed to be oblivious to the frantic pressures that usually overwhelm key figures in an imminent big-time movie production, like the one awaiting him in Boston.

"Nobody pushes Clint," said Bruce Ricker, the producer of *Piano Blues*, and one of Eastwood's battalion of longtime helpers. "Clint does what Clint decides to do in his own good time." Ricker is a bulky, fast-talking man who helped produce Eastwood's *Thelonious Monk: Straight, No Chaser*. As soon as Ricker arrived at the Mission Ranch—leading camera, sound, and lighting crews—he nervously scurried off to look for a baby grand piano that was to have been installed in the inn's former dairy barn, which is now used for weddings and parties.

Eastwood was already there, standing casually, six feet four inches tall, hands in his pockets, and watching a piano tuner plinking the keys. At seventy-two, he looks youthful, with bright-green eyes and high color in his cheeks. His hair is gray and white, full and uncombed, and that day he had on nondescript, loose-fitting gray pants, a tan cotton windbreaker, sneakers, and a blue-and-gray striped polo shirt, manufactured by his own clothing line, Teha̅ma.

He had driven over from his home in nearby Pebble Beach, where he lives with his thirty-seven-year-old wife, Dina; their six-year-old daughter, Morgan; their year-old pink-and-black pig, Penelope; three chickens; a fat black-and-white rat named Whiskers, who has ten new babies and a much older mate, Norbert; and a caged twenty-something yellow-naped Amazon-green female parrot named Paco, who likes to say, among other things, "Happy birthday" and "I love you."

Eastwood greeted Ricker with a calm nod and a grin. "Piano sounds O.K.," he said.

Ricker looked somewhat reassured. "Everybody's here," he said quickly. "The crew is unloading the equipment and will be setting up. Pinetop

Perkins and Jay McShann"—the Chicago bluesman and the Kansas City jazz player—"are both here. They made it."

Eastwood grinned again, and gave the piano a pat.

"Pinetop looks good; he's eighty-nine, you know," Ricker said.

"Eighty-nine?" Eastwood said. "I wonder what he eats."

Ricker looked as though he'd just been paid a personal compliment. "And Jay is eighty-six," he said.

"We'll have some good Kansas City and Chicago stuff," Eastwood said. "We'll try to find out who influenced the great players—blues, boogie, and beyond."

"We're bringing Pinetop and Jay to meet each other for the first time," Ricker said eagerly. "They never played together before."

"I always felt that jazz is the only original art form we have," Eastwood said. "It was very influential in creating the blues, and even rock is a spinoff."

"The blues tempo is the connecting link," Ricker said. "It's what both Pinetop and Jay come out of. We can establish that in the film."

"I want to keep it pure," Eastwood said. "Let the music speak for itself. Nothing fancy."

Mission Ranch sits on twenty-two acres of meadowland overlooking the Pacific Ocean, at the mouth of the Carmel River. Half a dozen chubby sheep graze dreamily on the meadow. Eastwood bought the place in 1986; it was built in the eighteen-fifties and has gone through various incarnations, including a dairy ranch and an officers' club during the Second World War. Eastwood rescued it from developers. The guest quarters are in small, renovated white clapboard cottages that resemble dollhouses, with paned windows, white lace curtains, flower boxes, and high-backed white rocking chairs on porches overlooking the sheep. Pinetop Perkins was accommodated in the Honeymoon Cottage.

Eastwood had crossed into the new century with some forty films on his résumé, several of them produced and directed by him, and some with music composed by him. On March 9th, he received the Screen Actors Guild Life Achievement Award. He has come a long way from his *Dirty Harry* roles of the nineteen-seventies. Among other things, he directed and played opposite Meryl Streep in *The Bridges of Madison County*. For that, he composed the theme "Doe Eyes," which became very popular, and which telephone callers to the Mission Ranch are obliged to listen to when they are put on hold.

Ricker told Eastwood that they could start filming late that afternoon, and then the two climbed into Eastwood's 1976 Mercedes sedan. "Let's go to my house," Eastwood said. "Mumsy will be there. She's ninety-four. Mumsy and I talk every night on the telephone. Last night, I took her to dinner at my golf club; it's called the Teha̅ma, too, after an extinct tribe of California Indians. I built it three years ago because it was so difficult to get tee times at the Pebble Beach club."

On the way, Eastwood stopped at a wooden shack in Carmel Valley that looked like a leftover from one of his *Unforgiven* sets. A sign on the roof read "Hacienda Hay and Feed." The proprietor, a spare fellow with spectacles, also looked left over from an Eastwood film set.

"Do you have one of those water bottles for animals?" Eastwood asked politely. "Where's George?" he said, looking around. "I don't see George."

"Dunno, haven't seen him," the proprietor said.

Eastwood walked over to a back door leading into a small yard. A goat munching on something lifted its head immediately and bounded over to him. Eastwood petted it, murmuring something friendly, then turned away. "Ah, there's George!" he said, raising his voice slightly for the first time that day. He bent down and picked up a spectacularly clean white rooster. "Glad to see you, George," he said, cradling the chicken against his chest. He set George down gently on the ground and went back inside to the proprietor, who handed him the bottle and said it cost three dollars and twenty-three cents. Eastwood counted out three dollar bills and a quarter, slowly picked up two pennies in change, and, clutching the bottle, headed back to his car.

The baby bottle, he said, was for Whiskers and her ten babies. "Dina is sort of an animal freak," he said. "Penelope, our pig, was the sick runt of a litter. Dina thought she was going to die, so she brought the pig into the house, and now Penelope is so strong and bold. When she was in the house, she would always be pushing our furniture around, out of place, from one room to the other." He looked very content, driving slowly. "Dina is everything I ever wanted and never found anywhere before," he said. "I'm very lucky. I've got a great girl. She's completely unselfish," he said, with a sudden passion. "It was a wonderful romance. We went together four or five months. Then I knew I could get married again. Instinctively, I knew she was the right person. I was never a guy on a white horse. She's a self-feeder."

The former Dina Ruiz is Eastwood's second wife. When they met, she was working as a news anchor at an NBC TV affiliate. His first wife was the former Maggie Johnson, whom he married in 1953, when he was twenty one. They divorced thirty years later. They have two children—Kyle, now thirty-four, a jazz bassist, and Alison, thirty, an actress, who recently posed for *Playboy*. Eastwood has several other children: Kimber, thirty-eight, the daughter of Roxanne Tunis, is married and lives with her husband; Scott, seventeen, and Katie, fifteen, live with their mother, Jacelyn Reeves, in Hawaii; and Francesca, who is now nine, is the daughter he had with the actress Frances Fisher. "Dina has embraced everybody," Eastwood said. "She brought the whole family together, with no territorial demands, no big ego, none of that. Francesca and Morgan are great friends. The kiddies— and their mothers—visit each other regularly. I take some of the kids, and Mumsy, too, on our vacations, to Sun Valley or Hawaii, wherever. That's the way Dina feels it should be."

He headed for Pebble Beach, passing several thousand of his own acres here and there. "I never bought any real estate I didn't really like," he said. "I like land, the land out here. I first came here when I was twenty-one and stationed at Fort Ord. I liked it. When everybody was going crazy with stocks and investments not long ago, I stayed with the land. I like the tangible. I like to enjoy things, and I enjoy this land."

He ran for mayor of Carmel, and won, in 1986, he said, because he didn't like the way the City Council was handling land, building, and water problems. He served for two years. "I enjoyed it," he said. "I enjoyed presiding over the council meetings, repairing the roads, deciding on water allotments. I liked doing things for people who can't stand up for themselves."

Eastwood's house—with eight rooms, two pianos, and a fully equipped gym—is a one-story, seventy-five-year-old adobe-and-wood hacienda, with a courtyard that encircles a huge oak and a stand of eucalyptus and palm trees. He parked alongside a black GMC pickup truck, circa 1951, that was, he explained, the one he drove in *The Bridges of Madison County*. One of the doors still bore the name of the character he played: "Robert Kincaid— Photographer—Bellingham, Washington."

Eastwood's appearance in the kitchen, where Paco the parrot greeted him with repeated "I love yous," didn't seem to slow down the lunch preparations that were under way. He introduced Dina, an ebullient, dark-haired woman. Morgan, a curly-haired miniature of her mother, was helping her make a huge salad. Dina's mother, a pretty, red-haired youngish woman, was cooking cheese quesadillas. Eastwood's sister, Jeanne, with her husband, was preparing a platter of rice and beans. His mother, Ruth, alert and trim in a gray warmup suit, was smiling benevolently at everybody. Additional husbands, some wearing pastel-colored pants with conservative, long-sleeved shirts, materialized. The dishes were placed, buffet style, on available countertops.

Eastwood took his plate to a corner of the kitchen table, sat down, and pointed to the rats' cage nearby. "I put up the bottle," he said softly to his wife.

"Daddy gives the rats vegetables the way he does us," Morgan said.

"Clint believes in eating vegetables, fruits and vegetables," Dina said. "He's the first one up every morning. He makes fruit smoothies for himself and everybody else."

"He makes a waffle for me," Morgan said. "And a smoothie."

"Clint believes every animal should eat what we eat—the pig, the parrot, the rats," Dina said. "He believes a bug has as much right to be on this earth as anybody else."

Eastwood, chewing, looked thoughtful.

"He's been this way all his life," Ruth Eastwood said. "One time, he had thirteen snakes. When he was four, we discovered he was allergic to dogs and cats, so he collected snakes. I guess he's kind of a supernatural person."

"My grandmother had a small farm, where I stayed as a boy," Eastwood said. "Sometimes when you move a lot as a little kid, animals are your best friends. Animals just like you for you."

He looked at his wristwatch and, motioning to Bruce Ricker, said there was time, before the filming for *Piano Blues* started, to look in on the Forty-fifth Annual Monterey Jazz Festival, which was taking place that weekend at the Monterey Fairgrounds, a short drive away. Ricker said that Marcia Ball, the blues pianist and vocalist, and the jazz pianist Dave Brubeck would be there, and they could try to find them and remind them to come over to the Mission Ranch for the filming. Neither Pinetop Perkins nor Jay McShann had ever met Dave Brubeck.

"If we get them playing together, it will also show the timelessness of the blues," Ricker said. "Maybe we'll even get some four-handed stuff!"

"That's the idea," Eastwood said.

Back at the Mission Ranch later that afternoon, Perkins and McShann were in the former milk barn, waiting near the piano. They were similarly attired, in white shirts and dark-blue suits. Perkins, dark-complexioned, with a white brush mustache and large round eyeglasses, was impish and restless, and had a black fedora perched on his head, along with a necktie decorated with a piano-key motif. McShann, who has light-brown skin, walked with the help of a cane. Both men watched alertly as the crew got lights, camera, and sound equipment ready.

Ricker told Eastwood that some of the other directors of Scorsese's blues series were shooting with handheld cameras, and using gels and smoke for atmosphere. Eastwood said he didn't want any gimmicks. "A good recording of the music is the most important thing," he said.

He pulled on a blue blazer over his sports shirt and walked over to the piano. Nodding a "Let's go!" to the crew, he sat down at the piano, beside Pinetop Perkins.

"Pinetop, you look fantastic!" he said. "You got a diet I should follow?"

"Heh-heh-heh!" Pinetop laughed, his face breaking up into dozens of creases. He pushed his fedora up on his head a bit, sat down at the piano, and fingered out a sharp, attention-getting "Shave and a haircut, two bits!" Eastwood laughed along with him and then began to ask deferential questions about the origin of the piano blues.

"We're trying to find out who the great influences were," he said.

Pinetop gave answers in words and in music. "My real name is Joe Willie Perkins," he said. "I used to listen to Pinetop Smith playin' his 'Boogie Woogie.' I tell ya, he was great, so when he died I took the name Pinetop."

"My idea of something to do when I was a kid was to put on Jay McShann playing 'Hot Biscuits,'" Eastwood said. "Didn't Tommy Dorsey take Pinetop Smith's 'Boogie Woogie'—sort of ripped it off, as I recall? Dorsey made a record of it, and it was a big hit."

"Yeh, heh-heh," Pinetop responded, and then he played some boogie and sang, "Come back, baby, please don't go…"

He stopped and said that he couldn't get the bass notes rolling with his left hand, because, some years ago, a woman had stabbed him in that hand.

Eastwood said that he couldn't get the bass notes rolling in his left hand, either. "And I wasn't even stabbed," he said, laughing.

When Jay McShann sat down at the piano, he showed how he got a steady rhythm going with his left hand while improvising with his right.

McShann said that he was born in Muskogee, Oklahoma. He told Eastwood, "My dad worked in a furniture store, and he'd bring his truck home, and there'd be broken records in it. One day, I picked up the pieces of a broken record and stuck them together. That's how I heard Bessie Smith for the first time, singin' 'Backwater Blues.' That particular record, with her hollerin', 'I can't move no more…. There ain't no place for a poor old girl to go.' It got to me. It sure sounded good to me."

Eastwood said, "When I was a kid, my mother, when Fats Waller died, brought home his records and said, 'That's what I call real piano playing.' I listened to 'Your Feet's Too Big' and 'Ain't Misbehavin'' for the first time. I was always trying to save up money to go to Fifty-second Street in New York, but I never could. Give us a taste, Jay. 'Hootie's Blues.'"

With a very light touch, in contrast to Pinetop's barrelhouse, McShann played and sang:

> She calls me her lover
> And I beg her to
> Ain't you sorry
> That little girl ain't you?

Then he played another version and sang, "She called me her lover; she called me her beggar, too…"

"I know those words," Eastwood said, laughing again. "I've used them. I've been in that position many times. You don't know how many lovely young ladies I've met by being able to copy your playing."

McShann started again, improvising.

"Beautiful," Eastwood said. He put his hand on McShann's upper back and rubbed it. "Would you describe yourself as happy, Jay?"

"Pretty much," McShann said. "But sometimes you can't see for lookin'."

They both went "Heh-heh-heh," and gave each other understanding looks.

Two weeks later, Eastwood was in Boston, directing *Mystic River*. He planned to pick up *Piano Blues* again in a few months, when he would be going to New Orleans. After that, Ricker said, they would film Ray Charles, in his studio in Los Angeles. In the meantime, ensconced in Boston's Ritz-Carlton hotel, Eastwood said that he could still hear the blues playing in the back of his head, as he contemplated what he might want to do with the score for *Mystic River*.

"I can do quite a bit simultaneously," he said. "As soon as I can get back to my piano at home, I may write some music of my own that will be suitable for this movie."

During the seven-week *Mystic River* shoot, Eastwood regularly spent an hour, after a day's filming, in the hotel's gym, where, among other routines, he bench-pressed two hundred pounds. As soon as he arrived in Boston, he went to a Whole-Foods market and stocked up on health foods. He installed a blender and a refrigerator in his hotel suite, and made smoothies every morning. When Dina and Morgan visited, a few weeks into the filming, he made smoothies for them, too.

*Mystic River* is a co-production of Warner Bros. and Eastwood's company, Malpaso, a Spanish word that means "bad step"; it was named after a creek in Carmel. His crew included many people who had worked with him during the past thirty years.

"They know the shorthand," he said.

Nobody ever broached the subject of Eastwood's retiring. He told me that he once discussed the topic with Jack Nicholson.

"About ten years ago. I was with Jack, driving out to the golf range," he said. "Jack said he was going to do just one more movie, *The Crossing Guard*, and that would be his last. I said I would do *In the Line of Fire* and *A Perfect World*, and that would be it. Well, he went on to act in about ten more movies, and I went on to act in or direct six more." Then he grinned and added, "They keep saying yes to you, so you keep on going."

*Mystic River* centers on three working-class friends—Jimmy, played by

Sean Penn; Dave, by Tim Robbins; and Sean, by Kevin Bacon—and how their lives have been haunted by an incident of sexual abuse in the past.

"These actors are so good and so enthusiastic, and they've all worked and prepared so hard, it's for me alone to screw up," he said. "There are so many characters, and the story weaves back and forth in time, so those are the only difficult aspects for me to deal with. I stay close to the impression of the story I got when I first read it. Sometimes embellishments just come. The actors bring them to me.

"I've even learned from my screenwriters. Seventeen years ago, when I produced, directed, and starred in *Heartbreak Ridge*, as Marine Gunnery Sergeant Tom Highway training a platoon of jarheads, I say, 'You improvise! You adapt! You overcome!' Helpful words to remember. I always equate a movie director with a platoon leader: he's only as good as the cast and crew behind him."

Someone on the set asked Eastwood how it felt to produce and direct the film, but not to act in it.

"It feels great!" he said. "This is much more fun. As an actor, I'm constantly being fiddled with. I'm being told, 'You gotta do this, you gotta do that.' Somebody is always fussing over my hair, somebody else is tampering with my skin. I'm told to go to wardrobe and put on these clothes or those other clothes. Here, I come to the set in my T-shirt and jeans and sneakers, and nobody cares what I look like. I'm getting the scenes I want, and it makes me very happy. I'm free, free of extra pressure, the constant worry over how I'm doing and what I'm doing. As the director, I want to be watching my actors—it's fun to watch the emotions in my actors unfold. If it weren't fun, I wouldn't be doing it."

One day, while directing *Mystic River*, Eastwood watched Sean Penn do a scene in which Penn's character comes upon the body of his murdered teenage daughter. The members of the crew who were watching were visibly shaken by the performance. Someone asked Eastwood how he felt about the shot.

"It's important to follow what you have in mind," he said. "I try to get what I have in mind, but if an actor does what he has in his mind, and if it's anything like what I just saw here with Sean, I'm very grateful to take it. It's like going to a store and looking at all the suits on the rack and seeing one that makes you feel, 'That's exactly what I have in mind.' I never had to work with someone like a Marilyn Monroe, who, I've heard, made everybody wait three hours before showing up, that sort of thing—that would drive me fruitcake."

The actors seemed grateful, too. "He's the least disappointing icon in American film," Sean Penn said.

"The actors have never been on a set like this before," one of Eastwood's longtime assistants said. "Nobody's yelling. Nobody calls out, 'Lights! Camera! Action!' Once in a while Clint says, '*Actione*,' perhaps as a tribute to his Sergio Leone days. Usually, he just kind of mutters, 'Go ahead.' He never shouts, or even says, 'Cut!' He just mutters, 'O.K.' or 'Stop.'"

When Eastwood is directing, instead of peering with the cinematographer through the lens, he uses a digital, battery-operated handheld monitor; it has a seven-inch screen, which is linked to the steadicam lens. In Boston, he didn't follow the usual routine of watching video playbacks on the set or having the actors watch or worry about their performances.

"It's like being on a Zen retreat," Marcia Gay Harden, who played Tim Robbins's (Dave's) wife, said. "Everything is so quiet and peaceful."

Buddy Van Horn, Eastwood's stunt coordinator, golfing partner, expert horseman, and second-unit director, started working with him in 1968, on the movie *Coogan's Bluff*. A former stuntman, Van Horn has the kind of weather-beaten, deeply lined face that moviegoers have spotted for ages wrecking wagons, fencing in *Zorro* pictures, starting bar scuffles, and finishing fights. He has also directed some of Eastwood's films, including *Pink Cadillac* and *Any Which Way You Can*. He was born on the backlot of Universal Studios, where his father worked as a veterinarian for the live animals until Buddy was two. He has seven grandchildren.

"Clint is really good with actors," Buddy says. "He knows actors' problems and lets them do their thing. If they need direction, he gives it to them."

Steve Hulsey, who has been Eastwood's driver since 1986, drove the director's nineteen-year-old motorhome, a silver Prevost that he likes to use as a trailer on the set, from California to Boston, taking six days to make the trip. "It's got a queen-size bed, a kitchen, a dinette, a TV, and a VCR. We lent it to the Pope in 1984, when he visited Monterey," Hulsey said. "It's in mint condition, with only 62,768 miles on it." Everybody seemed to look upon the Prevost as a sacred family heirloom. (Alana, the twenty-three-year-old daughter of another driver, followed in Malpaso's fuel truck, a one-ton Chevy Crew Cab Dually.)

The movie's production designer, Henry Bumstead, who is eighty-eight and a winner of two Oscars—for *To Kill a Mockingbird* and *The Sting*—scouted locations for *Mystic River* last summer and built the sets for all the interiors. He is known as Bummy to the rest of the crew.

"I wouldn't be working for anyone else at my age," Bummy said. "Clint takes the B.S. out of making movies."

A common pastime on the set, during all the waiting that is an integral part of moviemaking, was swapping Clint lore: "For recreation, Clint reads medical journals." Or, "When Clint first tried to get a job at Universal, in 1953, they told him he was too tall, that his Adam's apple was too obvious." Or, "Clint flies his own helicopter. He's had it for twelve years." Or, "He jumps out of a helicopter wearing his skis."

One evening after a day's work on the set, Eastwood was sitting in the hotel restaurant with some friends. He had completed his workout in the gym, had made a smoothie for himself in his room, and was nursing a single beer. Someone brought up Bummy and what he said about Eastwood taking the B.S. out of moviemaking.

"That's flattering, coming from him," Eastwood said. "I guess Bummy means all the moviemaking organization. Bummy knows his stuff. As a designer, he's still the best, still putting out, at his age. The actual ages of these people, the ones who can do what he does on that level, don't mean a thing. He knows how it was with some of the special people I worked with, too, in what might be called the great era of moviemaking. They were terrific people, like John Calley and Don Siegel. They read a lot. They knew a lot. If you asked one of them a question, you got an answer.

"Today, there are many differences. We have a lot more technology, a lot of toys to play with, but they don't necessarily do anything to make movies better. Unfortunately, today, when a movie is successful, they try to make twenty more like it," he went on. "Some people, for example, have wanted me to do *Dirty Harry* again. Harry or Josey Wales were just characters, and they came with a dramatic situation. They weren't like me, and the less they were like me, the more fun it was to do them. However, at some point in your life that kind of thing becomes less challenging. You have to start to grow within yourself, or else you'll start going backwards. I don't understand Sylvester Stallone. I hear he's going to do *Rocky* again. For me, it would look like you're doing it for a paycheck."

"I like to move on," he said. "I enjoyed making *The Bridges of Madison County*. I hadn't read the book. One day, the producer Lili Zanuck called me and told me to read it. She said, 'You're in it.' I hung up. The phone rang again. It was Terry Semel, who was then co-head of Warner Bros. He said, 'There's a lot of you in the character.' So I read the book and fought my way through the fancy, pretentious writing.

"I could see the story. In my mind, however, I saw it as the woman's story. So that's what it became as a movie. What often has set me off in making a movie is a song. I did it once before, in *Play Misty for Me*. In *Bridges*, for the love scene in the kitchen, where I—the photographer, Robert Kincaid—dance with Meryl Streep, I used the song 'I See Your Face Before Me,' by Johnny Hartman. Music often leads me into the sequence."

Eastwood gave no sign of being tired, even though other tables in the room had become deserted and he, like others in the crew, had an early-morning call. "Many people now making movies have been conditioned by television," he said. "I like using closeups. I'm fond of them. But people today use all closeups. A lot of them are claustrophobically hard to watch. They crank them in so tight I lose interest. Some of those old black-and-white movies have scope and size. My six-year-old daughter, Morgan, likes them. We were dialing around on television the other night, and we stopped on *Mildred Pierce*, with Joan Crawford. Morgan liked that movie, especially since it had a little girl her age in it. Dina and I took her with us the other night to see *Catch Me If You Can*. She sat there and sat there, expectantly, fifteen minutes into the movie, and then she asked, impatiently, 'When does the movie start?' She wanted some action, instead of closeups of heads. The other night, we dialled to *In the Line of Fire* on television, and Morgan said, 'Hey! That's you!' But she didn't want to watch it."

The South Boston neighborhood people gathered in small, respectful huddles to watch *Mystic River* being filmed. They gave Eastwood dozens of

T-shirts bearing the logos of local organizations—policemen, firefighters, Teamsters, Southies, Celtics, Red Sox—and he wore one to the set almost every day.

"You don't need to bring your own clothes when you work here!" Eastwood announced to his agent, Leonard Hirshan, during the latter's obligatory visit early in the filming. Hirshan regarded the T-shirts with detachment. He was neatly attired in the garb of agentry—blazer, gray flannel trousers, cashmere sweater, and well-worn white sneakers. He announced that he had given up agenting in favor of business managing, which he did exclusively for Eastwood. "In 1961, I became Clint's agent and Walter Matthau's agent, and now I'm wearing Walter's old Mephisto sneakers, which I inherited," he said. He stayed long enough to tell a number of people that the only independent moviemakers who have controlled their own pictures were Charlie Chaplin, Woody Allen, and Clint Eastwood. He reminded Sean Penn, "I used to get jobs for your father, Leo Penn." He pointed out that "Clint never says yes unless he intends to make the picture." He also stated, "I always say, 'Clint doesn't make deals, Clint makes movies.'" Then, looking around, he said, "Everything looks good here," and he left to return to Los Angeles.

Bruce Ricker, who lives in Cambridge, came to the set on every one of the production's thirty-nine days, to watch Eastwood direct and to eat lunch with the crew. (Eastwood has used the same set caterer, a Los Angeles outfit called Tony's, which leans toward steamed vegetables, for three decades.) As the filming neared the end, Ricker made a few musical suggestions for the score. Eastwood said he wanted to see what he might compose himself. "I want to write something that will be in tune with the feeling of the lives of these people," he said.

When *Mystic River* wrapped, Eastwood went home to Pebble Beach. In his office at the Mission Ranch, he worked with Joel Cox, digitally editing the footage from the movie. When they finished, Cox took it with him to Los Angeles, to have it put on film for additional editing.

One afternoon in his living room, Eastwood sat down on the bench of his Chickering baby grand and started working out possible melodies for the movie. "I was improvising one melody and fooling around with another," he said. "Then Dina came into the room to listen to what I was playing, and she said she liked the first one. So I got that one on the road. I put it in the picture. There's no jazz in it. And there's no blues. It's more on the classical side, to be played by a full orchestra, eventually—by the Boston Symphony Orchestra, as it turns out. If I had to describe it, I'd say it's something bittersweet. It's like life, where you're constantly adjusting to everything. It's all improvisation."

## Tony Again

September 29, 2003

Guests at last week's special screening of the re-released movie *Scarface*—about a Cuban immigrant named Tony Montana who becomes a powerful, wealthy, and very profane drug lord—seemed noticeably liberated after watching the film at City Cinemas, across from Bloomingdale's. When it was over, they moved on to the Metropolitan Club to toast its twentieth anniversary.

"Why the fuckin' snob Metropolitan Club?" a young employee of City Cinemas asked.

"This movie is so like fuckin' life," his companion said. "I've seen it thirty times. When you see it, you never let it go."

*Scarface* features Al Pacino, Steven Bauer, Michelle Pfeiffer, and Mary Elizabeth Mastrantonio, among others. It has inspired many imitations and has been accorded a cult of followers around the world, including rappers and young men in the business of high finance. The screenwriter was Oliver Stone, the director Brian De Palma, the producer Martin Bregman. At the Metropolitan Club, a number of these folks celebrated over a huge spread of food and drink, while the movie's oft-repeated message, "The World Is Yours," was projected in colored streams of lights across the marble halls and walls. Samplings of Hollywood agents, producers, managers, publicists, and distributors joined in. They lined up to congratulate Pacino, who was wearing a black suit and a thin gold chain over a black T-shirt. He had a scraggly gray beard, because, he explained, he just hadn't felt like shaving for a week. Hand-shaking kept him from getting hold of a first forkful of pasta and salad, and from talking to his table companion, Lee Strasberg's widow, Anna, who was trying to tell him about her new grandchild. Pacino stood up politely for the well-wishers.

"It's a truly fucking great film," a man from an entertainment publication told him.

"Well done," James Lipton, the host of *Inside the Actors Studio*, said, with teacherly restraint, gently patting Pacino on the back.

"It's on another level—it's operatic," Jeff Berg, the chairman of I.C.M., said.

Mary Elizabeth Mastrantonio, who plays Tony's sister, Gina, in the movie, had flown in from London for the occasion. "It's puzzling," she said. "With all the work I've done in my life, this is the one I'm known for."

"You're big with the rappers now," someone told her. "They love this movie."

"I'm really curious about what their ideology is," she said.

"The movie is dedicated to Howard Hawks and Ben Hecht, so maybe the thread started there," someone else said.

"When Tony shoots the crooked cop and says, 'So long, Mel, have a good trip!'—that's seminal," an elderly gentleman said.

Some of the guests rendered Tony Montana impersonations:

"You're all a bunch of fucking assholes! You need people like me. So you can point your fucking fingers and say—'That's the bad guy!'"

"I always tell the truth, even when I lie."

"I'm Tony Montana from Cuba, and I want my fucking human rights now!"

One man, who said he worked on Wall Street, told Pacino that the line he and his colleagues loved best was "Why don't you try sticking your head up your ass, see if it fits?"

Their second favorite, he went on, was one recited by Frank, a drug boss whom Tony orders killed: "Lesson No. 1, 'Don't underestimate the other guy's greed.' Lesson No. 2, 'Don't get high on your own supply.'"

Pacino welcomed all these recitations with a friendly grin. His pasta, on the table, was starting to congeal. Steven Bauer, who plays Tony's friend Manuel Ray in the movie, came over, and the actors hugged each other.

"You told me when we made the movie it would come back big," Bauer said.

"It's a different thing," Pacino said. "It's a movie, because it's on film. But it's a different kind of movie."

"You said, 'Trust me, trust me.' You said, 'This one is different, and it will always be different.'"

"It was that combination of Oliver Stone and De Palma that did it," Pacino said.

"And you," Bauer said. "For years, people have been coming up to me on the street and yelling, 'Hey, Manolo! Shoot that piece of shit!' In Miami, kids come over and say, 'Every Halloween, I'm you.'"

An elegant older woman walked over to Pacino and looked with astonishment at his still untouched dish of pasta.

"What the fuck are you eating?" she asked.

"I love it when you talk dirty to me," Pacino said, his face behind the beard looking as pure as they come.